SOVEREIGNTY
AS
RESPONSIBILITY

Publications of the Brookings Institution's Conflict Resolution in Africa Project

Conflict Resolution in Africa, edited by Francis M. Deng and I. William Zartman (1991)

South Africa: The Struggle for a New Order, Marina Ottaway (1994)

The New Is Not Yet Born: Conflict Resolution in Southern Africa, Thomas Ohlson and Stephen John Stedman with Robert Davies (1994)

Somalia: State Collapse, Multilateral Intervention, and Strategies for Political Reconstruction, Terrence Lyons and Ahmed I. Samatar (1995)

War of Visions: Conflict of Identities in the Sudan, Francis M. Deng (1995)

Governance as Conflict Management: Politics and Violence in West Africa, edited by I. William Zartman (1996)

Sovereignty as Responsibility: Conflict Management in Africa, Francis M. Deng, Sadikiel Kimaro, Terrence Lyons, Donald Rothchild, and I. William Zartman (1996)

SOVEREIGNTY
AS
RESPONSIBILITY

Conflict Management in Africa

Francis M. Deng
Sadikiel Kimaro
Terrence Lyons
Donald Rothchild
I. William Zartman

The Brookings Institution
Washington, D.C.

Copyright © 1996

THE BROOKINGS INSTITUTION

1775 Massachusetts Avenue, N.W., Washington, D.C. 20036

Library of Congress Cataloging-in-Publication data
Sovereignty as responsibility : conflict management in Africa /
  Francis M. Deng [et al.].
      p.   cm.
  Includes bibliographical references (p.) and index.
  ISBN 0-8157-1828-4 (c :alk. paper). — ISBN 0-8157-1827-6 (pa:
alk. paper)
    1. Africa—Politics and government—1960–   2. Conflict management
—Africa.   3. Sovereignty.   I. Deng, Francis Mading, 1938–   .
DT30.5.S667   1996
327.1—dc20   96-14159
                                                                            CIP

9 8 7 6 5 4 3 2 1

The paper used in this publication meets the minimum
requirements of the American National Standard for
Information Sciences—Permanence of Paper for Printed Library
Materials, ANSI Z39.48-1984

Set in Palatino

Composition by Harlowe Typography
Cottage City, Maryland

Printed by R. R. Donnelley and Sons Co.
Harrisonburg, Virginia

Foreword

AFRICA has been the site of some of the most brutal and difficult-to-manage conflicts in the 1990s. The human costs and challenge to the international community in general and the United States in particular of genocide in Rwanda, state collapse in Somalia and Liberia, decades of internecine civil war in Sudan and Angola, and the worrisome potential for chaos in Zaire and Nigeria compel attention both on humanitarian grounds and because pervasive and persistent civil unrest undermines the regional legal order. These tragic cases are balanced, happily, by others. Several African states have initiated far-reaching reforms that offer hope of breaking the vicious cycle of conflict, authoritarianism, and economic decline. The end of thirty years of conflict in Ethiopia/Eritrea, efforts to rebuild the state in Uganda, termination of decades of internal fighting in Mozambique, economic reform in Ghana, the emerging democracy in Benin, and, most encouraging of all, the transition to multiracial democracy in South Africa suggest that Africa provides models of relatively successful governance and conflict management along with the more dramatic cases of chaos and collapse.

According to Francis M. Deng, Sadikiel Kimaro, Terrence Lyons, Donald Rothchild, and I. William Zartman, sovereignty should no longer be seen as protection against external interference in a state's internal affairs. Rather the state must be held accountable to domestic and external constituencies. In *Sovereignty as Responsibility* the authors develop a framework to guide national governments and the international community in discharging their respective responsibilities. They examine identity as a potential source of conflict, governance as a matter of managing conflict, and economic tools as a possible means of deterring conflict. They analyze the opportunities that exist for making sovereignty more responsible and improving the management of conflicts at the regional and international levels, in support of their assertion that sovereignty as responsibility is both a national obligation and a global imperative.

Since its creation in 1988, the Brookings Institution's Africa Project has focused on the continent's challenges in conflict resolution, human rights, democracy, and sustainable development. The project's agenda emphasized conflict resolution, and studies were initiated to analyze conflict in Africa and suggest what policymakers in Africa, the United States, and elsewhere might do to improve conflict management. The published studies are listed in the front matter of this volume. This volume, *Sovereignty as Responsibility: Conflict Management in Africa*, concludes the series.

Francis M. Deng is a senior fellow in the Foreign Policy Studies program of the Brookings Institution. Sadikiel Kimaro is deputy division chief, Africa Department, of the International Monetary Fund. Terrence Lyons is a research associate in the Foreign Policy Studies program of the Brookings Institution. Donald Rothchild is a professor of political science at the University of California, Davis. I. William Zartman is a professor of conflict resolution and African Studies at the School of Advanced International Studies, Johns Hopkins University.

Michael Chege, Gilbert Khadiagala, Marina Ottaway, and Stephen John Stedman read early versions of the manuscript. Theresa Walker, Tanjam Jacobson, and Deborah Styles edited the final manuscript; Michael Donovan, Gary Gordon, Susan Hardesty, Cynthia Iglesias, Jennifer McLean, Mark Strauss, and Gerard Trimarco verified it, and Andrew Solomon coordinated the verification. Kris McDevitt, Maureen Merella, and Susan Blanchard provided administrative assistance, and Princeton Editorial Associates prepared the index.

The Conflict Resolution Project was made possible by a grant from the Carnegie Corporation of New York. Other activities supporting the project were funded by the Rockefeller Brothers Fund and the Rockefeller Foundation. Brookings gratefully acknowledges this support.

The views expressed in this book are those of the authors and should not be ascribed to the people whose assistance is acknowledged above, to the organizations that supported the project, or to the trustees, officers, or staff members of the Brookings Institution.

April 1996
Washington, D.C.

Michael H. Armacost
President

Contents

x   Contents

Preface

As the twentieth century nears its end, sovereignty is increasingly under attack. The nation-state paradigm has been frequently analyzed for its inadequacies in the post–World War II period, since neither the institution itself nor the myths by which it endures are fully appropriate to the current conditions.[1] But even as the traditional concept of sovereignty erodes, there is no presumptive, let alone adequate, replacement for the state. The locus of responsibility for promoting citizens' welfare and liberty, for organizing cooperation and managing conflict, when not exercised by society itself, remains with the state. Until a replacement is found, the notion of sovereignty must be put to work and reaffirmed to meet the challenges of the times in accordance with accepted standards of human dignity.

A cursory look at conditions on the African continent reveals several crisis areas and correlative policy themes: conflict management, human rights protection, democratic participation, and sustainable development. Although the priority is obviously debatable, there is a logic to the sequence. Because a situation of conflict, especially one involving mass violence and a breakdown of order, often implies gross violation of human rights, denial of democratic liberties, and frustration of socioeconomic development, conflict management claims a rightful place on top of the list. But it is perhaps more appropriate to emphasize the interconnectedness of these policy areas and their overlapping values.

Since October 1989, the Africa Project of the Brookings Institution's Foreign Policy Studies program has conducted research on these interrelated themes. Much of the research agenda has focused on conflict analysis, management, and resolution. This volume, the last in the series, draws major conclusions from the work already done and provides guidance on future work in this field. The premise is that internal conflicts are the principal source of human suffering, gross violations of human rights, and massive destruction of civilian lives and productive capacity. Internal conflicts often involve racial, ethnic, cultural, or religious cleavages that reflect severe, sometimes zero-sum, crises of national identity, usually manifested in a wide discrepancy between group identities and the official identity structures of the state.

Those who suffer the humanitarian consequences of conflict fall into a moral vacuum left by the state's failure, deliberate or imposed, to fulfill its normal responsibilities. To fill this vacuum the international humanitarian agencies are often called upon to step in and provide the necessary protection and assistance.

Whether conflicts result from the crisis of national identity, disparities in political participation, or inequities of distribution, the critical factor is one of management through governance. Different regions and countries of Africa differ in their level of success or failure. The apartheid system in South Africa, as is now obvious, was untenable. Despite ongoing concern for the future, the establishment of majority rule with power-sharing arrangements that ensure the inclusiveness of all racial and ethnic groups makes the postapartheid South Africa a success story. The crises of conflicts in the Horn of Africa have ranged from the collapse of the Somali state, to the independence of Eritrea from Ethiopia, to developments in Ethiopia itself, where the policies of democratization based on ethnically defined regions represent a precarious experiment in restructuring politics and identity. In Kenya, a fragile, imperfect democracy is struggling under President Daniel arap Moi's heavy-handedness, and Sudan remains one of the extreme cases of the national identity crisis on the continent. In West Africa, Côte d'Ivoire, Ghana, and Nigeria historically have reflected a higher level of success in the management of ethnic conflict, although recent repression in Nigeria in particular makes the situation there dangerously explosive. In the southern African region, Botswana is acclaimed as a highly successful example of democracy, economic growth, equitable distribution, and overall stability.

If conflict management, political stability, economic growth, and social welfare are functions of governance, then the responsibility for failed policies and their disastrous humanitarian consequences must rest with the governments concerned. Although accountability for such responsibility rests with the people of the country, when people are oppressed, their power to hold their governments accountable becomes very limited. To the extent that the international community is the ultimate guarantor of the universal standards that safeguard the rights of all human beings, it has a corresponding responsibility to provide innocent victims of internal conflicts and gross violations of human rights with essential protection and assistance. The normative code that should guide such international action should be the universal standards of human dignity, as embodied in the Universal Declaration of Human Rights, elaborated in the International Covenant on Civil and Political Rights and the International Covenant on Economic, Social, and Cultural Rights, and a wide array of other human rights instruments. From a pragmatic point of view, human dignity is conceived of not as a utopian vision, but in its minimum content, as a political demand for which people are often prepared to risk their lives. The quest for human dignity usually translates into a struggle for recognition, respect, and equitable participation in the political, economic, social, and cultural life of the country.

Magnitude of the Crisis

In the post–cold war era the proliferation and intensification of internal conflicts have resulted in unprecedented human tragedies and, in some cases, have led to partial and even total collapse of states. This state of affairs has brought pressures for global humanitarian action, sometimes even forced intervention, as well as an urgent quest for peacemaking and peacekeeping. The response of the international community has inevitably contributed to an erosion of traditional concepts of sovereignty in order to ensure international access to the affected population within state borders. Culpable states have responded by trying to reassert sovereignty and territorial integrity. The resulting tug-of-war is acquiring a crosscultural dimension that confronts the international community with severe dilemmas. But the war is certainly not being won by those governments that are attempting to barricade themselves against warranted international scrutiny.

The events in the former Yugoslavia and the former Soviet Union demonstrate that the crisis of internal conflicts and their humanitarian consequences is global. As UN Secretary General Boutros Boutros-Ghali observed in *An Agenda for Peace*: "Poverty, disease, famine, oppression and despair abound, joining to produce 17 million refugees, 20 million displaced persons and massive migrations of peoples within and beyond national borders," all of which "are both sources and consequences of conflict that require the ceaseless attention and the highest priority in the efforts of the United Nations."[2] Since the secretary general wrote, estimates of refugees and internally displaced persons have exceeded 20 million and 30 million respectively.

Although the global dimension of the crisis needs to be stressed, some regions are more affected than others. Africa is perhaps the most devastated by internal conflicts and their catastrophic consequences. Of the estimated 30 million internally displaced persons worldwide, about 16 million are African, as are 7 million of the 20 million refugees in the world. African leaders, diplomats, scholars, and intellectuals have recognized the plight of their countries and their people and are demonstrating a responsiveness commensurate to the challenge, recently culminating in a series of interrelated initiatives. Among them are the Africa Leadership Forum's proposed Conference on Security, Stability, Development and Cooperation in Africa (CSSDCA), embodied in the Kampala Document in May 1991; the International Peace Academy (IPA) Consultations on Africa's Internal Conflicts, first launched at Arusha in March 1992; and the Secretary General's Proposals for an OAU Mechanism for Preventing, Managing, and Resolving Conflicts, which was first endorsed by the Council of Ministers and the Assembly of Heads of State and Government in Dakar, Senegal, in June 1992.

Secretary General Salim Ahmed Salim introduced the item to the Council of Ministers at Dakar in 1992 by emphasizing that:

Conflicts have cast a dark shadow over the prospects for a united, secure and prosperous Africa which we seek to create. . . . conflicts have caused immense suffering to our people and, in the worst case, death. Men, women and children have been uprooted, dispossessed, deprived of their means of livelihood and thrown into exile as refugees as a result of conflicts. This dehumanization of a large segment of our population is unacceptable and can not be allowed to continue. Conflicts have engendered hate and division among our people and undermined the prospects of the long term stability and unity of our countries and Africa as a whole. Since much energy, time and resources have been devoted to meeting the exigencies of conflicts, our countries have been unable to harness the energies of our people and target them to development.[3]

To compound the crisis, fundamental human rights, democratic freedoms, and economic and social development are gravely compromised as civil order breaks down and insecurity becomes rampant. What is more, although most of the conflicts are internal, they spill over into neighboring countries with the influx of refugees and political dissidents, thereby causing widespread regional insecurity and instability. Regional and international response to the consequence of conflict is therefore motivated as much by common interest in global peace and security as by humanitarian concerns. This in essence poses serious dilemmas for sovereignty and a major challenge to the international community.

Dilemmas of Sovereignty

The very notion of sovereignty paradoxically implies an international system that imposes international responsibilities on the state in the mutual interest of the state and the international community. Both the 1648 Treaty of Westphalia, which created the modern state in the European context, and the 1885 Berlin Conference, which carved up Africa into European colonial territories, were indeed motivated by the interest of the European powers in promoting conditions of domestic law and order within territorially defined states. They thereby hoped to facilitate peaceful political and commercial relations among the principal actors in the European-centered international system.[4]

In the contemporary international climate, two seemingly contradictory, but in fact complementary, trends characterize the post–cold war era. One is the visible but ambivalent erosion of sovereignty in favor of human rights protection and humanitarian intervention. The other is the isolationist tendency emerging within the major powers.

Rwanda in 1994 is an example of this paradox. In the face of genocidal ethnic conflict the United Nations withdrew its peacekeeping forces from the country at precisely the time of its greatest need for humanitarian intervention. Then, as though to compensate for this gross failure to meet an urgent humanitarian challenge, the international community returned with a massive emergency assistance program, especially for the refugee and internally displaced populations, costing hundreds of millions of dollars.[5] The humanitarian operations were conspicuously conducted by foreigners, well equipped with vehicles, communications systems, and other supplies in an atmosphere in which the newly established government lacked the basic needs—authority, infrastructure, and resources—for running the state. Inevitably, the government responded ambivalently to international humanitarian operations to a degree that began to threaten the continuation of relief assistance programs, especially to the internally displaced.

Whether international involvement in a domestic problem is strategically motivated or driven by humanitarian concerns, it nearly always evokes a reaction that is both appreciative of assistance and hostile to foreign intervention. It could indeed be conjectured that when the state fails to honor the responsibilities of national sovereignty, the people will retain their consciousness of pride, honor, and independence, despite their need for external help. If certain parties claim to be the custodians of the identity and pride of the country, those parties must also assume the concomitant responsibilities. If militia leaders claim to be such custodians, as happened in Somalia, then the responsibilities of state sovereignty logically fall upon them. The withdrawal of the international community from Somalia was a way of telling the people and their militia leaders that they were responsible for the sovereignty that they were so sensitive about. After the withdrawal of UN peacekeeping forces relief operations continued but not with the same degree of moral commitment that marked the U.S. Operation Restore Hope.

This is an important message for the Africans to heed, whether they are governments, rebel leaders, militia leaders, civil society, or the general population. If they fail to discharge the responsibilities of sovereignty, whether through the state or alternatives to it, they cannot legitimately complain against international humanitarian intervention or against its withdrawal and neglect.

Not all governments are deficient in discharging the responsibilities of sovereignty, in providing protection and assistance for their affected population, or in requesting the international community to supplement their national efforts. Some are clearly more responsive than others, and some may even meet high levels of expectations within their means. Nevertheless, where human tragedies prevail, there is usually a significant gap between what is desirable and what the governments do.

Responsibility and Accountability

The sovereign state's responsibility and accountability to both domestic and external constituencies must be affirmed as interconnected principles of the national and international order. Such a normative code is anchored in the assumption that in order to be legitimate, sovereignty must demonstrate responsibility. At the very least that means providing for the basic needs of its people. Most governments under normal circumstances do discharge that responsibility. When they cannot do so because of incapacity, they can legitimately call upon the international community to assist them. Sometimes governments fail to discharge this responsibility and refuse to call for help even under those exceptional circumstances. Masses of citizens may suffer and even die as a result. Then the international community can be expected to step in to provide the needed remedies.

These circumstances usually involve the breakdown of peace, security, and stability, which the state was created to establish and preserve. In a desirable and normal situation the system of law and order is responsive to the needs of the national population for justice and general welfare. When things fall apart and peace, security, and stability cannot be guaranteed, the prevailing order may be challenged by a rebellion that can claim significant legitimacy and effectiveness. Under those circumstances, the authority of those entrusted with sovereignty falls into question. Between these two extremes are many cases where internal conflict is endemic, societal needs and demands are unmet, and government is seen as a private function. Although law and order are overriding objectives, they cannot be seen as concepts of value-free control and authority. Rather they are elements of an exercise of power legitimized by the pursuit of the common and overriding objectives of the community or the nation.

The normative principles of sovereignty, responsibility, and accountability have internal and external dimensions. The internal dimension has to do with the degree to which the government is responsive to the needs of its people, is accountable to the body politic, and is therefore legitimate. The international dimension has to do with the cooperation of sovereign states in helping or checking one another when a fellow state loses or refuses to use its capacity to provide protection and assistance for its citizens.

Traditionally, sovereignty implies a supreme, independent, original authority, but in an age imbued with democratic ethos, it should mean that a people governs itself. Sovereignty, even in its traditional sense, refers not only to the inviolability of the state but to its ability to carry out its functions of government. Sovereignty is not merely the right to be undisturbed from without, but the responsibility to perform the tasks expected of an effective government. Normatively, to claim otherwise would be to lose sight of its purpose in the original context of the social contract, taking the means for the end. Sovereign authority is only the means for making harmony and solving problems when harmony does not exist on its own, and conflicts are not worked out by society.

The obligation of the state to preserve life-sustaining standards for its citizens must be recognized as a necessary condition of sovereignty. And indeed although this normative principle is not yet fully or consistently observed in practice, it is becoming increasingly recognized as the centerpiece of sovereignty. The state has the right to conduct its activities undisturbed from the outside when it acts as the original agent to meet the needs of its citizens. But that right is not license. It is merely—and normally—the obligation of the first resort, and it is dependent on the performance of the agent. If the obligation is not performed, the right to inviolability should be regarded as lost, first voluntarily as the state itself asks for help from its peers, and then involuntarily as it has help imposed on it in response to its own inactivity or incapacity and to the unassuaged needs of its own people.

On the international level, then, sovereignty becomes a pooled function, to be protected when exercised responsibly, and to be shared when help is needed. Operations would become hard to manage and responsibility hard to define if the normal functions of sovereignty were to be shifted from the national to the global level. It is best to think of the international exercise in terms of layers of assistance. The state exercises sovereignty at home. It can then turn to its neighbors for assistance, next to its regional partners, and finally to the global organization, the United Nations. In between, it may also seek bilateral assistance as it chooses, from a distant great power or from a foreign state with which it entertains special relations—such as a former metropole.

The response of the international community to internal crises is becoming less prone to intervention than in the past, however, as the end of great power rivalry and the rise of budgetary constraints make it harder for governments to pursue activist policies outside their national borders. Although often driven by humanitarian concerns to deliver needed assistance, and occasionally taking military action to facilitate that mission, the international community invariably fails to give the sustained attention that is needed to address the political dimensions at the root of the crises. Increasingly, the message to Africa is that even when the international community is prepared to assist, the primary responsibility must fall on the Africans themselves.

Consequently, the sharing of sovereignty begins on the subregional and regional levels. The role played by the Economic Community of West African States (ECOWAS) in Liberia, the Southern African Development Community (SADC) in Lesotho and Mozambique, the Intergovernmental Authority on Drought and Development (IGADD) in the Sudan and Somalia, and the Arab-Maghrib Union (UMA) in the Western Sahara are indicative of new attempts to exercise subregional responsibility and accountability within the regional framework. This learning experience is welcome in an international atmosphere that is becoming increasingly isolationist, except for the most compelling humanitarian need for international responses. Although none of them proved conclusive, such regional responses offer a potential that can grow to encompass a wide range of contexts requiring cooperation, from the search for peace to regional economic arrangements, that in themselves could be an effective preventive measure against human tragedies.

Although it is important to emphasize the primary responsibility of subregional and regional organizations, it would be a major strategic mistake to absolve the international community of its regional responsibilities. Secretary General Salim Ahmed Salim of the OAU has repeatedly stated that Africa is part of the international community, has played an effective role in many UN peacekeeping operations around the world since their inception, and has the right to expect from the international community both the privileges and obligations of membership. Africa's involvement in the international system, as a source of support and as an obligation, is inherently in the interest of global order.

Responsibility and Conflict Management

One of the indirect objects of sovereign responsibility has been identified, as responsibility *to* its citizens, but another needs to be further clarified. Responsibility *for* what? The job of the state is to ensure that the basic needs and demands of its people are provided for and that the conflicts arising among them are managed.

As the social contract literature of Hobbes, Locke, and Rousseau tells us, conflict management is the reason why free and conflicting individuals gave up their liberty to create a state. Conflict is often inevitable and may at times even be healthy in a society. Conflict has been variously defined by the prominent authorities on the subject as "perceived divergence of interest" or a situation where "parties' current aspirations cannot be achieved simultaneously," "a problem in identifying and reaching common goals," "incompatible or mutually exclusive goals or aims or values," "action seeking inconsistent goals," "opposition between groups and individuals for the possession of goods . . . in short supply or the attainment of mutually incompatible values," or "a struggle over values and claims to scarce status, power and resources in which the aims of the opponents are to neutralize, injure or eliminate their rivals."[6] The common elements are a zero-sum situation of desired items among competing drives for their possession or attainment.

These incompatibilities, inequalities, and deprivations are the bases or grounds for conflict. When needs and demands clash in a zero-sum relation and become the elements of political actions that confront each other, they turn into conflict. If ignored, they can escalate into violent conflict. Unmanaged, these elements have a great destructive effect. This threat of worsening serves as the greatest incentive to undertake measures of conflict reduction. But managed, conflict can produce involvement, direction, production, competition, and improvement, rather than alienation, disorder, stalemate, violence, and degeneration.

"Political stability and a minimum degree of social harmony," Richard Sandbrook's basic conditions for good governance, are not produced by the absence of conflict but by successfully managing conflict; they are dynamic results, not static conditions.[7] A society without conflict is as utopian a condition as a government without need for accountability, and accountability necessarily involves conflict. But, like conflict, accountability can get out of hand and destroy its own purposes, leading to stalemate and then government overthrows, as in the democratization processes in Benin and Zambia or the political stalemates in Zaire and Cameroon. Yet, like accountability, conflict over local demands unheeded, as in Eritrea before independence from Ethiopia, or class demands unsatisfied, as in Algeria or Nigeria, can impede governance, progress, and development. Yet, like accountability, local and class demands provide the motor for governance when they are managed productively.

The failure of regimes to manage conflicts may generate conditions of violence that are not only destructive to society but can degenerate into a widespread breakdown of civil order and even the collapse of the state as Liberia, Rwanda, and Somalia have so tragically demonstrated. Then follow human tragedies which in turn require sharing the responsibilities of sovereignty to contain them.

Questions and Assumptions

From the perspective of both national and international responsibility, a series of questions pose themselves: To whom is the government accountable when it fails to discharge its responsibility toward its citizens? To argue that it is the people of the country would be to give an obvious but only partial answer. The mere fact that a government that has failed dismally remains in power indicates the limits of national accountability. The alternative leverage can only be external. But to whom among the external actors or sources of influence, persuasive or coercive, can the people turn for remedies? What are the bases for such international responsibility? And to whom are the external actors responsible and accountable?

Any effort to address these issues in the context of both the assumed national sovereignty and international concern must build on several basic assumptions. First, although the state is under pressure from above and below, it will continue to be a central factor in national and international affairs. The state, however, has both international and national dimensions. The global dimension embraces subregional, regional, and international contexts, while the national dimension envisages internal structures: central, provincial, district, and local. Humanitarian and human rights problems emanating from internal conflicts need to be analyzed and responded to at each of these levels.

Second, the national structure is dominated by the laws, policies, and actions of the central government that, although pertinent to the maintenance of law and order, favor the status quo. Grossly disadvantaged citizens are therefore forced to choose between conformity and various forms and degrees of opposition, sometimes culminating in armed rebellion. Rather than being seen by the government as citizens to be protected, civilians who sympathize or are otherwise identified with such rebellion or opposition are perceived as adversaries. For people falling into the cracks of national identity or orphaned by state collapse, the only alternative source of protection, relief assistance, and rehabilitation toward a self-reliant development is the international community, both intergovernmental and nongovernmental.

Third, the existing legal and institutional frameworks for making these alternative sources available are fundamentally constrained by the state orientation of the international system and its commitment to national sovereignty. This presents something of a dilemma. On the one hand, the cooperation of the states is needed to move the international system to respond to the call of the needy within the framework of national sovereignty. On the other hand, the mere fact that the international community is needed implies the failure of national sovereignty and inadequacy of exclusive dependence on the state for the welfare of its citizens.

The fourth assumption logically flows from the third: as long as the international system remains state oriented, any policies and strategies to help a population within the framework of national sovereignty must first aim at winning the cooperation of the government. When a government refuses to cooperate, thereby exposing large numbers of citizens to suffering and perhaps death, the international community, intergovernmental or nongovernmental actors, must make it clear that such a state of affairs ultimately threatens global order and will not be tolerated. Seeking policies, norms, and strategies that strike the delicate balance between what is expected of the state in exercising the responsibilities associated with sovereignty and international measures aimed at complementing national efforts or remodeling the failures of governments to live up to their responsibilities becomes the challenge.

As noted earlier, the guiding principle for reconciling these positions is to assume that under normal circumstances, governments are concerned about the welfare of their people. Governments will provide their people with adequate protection and assistance, and if unable, will invite or welcome foreign assistance and international cooperation to supplement their own efforts. Controversy arises only in the exceptional cases when the state has collapsed or the government is unwilling to invite or permit international involvement, even though the level of human suffering and loss of lives dictates otherwise. This emergency often occurs in civil conflicts characterized by racial, ethnic, or religious crises of national identity in which the conflicting parties perceive the affected population as part of "the enemy." To fill the vacuum of moral responsibility created by such cleavages, international intervention becomes a moral imperative.

In sum, the perspective that sovereignty is shared responsibility means attention to the domestic performance of governments. It also means invoking states' accountability to the international community in its various forms from the United Nations to other intergovernmental organizations to the wide array of nongovernmental organizations at subregional, regional, and global levels.

Approaching conflict management or resolution in terms of the responsibilities of sovereignty is important. That viewpoint can deepen understanding of the domestic performances of governments and clarify states' accountability to domestic and international constituencies. Rewarding positive national performance through international programs of security, economic, and humanitarian cooperation should provide an incentive for governments to score high marks. Sovereignty as responsibility is therefore as much a national obligation as it is a global imperative.

SOVEREIGNTY
AS
RESPONSIBILITY

1

Normative Framework of Sovereignty

*T*HE premise of the normative analysis in this volume is to recognize internal conflicts and their consequences as falling within the domestic jurisdiction and therefore national sovereignty of the country concerned. However, it is also recognized that sovereignty carries with it certain responsibilities for which governments must be held accountable. And they are accountable not only to their national constituencies but ultimately to the international community. In other words, by effectively discharging its responsibilities for good governance, a state can legitimately claim protection for its national sovereignty.

The challenges posed by internal conflicts have two aspects. One is establishing and applying an effective system of conflict prevention, management, and resolution nationally, regionally, and globally; the other is providing protection and assistance to those affected by conflict, whether through the violation of their fundamental human rights or by being deprived of basic survival needs. In both cases, the state, the centerpiece of the international system, is often not capable or willing to provide adequate solutions or remedies, especially as the government is in most cases a party to the conflict and a principal target of the demands for human rights protection and humanitarian assistance. And because it is partisan, the government often acts as a barrier. It prevents the international community from providing protection and assistance to the needy and helping in the search for an end to destructive violence. Such resistance to outside involvement is often justified by the invocation of national sovereignty.

Genesis of Sovereignty

Since its inception, sovereignty has developed through several overlapping phases, which may not be neatly delineated historically but which nonetheless signify an evolution. The first, represented by the Treaty of Westphalia, is the initial phase when the sovereign reigned supreme domestically and in its relations with the outside world. The second, following World War II, marks the erosion of sovereignty with the development of democratic values and institutions internally and with international accountability on the basis of human rights and humanitarian standards. With the greater assertion of these values following the end of the cold war, the third phase emerged as a reactive assertion of sovereignty by governments whose domestic performance renders them vulnerable to international scrutiny. The fourth is the contemporary pragmatic attempt at reconciling state sovereignty with responsibility. Given the racial, ethnic, and religious diversity that characterizes the African state, the tensions of fostering national unity out of such diversity, the repression that has marked postcolonial trends, and the more recent pressures for democratization across the continent, these phases have particular relevancy to the African context.

Sovereignty in legal and political theory was initially conceived in Europe as an instrument of authoritative control by the monarch over feudal princes in the construction of modern territorial states. It was believed that instability and disorder, seen as obstacles to a stable society, could only be overcome by viable governments capable of establishing firm and effective control over territory and populations.[1] The sovereign, as the lawmaker, was considered above the law. Indeed, law according to the "command theory" of the leading positivist jurist, John Austin, is "a rule laid down for the guidance of an intelligent being by an intelligent being having power over him."[2] According to this theory, law is considered the command of the sovereign who is habitually obeyed by his subjects. The power of the sovereign is supposedly not limited by justice or any ideas of good and bad, right or wrong.[3] "For Austin . . . any legal limit on the highest lawmaking power was an absurdity and an impossibility."[4] Even in contemporary literature, it is still argued that "sovereignty is a characteristic of power that relegates its holder to a place above the law. A sovereign is immune from law and only subject to self-imposed restrictions."[5] Although the form of government might vary among monarchy, aristocracy, or democracy, it is considered essential that governments maintain order through an effective exercise of sovereignty.

A corollary of the supremacy of the sovereign as the lawmaker is the postulated supremacy of the law, which allegedly places it above the scrutiny of morality. A sharp debate has persisted among legal theorists on the issue of supremacy of or "fidelity to law." This debate, initiated by H. L. A. Hart of Oxford and Lon L. Fuller of Harvard in two classic articles published by the *Harvard Law Review* in 1958, originally focused on offenses committed under the Nazi regime in Germany that were allegedly in conformity to Nazi law. Hart, following in the positivist tradition of Jeremy Bentham and John Austin, argued that the alleged offenders could not be held liable for acts that were legal according to the prevailing system unless retroactive legislation provided otherwise. Fuller, however, argued that there is an internal morality to law and that a legal system that so fundamentally violates that morality, as did the Nazi system, loses its legitimacy as law. "When we recognize this simple fact of everyday legal experience, it becomes impossible to dismiss the problems presented by the Nazi regime with a simple assertion: 'Under the Nazis there was law, even if it was bad law.' We have instead to inquire how much of a legal system survived the general debasement and perversion of all forms of social order that occurred under the Nazi rule, and what moral implications this mutilated system had for the conscientious citizen forced to live under it."[6]

In another context, Fuller was even more explicit in subjecting a legal system to the superior standards of his postulated internal morality of law.

To me there is nothing shocking in saying that a dictatorship which clothes itself with a tinsel of legal form can so far depart from the morality of order, from the inner morality of law itself, that it ceases to be a legal system. When a system calling itself law is predicated upon a general disregard by judges of the terms of the laws they purport to enforce, when this system habitually cures its legal irregularities, even the grossest, by retroactive statutes, when it has only to resort to forays of terror in the streets, which no one dares challenge, in order to escape even those scant restraints imposed by the pretense of legality—when all these things have become true of a dictatorship, it is not hard for me, at least, to deny to it the name of law.[7]

When Hart and Fuller debated the issue of fidelity to law with reference to the Nuremberg trials, they both agreed that Nazi war criminals should not be exonerated from guilt because they acted in accordance with German law. What they debated was whether, as Hart argued, a new law should have been passed to make illegal retroactively the Nazi laws under which those crimes had been committed, or, as Fuller contended, those laws had so violated the fundamental principles of morality and human dignity as to have ceased to be law.

Although foreign intervention on behalf of national or religious minorities is a well-established historical phenomenon, the Nuremberg trials and the mounting humanitarian and human rights movement following World War II represent a clear demarcation line for the erosion of sovereignty. Since then, the dilemmas of sovereignty and interdependence are clearly being resolved in favor of an international response system, which, though not fully developed, is normatively grounded in the fundamental values of human dignity. Although the details of these norms vary considerably, the principles involved are universal and have become largely adopted by the international community. For the most part, they are enshrined in the International Bill of Human Rights, composed of the Universal Declaration of Human Rights, the International Covenant on Civil and Political Rights, and the International Covenant on Economic, Social, and Cultural Rights. These documents represent the corpus of human rights law, which recognizes the inherent dignity and equality of all human beings and sets a common standard for their rights.[8]

The basic proposition of international human rights law is that "to qualify for the name of government, a government now has to meet certain standards, all of which involve restraints on the use of power: no torture, no brutalization; no seizure of property; no state terror; no discrimination on the basis of race, religion, or sex; no prevention of people leaving a particular country, and so on."[9] For assessing the responsibilities of sovereignty, Richard B. Lillich advances three major premises. One, " 'Humanity'—is the *raison dêtre* of any legal system." Two, "the international system for over 300 years, since the Peace of Westphalia, has not been fulfilling what should be its primary function, namely, the protection and development of the human dignity of the individual." Three, "Any proposed 'new world order' should be structured so as to maximize benefits not for States but for individuals living within States, all the way from freedom of speech and elections, on the one hand, to freedom from hunger and the right to education on the other hand."[10]

The argument that the interests of individuals should be paramount and the interests of the states subordinate and that the primary purpose of the state is to protect the interests of the individual is of course an ideologically controversial proposition. Essentially, it pits the individually oriented capitalist tradition against the communally oriented socialist tradition. In the African context, the tendency in anthropological literature has been to emphasize the communal aspect of the African traditional social systems. In the modern context, this aspect has been alleged to lay a theoretical foundation for the so-called Marxists and other socialists as a pretext for importing "scientific socialism" to Africa.

Quite apart from the individual orientation of the universalizing values behind the human rights movement, it can be argued that even in the indigenous African value system, the individual is ultimately the core of the social order. The community or the society that the state represents and protects is essentially the aggregation of all its individuals. Vicarious responsibility so characteristic of traditional African law of wrongs is essentially founded on the reciprocal interdependence between the individual and the group. The protection of every individual member is as important to the group as the group solidarity is a source of security for the individual. Where the individual acts in a manner detrimental to the interests of the community, it becomes a case of one individual against the collectivity of many individuals who constitute the community. Under those circumstances, the primacy of the community's interest is not that of an abstract notion of the state, but of the higher value of the greatest number of individuals who constitute or represent the collective interest of the whole. Only in that sense can or should the interest of the society be regarded as overriding the interest of the individual who, though of prime concern to the society, cannot be recognized as absolute.

Since the threat of the individual to the community is minimal compared with the danger that the awesome power of the state represents for the individual, the normative principles of governance should emphasize state protection for the individual. At the basic level, this consideration demands the provision of the essential requirements of life—physical security, food, shelter, medical care, gainful occupation, and family integrity. At the level of civil and political rights, it calls for democratic participation in the process of governing the larger society and in the making of its laws.

These principles impose on the international community a correlative responsibility for their enforcement. Indeed, it can be argued that the discovery of "the internal morality of law" in the Nazi regime, which Fuller advocated for the Nuremberg trials, would not have been possible without the intervention of external powers following the defeat of Germany. Herein lies the paradox of the supposed supremacy of sovereignty and the legitimizing function of the international order. That paradox was indeed inherent in the settlement of Westphalia, from which time "sovereignty created both the territorial state and the international system."[11]

The crisis of the legitimacy of a legal system is even more acute when a country suffers from the incompatibility of identities and the cultural and legal values that they postulate for the nation, a common feature of the pluralistic condition of the African state. If law is an expression of the distinctive values and institutional practices of a people organized politically into a nation or a state, then the coming of diverse peoples into one political framework requires a system that can accommodate them on more or less equitable terms. Otherwise the country may face a zero-sum conflict and possible disintegration.

The post–World War II erosion of sovereignty was expanded by the application of the right to self-determination, which provided the basis for the process of decolonization. One of the effective measures in contravention of the narrow concepts of absolute sovereignty was that of international sanctions against apartheid South Africa. Undoubtedly, the combination of internal and external pressures eventually culminated in the collapse of apartheid. The increasing wave of democratization that is sweeping the world constitutes another contemporary challenge to sovereignty. The evolution of increasing demands for democratic values, institutions, and practices has devolved the classic notion of sovereign will and authority to the people, who are increasingly becoming intolerant of the dictatorship of unaccountable government. It is becoming concomitantly recognized that the will of the people, democratically invested in the leaders they elect freely or otherwise accept as their representatives, entitles authorities to value and uphold the sovereignty of a nation. As W. Michael Reisman has written with reference to the illegitimacy of military dictatorship:

> It should not take a great deal of imagination to grasp what an awful violation of the integrity of the self it is when men with guns evict your government, dismiss your law, kill and destroy wantonly and control you and those you love by intimidation and terror. When that happens, all the other human rights that depend on the lawful institutions of government become matters for the discretion of the dictators. And when that happens, those rights cease. Military coups are terrible violations of the political rights of all the members of the collectivity, and they invariably bring in their wake the violation of all the other rights. Violations of the right to popular government are not secondary or less important. They are very, very serious human rights violations.
>
> International human rights, it bears repeating, are matters of international concern. They are not shielded by domestic jurisdiction. Indeed, this aspect of the international law of human rights has even affected the law of recognition. A verifiably popular government has become an important component of the international legitimacy of an elite.[12]

Devolving power through an extensive system of decentralization is one of the ways of sharing sovereignty with the national population.[13] Domestic distribution of power and the demand for government accountability to the people clearly defuse the exercise of sovereignty by the state.

It has been argued that sovereignty derives from three principal sources: the degree of respect merited by an institution, the capacity to rule, and the recognition that the authority acts on behalf of and for the benefit of the people.[14] These principles are not only demanded by the population of the state concerned but also sanctioned by the international community, primarily in the name of fundamental human rights. Indeed, since the signing of the UN Charter and the adoption of the Universal Declaration of Human Rights, boundaries of state sovereignty have become more and more porous. Areas that were previously considered within the domestic domain of states, such as minority and individual rights, have become open to external scrutiny. The vast range of human rights agreements signed by UN member states not only oblige governments to protect the human rights and welfare of their citizens, but also require them to allow other governments to review their records. When governments do not fulfill their obligations, it is understood that they open themselves up to on-site monitoring and visits, criticism, condemnation, sanctions, and even armed intervention where regional or international peace is threatened. They also open themselves up to the forced delivery of humanitarian assistance to besieged civilians.[15] Under the leadership of the United States, particularly in the 1970s, international scrutiny of states on the basis of their human rights record was asserted more strongly. Indeed, the "internationalization of human rights," which President Jimmy Carter enunciated when he "startled the world with his insistence that the United States would henceforth take seriously its commitment to the advancement of human rights without controversial regard for national boundaries" has become commonplace, if still controversial, practice and wanting in enforcement procedures.[16]

Post–cold war dynamics appear to be reinforcing the universality of humanitarian values and the need for subordinating conventional notions of sovereignty to the imperatives of those values.[17] As has been observed:

> In the post–Cold War world . . . a new standard of intolerance for human misery and human atrocities has taken hold . . . Something quite significant has occurred to raise the consciousness of nations to the plight of peoples within sovereign borders. There is a new commitment—expressed in both moral and legal terms—to alleviate the suffering of oppressed or devastated people. To argue today that norms of sovereignty, non-use of force, and the sanctity of internal affairs are paramount to the collective human rights of people, whose lives and well-being are at risk, is to avoid the hard questions of international law and to ignore the march of history.[18]

The conclusions of a 1992 international conference on human rights protection for internally displaced persons underscored the extent of changes in perspectives on the confrontation between the universal standards of human rights and the parochialism of traditional ideas of sovereignty. The report on the conference states that the "steady erosion" of the concept of absolute sovereignty is making it easier for international organizations, governments, and nongovernmental organizations to intervene when governments refuse to meet the needs of their populations and substantial numbers of people are at risk. The concept of sovereignty, it continues, is becoming understood more in terms of conferring responsibilities on governments to assist and protect persons residing in their territories; "If governments failed to meet their obligations, they risked undermining their legitimacy."[19] The scrutiny of world public opinion as represented by the media makes it difficult for governments to ignore these obligations or defend their failure to act. The report noted, "Participants considered it essential for the international community to continue to 'chip away' and 'pierce' narrow definitions of sovereignty so that sovereignty would not be as great a barrier to humanitarian intervention."[20]

Scholarly opinion is also rallying behind a radical reassessment of the place and value of sovereignty in the contemporary world. Louis Henkin, for instance, has argued that "we might do well to relegate the term to the shelf of history as a relic from an earlier era. . . . As applied to a State, elements long identified with 'sovereignty' are inevitably only metaphors, fictions, fictions upon fictions."[21] In another context, Henkin pursues the same argument and declares "that it is time to bring 'sovereignty' down to earth, cut it down to size, discard its overblown rhetoric; to examine, analyze, reconceive the concept and break out its normative content; to repackage it, even rename it, and slowly ease the term out of polite language in international relations, surely in law."[22]

W. Michael Reisman sees "sovereignty" as "popular," and not as "state" sovereignty. As he said in the context of international intervention in Haiti, "In modern international law, what counts is the sovereignty of the people and not a metaphysical abstraction called the state. If the de jure government, which was elected by the people, wants military assistance, how is its sovereignty violated? And if the purpose of the coercion is to reinstate a de jure government elected in a free and fair election after it was ousted by a renegade military, whose sovereignty is being violated? The military's?"[23]

Although the substantive principles of international human rights and humanitarian law have become widely accepted, their implementation and international enforcement remain more of an aspiration than a reality, even though post–cold war developments have witnessed some dramatic, if selective, exceptions. Certainly, during the past several decades, through various monitoring and reporting procedures of the human rights bodies, the implementation process has progressed considerably.

The area of humanitarian intervention has witnessed the greatest erosion of sovereignty, mostly with the consent of the states but at times through forceful enforcement. Although the narrow concept of sovereignty remains a major obstacle to assisting and protecting victims of internal conflicts, it is no longer as insurmountable as it once was. There have been successful efforts by the UN agencies, other governments, and nongovernmental organizations to provide humanitarian assistance. One of the pioneering examples of major international humanitarian assistance in a civil war situation was Operation Lifeline Sudan, negotiated by the United Nations with the government of Sudan in 1989 and then agreed to by the rebel forces of the Sudan People's Liberation Movement and its army, SPLM/SPLA. This agreement enabled the United Nations and voluntary agencies to provide food, medicine, and needed relief to displaced populations throughout the country. Both sides also agreed on zones of peace or "corridors of tranquility" in the areas of conflict to enable the passage of humanitarian relief assistance.[24]

What was negotiated in Operation Lifeline Sudan was achieved by forceful international action in Iraq, where in the aftermath of the Persian Gulf War in 1991, the United Nations authorized a military operation to establish safe havens on Iraq's territory to enable the international community to assist and protect displaced Kurds. Similar measures were taken in Somalia, where, after the ouster of the military dictator, Siad Barre, clan-based militia leaders embarked on terrorist violence that blocked the delivery of humanitarian relief assistance to large numbers of the affected population. The same principles have guided international action in the former Yugoslavia and in Rwanda, where the humanitarian concerns justified intervention and where tribunals have been set up to try individuals charged with war crimes and crimes against humanity. Although these cases were characterized by total or partial collapse of the state or its severe incapacity to deliver, they illustrate the growing resolve of the international community to override sovereignty in support of international human rights and humanitarian intervention.

Nevertheless, mechanisms and procedures of implementation of the wide array of human rights and humanitarian standards remain undeveloped and grossly inadequate. As the international community has become more assertive, vulnerable governments have reacted more definitively against the erosion of state sovereignty. This indeed marks the third phase of the evolution of sovereignty. Governments that are threatened by the erosion of narrow concepts of sovereignty and are defensively trying to reassert it use the argument of cultural relativity and characterize the universality concept as a Western ploy to interfere in the internal affairs of other countries. Yet others invoke the need for unity as a national priority. Others simply assert national sovereignty as their shield.

In this war of cultures, African countries, along with other third world countries, appear to seek leadership from China. During the 1993 session of the Commission on Human Rights, in a discussion of the item on internally displaced persons, the representative of China submitted the most stringent defense of sovereignty, while simultaneously stressing that the promotion of human rights and fundamental freedoms is "a lofty goal of mankind." Citing the UN Charter and its insistence that the development of "friendly relations among nations be based . . . on the principle of sovereign equality of all members," China warned against interference in internal affairs of other countries by the "self-interested" concepts of human rights, values, and ideologies of "a few countries."[25]

The Chinese maintained that although the cold war had come to an end and the international situation had undergone significant changes, its vestiges were still affecting the work of the commission. "The practices of distorting human rights standards, exerting political pressure through abuse of monitoring mechanisms, applying selectivity and double standards have led to the violation of principles and purposes of the UN Charter, and the impairing of the sovereignty and dignity of many developing countries. Thus the beautiful term of human rights has been tarnished." The statement went on to say:

The urgent issue is to remove as soon as possible the imposition of their own human rights concepts, values and ideology by a few countries who style themselves as 'human rights judges': and the interference in internal affairs of other countries by using human rights as a means of applying political pressure. The victims of such practice are developing countries whose people suffered from violation of human rights and fundamental freedoms for a long time before and are now making great efforts to safeguard their sovereignty and independence for their survival and development.[26]

Another country that has championed the third world cause in the reassertion of sovereignty is Cuba. In the view of Cuba, "the Commission [on Human Rights] constituted an ideal forum from which to launch resistance to a 'new world order' in which 'humanitarian intervention' was merely a euphemism for attempts forcibly to impose certain ideological conceptions of human rights on a number of countries, chiefly, though not exclusively, in the third world."[27]

The view expressed by the delegation of the Sudan, whose government's human rights situation was under consideration by the commission, was identical to those of China and Cuba. Of all African countries, the Sudan is the one where the conflict between the universality and the relativity of human rights standards has been most pronounced. This is largely because Sudan applies Sharia law, with Islamic penalties of amputation of limbs for theft, flogging for consumption or possession of alcohol, stoning to death for adultery, and similar punishments that Gaspar Biro, the UN special rapporteur on the human rights situation in the Sudan, has declared in conflict with the provisions of relevant international human rights instruments to which the Sudan is a party.[28] The government of the Sudan saw the special rapporteur's criticism as totally inappropriate and unacceptable. The government's position was that Sharia laws were not only reflective of Sudanese cultural values but were the dictates of Islamic law. They were God-given and therefore could not be said to conflict with universal standards. If they were indeed in conflict, Islamic laws must prevail.[29] The statement in the report that the government objected to the most was the one that rejected culture or religion as a justification for the laws:

> Since the Sudan has ratified the International Covenant on Civil and Political Rights and the Convention on the Rights of the Child, the cultural argument that this practice is deeply rooted in the tradition of the country and is accepted by the people is irrelevant. The above-mentioned provisions, which are an integral part of the legislation of the State, were formally promulgated by the competent organs through a coherent and comprehensive Criminal Act and constitute in penal matters the supreme source of law of the

country. It does not matter in this context who the drafter is nor what the sources of inspiration of these norms are. In terms of human rights the only question is whether or not the national legislation is compatible with the existing international instruments to which the Sudan is a party.[30]

Construing this as an attack on Islam, Sudan tried to wage a major campaign against the special rapporteur, claiming that his "criticism and adverse comments on the Islamic Sharia echoed worldwide and generated protests all over the Islamic world."[31] Gaspar Biro, however, continued to enjoy the confidence and support of the international community and both the Commission on Human Rights and the General Assembly renewed his mandate as special rapporteur, clearly indicating the power of the international human rights agenda over the relativist claims of governments, however cloaked in religious garb they might be.

The mere fact that the Sudan proposed an annual compilation of the human rights records of all countries implies recognition of the limits of sovereignty. So does the Chinese recognition of human rights and fundamental freedoms as lofty goals of humankind. Nevertheless, the third world concern about the possible abuse of intervention is shared by some neutral observers. One has written, "It is well-known that the practice of intervention has diverged from international law with respect to 'less civilized,' 'non-Western,' 'developing' states, leaving intervention linked with imperialism and colonialism in historical memory."[32]

Even among the supporters of a more liberal interpretation of sovereignty, its erosion has been viewed with ambivalence, generating the need to reconcile sovereignty with responsibility. Former UN Secretary General Javier Perez de Cuellar highlighted the tension when he said in 1991: "We are clearly witnessing what is probably an irresistible shift in public attitudes towards the belief that the defense of the oppressed in the name of morality should prevail over frontiers and legal documents." But then he added the question, "Does [intervention] not call into question one of the cardinal principles of international law, one diametrically opposed to it, namely, the obligation of non-interference in the internal affairs of States?"[33] In his 1991 annual report, he wrote of the new balance that must be struck between sovereignty and the protection of human rights:

The principle of non-interference with the essential domestic jurisdiction of States cannot be regarded as a protective barrier behind
which human rights could be massively or systematically violated
with impunity. . . . The case for not impinging on the sovereignty,
territorial integrity and political independence of States is by itself
indubitably strong. But it would only be weakened if it were to carry
the implication that sovereignty, even in this day and age, includes
the right of mass slaughter or of launching systematic campaigns of
decimation or forced exodus of civilian populations in the name of
controlling civil strife or insurrection. With the heightened international interest in universalizing a regime of human rights, there
is a marked and most welcome shift in public attitudes. To try to
resist it would be politically as unwise as it is morally indefensible.
It should be perceived as not so much a new departure as more a
focused awareness of one of the requirements of peace.[34]

In place of exclusionary notions of sovereignty, de Cuellar called for
a "higher degree of cooperation and a combination of common sense
and compassion," arguing that "we need not impale ourselves on the
horns of a dilemma between respect for sovereignty and the protection
of human rights. . . . What is involved is not the right of intervention
but the collective obligation of States to bring relief and redress in
human rights emergencies."[35]

Current Secretary General Boutros Boutros-Ghali, in *An Agenda for
Peace*, wrote that "the time of absolute and exclusive sovereignty . . .
has passed," that "its theory was never matched by reality," and that
it is necessary for leaders of states "to find a balance between the
needs of good internal governance and the requirements of an ever
more interdependent world."[36]

In another context, Boutros-Ghali elaborated his views on sovereignty by highlighting the need to rethink the concept in the contemporary global context:

A major intellectual requirement of our time is to rethink the question of sovereignty—not to weaken its essence, which is crucial to
international security and cooperation, but to recognize that it may
take more than one form and perform more than one function. This
perception could help solve problems both within and among
states. And underlying the rights of the individual and the rights of

peoples is a dimension of universal sovereignty that resides in all humanity and provides all peoples with legitimate involvement in issues affecting the world as a whole. It is a sense that increasingly finds expression in the gradual expansion of international law.[37]

Living up to the responsibilities of sovereignty becomes in effect the best guarantee for sovereignty. As one observer commented, "Governments could best avoid intervention by meeting their obligations not only to other states, but also to their own citizens. If they failed, they might invite intervention."[38]

This was indeed the point made by the secretary general of the Organization of African Unity, Salim Ahmed Salim, in his bold proposals for an OAU mechanism for conflict prevention and resolution. "If the OAU, first through the Secretary General and then the Bureau of the Summit, is to play the lead role in any African conflict," he said, "it should be enabled to intervene swiftly, otherwise it cannot be ensured that whoever (apart from African regional organizations) acts will do so in accordance with African interests."[39] Criticizing the tendency to respond only to worst-case scenarios, Salim emphasized the need for preemptive intervention: "The basis for 'intervention' may be clearer when there is a total breakdown of law and order . . . and where, with the attendant human suffering, a spill-over effect is experienced within the neighboring countries. . . . However, preemptive involvement should also be permitted even in situations where tensions evolve to such a pitch that it becomes apparent that a conflict is in the making."[40]

The secretary general suggested that the OAU should take the lead in transcending the traditional view of sovereignty, building on the African values of kinship solidarity and the notion that "every African is his brother's keeper."[41] Considering that "our borders are at best artificial," Salim argued, "we in Africa need to use our own cultural and social relationships to interpret the principle of non-interference in such a way that we are enabled to apply it to our advantage in conflict prevention and resolution."[42] The secretary general's call challenges the organization to stipulate principles or norms for conflict prevention that would promote democracy, fundamental human rights, and good governance. These in essence are the principles that the proposed Conference on Security, Stability, Development, and Cooperation in Africa, the so-called Helsinki Process for Africa, which was initiated by General Olusegun Obasanjo and the Africa Leadership Forum, aims at promoting and which the new OAU mechanism has in part institutionalized.

The normative frameworks proposed by the OAU secretary general and the UN secretary general's *An Agenda for Peace* are predicated on respect for the sovereignty and integrity of the state as crucial to the existing international system. Human rights, however, are of transcendent importance as a legitimate area of concern for the international community. This is especially true when order has broken down or the state is incapable or unwilling to act responsibly to protect the masses of citizens. In that case international inaction would be quite indefensible. After all, internal conflicts in Africa as elsewhere often entail a contest of the national arena of power and therefore sovereignty. Every political intervention from outside has its internal recipients, hosts, and beneficiaries. Under those circumstances, there can hardly be said to be an indivisible quantum of national sovereignty behind which the nation stands united.

Furthermore, it is not always easy to determine the degree to which a government of a country devastated by civil war can be said to be truly in control, when, as is often the case, sizable portions of the territory are controlled by rebel or opposing forces. Oftentimes, as the civil wars in Angola, Mozambique, and the Sudan demonstrated, while a government may remain in effective control of the capital and the main garrisons, political order in much of the countryside in the war zone will have practically collapsed. How would such partial, but significant, collapse be evaluated in determining the degree to which civil order in the country has broken down? Indeed, the international community modifies its traditional ideas of sovereignty when it finds civilian populations in areas of states controlled by insurgent groups. Then the international community sometimes deals directly with those populations and insurgent movements. Increasingly, humanitarian agencies have been establishing dialogues with nongovernmental actors in order to reach persons on all sides of conflict situations, and nongovernmental organizations have been monitoring the compliance of nongovernmental actors with international humanitarian law. Direct contact with insurgent authorities has become an indispensable aspect of dealing with internal displacement and other humanitarian tragedies. The alternatives, therefore, as the case of the Sudan demonstrates, are not just the central government or the international community but nongovernmental actors as well. Somalia and Liberia have shown that this is particularly evident in failed states where there is no central governing authority and where UN agencies and others deal with local actors in charge of particular areas as well as with the local population directly.

It is most significant that the Security Council, in its continued examination of the secretary general's report, *An Agenda for Peace*, welcomed the observations contained in the report concerning the relationship between the humanitarian assistance and international peacemaking, peacekeeping, and peace building. In particular, the council established that under certain circumstances, there may be a close relationship between acute needs for humanitarian assistance and threats to international peace and security, which trigger international involvement. The council indeed "[noted] with concern the incidence of humanitarian crises, including mass displacements of population, becoming or aggravating threats to international peace and security."[43] It further expressed the belief "that humanitarian assistance should help establish the basis for enhanced stability through rehabilitation and development."[44]

Of course, despite increasing international response to domestic crisis situations, the tug of war between traditional notions of sovereignty and the evolving international society has not yet been decisively resolved, although considerable progress has been made. The conclusion of a conference on sovereignty noted:

From one point of view, we may be witnessing the very beginning of a period in which the balance between state sovereignty and international authority is shifting decisively. It is difficult to ignore the increasing resort to international intervention with or without government consent, or the structural changes that appear to be eroding the traditional authority of the sovereign state. Nevertheless, it is undoubtedly premature to declare that international society has moved beyond Westphalia and has overcome the idea of state sovereignty. The state system endures, even if states increasingly share authority with intergovernmental and nongovernmental organizations. The question remains an important one, and both scholars and practitioners are still forced to grapple with the complexity and ambiguity of the relationship between state sovereignty and international intervention.[45]

Nevertheless, the process of subjecting national authority to international standards of responsible sovereignty seems to be irreversibly advancing. As Burundi and Rwanda, and to a degree the Sudan have shown, this response is particularly true in emergency situations signifying the breakdown of the kind of public peace, security, and stability that the state was created to ensure and preserve. Effective sovereignty implies a system of law and order that is responsive to the needs of the national population for justice and general welfare. When things fall apart so that not only can peace, security, and public order not be guaranteed but the system becomes challenged by a rebellion with significant legitimacy and effectiveness, then the authority of those entrusted with sovereignty falls into question. Although law and order are overriding objectives, they cannot be seen as concepts of value-free control and authority. Rather they are elements of a legitimate exercise of power in pursuit of the common objectives of the community or the nation, and above all, of universal standards of human dignity. Can a country with a legal system like that of the Sudan be said to provide a national common ground responsive to the national quest for justice and equitable welfare? The Sudan is applying an Islamic legal system (Sharia) to a country of religious pluralism reinforced by entrenched racial, ethnic, and cultural diversity. What resort do the non-Muslims and the secularist Muslims have but appeal to universal standards and enforcement mechanisms? And can these appeals be effective without imposing limits on exclusionary notions of sovereignty?

Universality and cultural or contextual relativity was heavily debated at the Vienna World Conference on Human Rights in 1993 and although positions were sharply divided, a consensus emerged that reaffirmed the universality principle with the need for sensitivity to the particularities of cultures and national contexts. "All human rights are universal, indivisible and interdependent and interrelated. The international community must treat human rights globally in a fair and equal manner, on the same footing, and with the same emphasis. While the significance of national and regional particularities and various historical, cultural and religious backgrounds must be borne in mind, it is the duty of States, regardless of their political, economic and cultural systems to promote and protect all human rights and fundamental freedoms."[46]

The conference report emphasized the universality of human rights in a language that is clearly intended as a limitation on the use of sovereignty by vulnerable governments: "The promotion and protection of all human rights and fundamental freedoms must be considered as a priority objective of the United Nations in accordance with its purposes and principles, in particular the purpose of international cooperation. In the framework of these purposes and principles, the promotion and protection of all human rights is a legitimate concern of the international community. The organs and specialized agencies related to human rights should therefore further enhance the coordination of their activities based on the consistent and objective application of international human rights instruments."[47]

Anatomy of Conflict in Africa

Understanding the causes of internal conflicts in Africa, the required response to their humanitarian consequences, and the measures needed to prevent future conflicts and manage or resolve ongoing ones all pose practical questions about the assumptions and concepts of values that should guide national decisionmakers and the international community. In the search for normative principles it should be safe to reaffirm human dignity as an overarching goal to which all peoples and societies aspire and are committed, whatever the variations of their cultural perspectives on the details of the concept. Stated in political terms, the quest for human dignity is translatable into a demand for recognition and respect for human beings, both as individuals and as members of identifiable groups, for freedom from domination, equitable participation in political, economic, social, and cultural life, and for a fair share in the distribution of national wealth, services, employment opportunities, and resources for development. Human dignity demands, in other words, equal treatment with full rights and duties of citizenship. But, at a minimum, it requires basic protection and provision of survival needs—safety, food, shelter, medicine, family, and resources for a self-sustaining lifestyle.

In many parts of Africa, the threat to human dignity is often rooted in the politics of identity and competition for power and scarce resources, which often clash with the demands of nation building. On the one hand, individual and group identities and loyalties often rotate around such descent-oriented institutions as the family, the clan, the tribe (or ethnic group), language, and their correlative regional affiliations. On the other hand, forging national unity requires transcending these concepts and developing a more comprehensive community. The crisis of national identity emanates not only from the conflict between the exclusive and the inclusive notions of identity, but also from the tendency of the dominant, hegemonic groups to try to impose their identity as the framework for the national identity and a basis for power-sharing and resource allocation. This inevitably provides ground for discrimination, national integration, or both. As Stephen John Stedman has observed, "Conflict in Africa arises from problems basic to all populations: the tugs and pulls of different identities, the differential distribution of resources and access to power, and competing definitions of what is right, fair, and just."[48]

The myths of superiority associated with the dominance of the hegemonic groups nearly always run against the countermyths of self-esteem and defensive assertiveness of the disadvantaged minority or politically weaker groups. Studies of relatively isolated societies indicate that virtually all groups and individuals in their own specific cultural contexts not only demand respect as human beings, but ethnocentrically assume that they represent the ideal model. As has been observed, ethnocentrism essentially means, "One's own group is the center of everything, and all others are scaled and rated with reference to it. Folkways correspond to it to cover both the inner and the outer relation. Each group nourishes its own pride and vanity, boasts of itself as superior, exalts its own divinities, and looks with contempt on outsiders. Each group thinks its own folkways the only right ones, and if it observes that other groups have other folkways, these excite its scorn."[49]

It is only when members of different cultures come in contact and begin to interact with others and are adversely affected by the competition and conflict entailed in that interaction because of their relative military, economic, or other weakness that they begin to see themselves in less favorable light. The new hierarchy may become internalized and accepted as reality, or it may provoke an embittered and violent reaction that may take the form of armed rebellion or insidious criminal behavior. "In a political environment lacking an overriding consensus on values and issues, adversarial politics . . . can go beyond healthy competition and contribute to intense and highly destructive conflicts."[50]

In most African countries, the sources and causes of conflict are generally recognized as inherent in the traumatic experience of colonial state-formation, which brought together diverse groups that were paradoxically kept separate and unintegrated. Regional ethnic groups were broken up and affiliated with others within the artificial borders of the new state, with colonial masters imposing a superstructure of law and order to maintain relative peace and tranquility.

The independence movement was a collective struggle for self-determination that reinforced the notion of unity within the artificial framework of the newly established nation-state. Initially, independence came as a collective gain that did not disaggregate who was to get what from the legacy of the centralized power and wealth. But colonial institutions had divested the local communities and ethnic groups of much of their indigenous autonomy and sustainable livelihood and replaced them with some centralized authority and dependency on the welfare state system. Once control of these institutions passed on to the nationalists at independence, the struggle for control became unavoidable. The outcome was often conflict—over power, wealth, and development—that led to gross violations of human rights, denial of civil liberties, disruption of economic and social life, and consequent frustration of development.

As the cold war raged, however, some saw these conflicts not as domestic struggles for power and resources but as extensions of the superpower ideological confrontation. Rather than help resolve them peacefully, the superpowers often worsened the conflict by providing military and economic assistance to their allies.

Although the end of the cold war has removed this aggravating external factor, it has also removed the moderating role of the superpowers, both as third parties and mutually neutralizing allies. As Liberia, Ethiopia, Somalia, Mozambique, and Sudan illustrate, the results have been tragic brutalities and devastation.

It can credibly be argued that the gist of these internal conflicts is that the ethnic pieces that were put together by the colonial glue, and reinforced by the old world order, are now pulling apart and reasserting their autonomy or independence.

Old identities, undermined and rendered dormant by the structures and values of the nation-state system, are reemerging and redefining the standards of participation, distribution, and legitimacy. In fact, it may be even more accurate to say that the process has been going on in a variety of ways and within the context of the constraints imposed by the nation-state system.

The larger the gap in the patterns of participation and distribution based on racially, ethnically, or religiously determined forms of identity, the more likely the breakdown of civil order and the conversion of political confrontation into violent conflict. When the conflict turns violent, the issues at stake become transformed into a fundamental contest for state power. The objectives may vary in degree from a demand for autonomy to a major restructuring of the national framework to be captured by the demand-making group or to be more equitably reshaped. When the conflict escalates into a contest for the "soul" of the nation, it turns into an intractable "zero-sum" confrontation. The critical issue then is whether the underlying sense of injustice, real or perceived, can be remedied in a timely manner that avoids the zero-sum conflict and the consequent high level of violence. As the preliminary report of the Arusha Consultation on Africa's internal conflicts put it, "The general conviction was that, despite their apparently diverse causes, complex nature and manifold forms, internal conflicts in Africa were basically the result of denial of basic democratic rights and freedoms, broadly conceived; and that they tended to be triggered-off by acts of injustice, real or imagined, precisely in situations where recourse to democratic redress seemed hopeless."[51] The report summarized the challenge of conflicts as symbolizing a quest for justice:

> The most comprehensive set of "preventive measures" in this regard was thought to be the development and maintenance of a democratic state in which, among other things, civil society was vibrant, there was effective justice and the rule of law, there was equitable access to political power and economic resources by all citizens and groups, the various regions of the country were treated fairly and equitably in all matters of public concern, and there was sufficient economic growth and development to ensure reasonably decent livelihood or at least realistic hope for social progress.[52]

Viewing the crisis from the global perspective, UN Secretary General Boutros Boutros-Ghali observed in *An Agenda for Peace*: "One requirement for solutions to these problems lies in commitment to human rights with a special sensitivity to those of minorities, whether ethnic, religious, social or linguistic."[53] On the need to balance the unity of larger entities' respect for sovereignty, autonomy, and diversity of various identities, the secretary general noted: "The healthy globalization of contemporary life requires in the first instance solid identities and fundamental freedoms. The sovereignty, territorial integrity, and independence of States within the established international system, and the principle of self-determination for peoples, both of great value and importance, must not be permitted to work against each other in the period ahead. Respect for democratic principles at all levels of social existence is crucial: in communities, within States and within the community of States. Our constant duty should be to maintain the integrity of each while finding a balanced design for all."[54]

Where discrimination or disparity is based on race, ethnicity, or region, it can be combated by appropriate constitutional provisions and laws protecting basic human rights and fundamental freedoms. Conflicting perspectives on the national identity, especially ones based on religion, are more difficult to harmonize. In some instances, the Sudan being an outstanding example, religion, ethnicity, and culture become so intertwined that they are not easy to disentangle. The zero-sum conflicts they generate indeed challenge the very notion of sovereignty and the survival of the nation. For that reason, the report of the Arusha consultation states: "Two sociological factors were considered pivotal in the internal conflict equations in Africa. One was religious fundamentalism, the other, ethnicity. Both needed to be carefully monitored."[55] Monitoring them is indeed critical and urgent, since they are at the core of the challenge of nation building in countries that are religiously, ethnically, and culturally mixed, especially where these forms of identity correlate and deepen internal divisions.

African Policy Agenda

Internal conflicts and their consequences are primarily matters of internal concern. That is a basic assumption on which sovereignty as a pivotal, normative concept in the analysis of conflict is predicated. However, in the interdependent world of today, no matters, including resolving, preventing, and managing conflicts, can be exclusively the concern of any country. The interconnection of regional security situations, and in particular the spillover effects of conflicts, have direct impact on countries of the region concerned. Beyond the region, the tragedies that result from internal conflicts are nearly always the concern of the international community. All these impose responsibilities on governments, which limit their national sovereignty and make them accountable to both the national population and the international community.

The core of such responsibility is good governance, which implies the management of all internal affairs, including ethnic relations, the economy, and foreign policy. That implies opening the domestic conditions and governmental policies to multilevel scrutiny, which links interactive contexts. The very foundations of the African state imply a linkage of levels from local to global. A prominent feature of this linkage is the colonial experience. Since most countries in Africa have now been independent for several decades, however, it is becoming increasingly inappropriate to blame Africa's problems on colonial policies. Instead the focus should be on the postcolonial agenda of national governments, which bear the responsibilities of sovereignty, even though the external linkages created by the colonial legacy linger on. Among the principal elements on the postcolonial agenda are the national policy priorities, their operational implications, the current demand for reforms, and the required mechanisms and strategies for such reform.

The preoccupying policy objectives of independent Africa initially centered around nation building and accelerated economic and social development. It was believed by many that building the nation required a unitary form of government and a strong centralized authority. To these leaders, national unity was an assumed framework and its consolidation an overriding imperative. Since ethnicity or "tribalism" was perceived as a threat to national unity, it was at best pragmatically managed through disbursement of positions and material allocations and at worst repressed. For the same purpose of creating unity, political pluralism, as manifested in a multiparty system, trade union and professional movements, freedom of the press, and other institutional means of expressing opposition or dissent, was often discouraged, indeed repressed.

Economic and social development was expected as the immediate reward of independence and was seen in terms of rapid growth, equitable distribution, building of roads and communication systems, and provision of free education, health care, and other social services.

As the state was the only entity equipped to finance and manage development, central planning and state monopoly were considered the pillars of the economy. Bilateral security and economic assistance, although solicited and certainly welcomed by politically insecure leaders, was linked with neocolonial motivation by the politically conscious public. Such assistance was either resisted or accepted with the stipulation that there be no strings attached. In the Sudan in the early 1960s, public demonstrations against U.S. aid occurred, and Sudan rejected the Peace Corps.

The implication of these objectives was the adoption of policies and strategies that were to prove disastrous for the security and development of many African countries. Politically, one-party rule, authoritarianism, and military dictatorship became pervasive features of governance. Unity was misconceived as requiring uniformity and homogenization rather than acceptance of diversity. Political and civil liberties, fundamental human rights, and democratic principles were viewed as luxuries that the new nations could not afford. Economic mismanagement without transparency or accountability led to uncontrolled spending, corruption, and drastic deterioration in the economies of most countries. Far from pursuing equitable distribution, the political and economic system created new class structures with rapidly growing disparities between the rich, mostly in the urban centers, and the poor, composed of the rural masses and most of the urban populace.

Over the decades, the repercussions of the policies incrementally manifested themselves in mounting unrest, social tensions, civil violence, and ethnoregional conflicts. These repercussions in turn prompted more repression and militarization of politics, creating a vicious cycle of insecurity, instability, and even the collapse of states. This overall negative development has now entered a critical phase, which has generated the demand for reform and the reordering of the national policy agenda. The new agenda is emphasizing democratization, respect for fundamental individual and group rights, increasing the involvement of civil society in public life, a more efficient management of the economy, and above all, a leadership that is responsible, responsive, transparent, and accountable.

Although the state will continue to be pivotal to the welfare of the citizens, the excessive dependency on the state, which has grossly undermined the capacity of the population to generate a self-sustaining process of development from within, needs to be discouraged. Self-reliance can, in significant part, be encouraged through decentralization aimed at taking power to the people and tapping their local resources and resourcefulness. This objective will require encouraging the private sector, capacity building, access to capital, technology, and skills, and utilizing the indigenous structures, institutions, and organizations. A conducive climate must be created that ensures protection through the rule of law, respect for democratic freedoms and fundamental rights, and separation of powers. In particular the independence of the judiciary must be established.

These elements of the policy agenda can be said to be subsumed in the normative concept of human dignity, which is not merely a postulation of ideals but a phenomenon that drives the social processes of people seeking values. They may do so through institutions, using power or material resources to influence the outcome in terms of who gets what and how from the system. In this process, the equitable participation in the production and distribution (sharing) constitutes the overriding goal of promoting human dignity. Conversely, the denial of these fundamental values can be, and often is, a source of destructive conflicts resulting in widespread tragedies. Analysis of the trends in terms of the ideals of respecting human dignity is a policy perspective with significant implications as one examines the realities of who gets what from the system, on what basis, and with what consequences.

Articulating the normative framework of sovereignty is also important in policy analysis. Indeed, what makes the theme of sovereignty, responsibility, and accountability a useful tool of good governance is that it promises to set well-defined standards for gauging performance. The process provides an objective yardstick for evaluating one's own performance and the performance of others in the hierarchy of authority and control in the global system.

Ideally, from an instrumental or organizational perspective, problems should be addressed and solved within the immediate framework, with wider involvement necessitated only by the failure of the internal efforts. This means that conflict prevention, management, or resolution progressively moves from the domestic domain to the regional and ultimately the global levels of concern and action.

Those conflicts in which the state is an effective arbiter do not present particular difficulties since they are manageable within the national framework. The problem arises when the state itself is a party to the conflict. Under those conditions, external involvement becomes necessary. In the African context, it is generally agreed that the next best level of involvement should be regional organization such as the Economic Community of West African States (ECOWAS), the Intergovernmental Authority on Drought and Development (IGADD), and the Southern African Development Community (SADC). Next up the ladder would be the OAU. There are, however, constraints on these organizations. One has to do with the limitation of resources, material and human. But perhaps even more debilitating is the political will, since in the intimate context of the region, governments feel vulnerable to conflicts resulting from the problematic conditions of state formation and nation building and are therefore prone to resist any form of external scrutiny. And since the judge of today may well be the accused of tomorrow, there is a temptation to avoid confronting the problems. The result is evasiveness and neglect.

Beyond the OAU, the United Nations is the next logical organization as it represents the international community most broadly. But the United Nations also suffers from the constraints that affect the OAU, though to a lesser degree. It too has the problem of resources and the reciprocal protectiveness of vulnerable governments.

Mediating Sovereignty, Responsibility, and Accountability

Balancing between national sovereignty and the need for international action to provide protection and assistance to victims of internal conflicts would mean reaffirming the responsibility of sovereignty and accountability to the domestic and external constituencies as interconnected principles of the international order. To be legitimate, sovereignty must demonstrate responsibility, which means at the very least ensuring a certain level of protection for and providing the basic needs of the people.

But as UN Secretary General Boutros Boutros-Ghali stressed, "States and their governments cannot face or solve today's problems alone. International cooperation is unavoidable and indispensable. The quality, extent, and timeliness of such cooperation will make the difference between advancement or frustration and despair."[56]

Humanitarian intervention is the upper limit of reconciling sovereigny and responsibility with an affirmative exercise of international cooperation, accountability, and response mechanism. The choice for the state then becomes one of endeavoring to discharge its responsibilities or otherwise risk forfeiting its sovereignty. Rather than be perceived as a violation of sovereignty, humanitarian assistance in armed conflicts can and should indeed be seen as a complement and therefore fulfillment of national sovereignty.[57]

Invocations of sovereignty to justify the obstruction or denial of relief assistance to needy populations no longer command primacy over the needs of persons at risk. Humanitarian concerns have taken precedence over state imperatives, and governments are perceived as endangering their sovereignty by refusing to meet the humanitarian needs of their population.[58] The critical question, however, is under what circumstances the international community is justified in overriding sovereignty to protect the dispossessed population within state borders. The common assumption in international law is that to justify such action there must be a threat to international peace and security. The position now supported by the Security Council is that massive violations of human rights and displacement within a country's borders may constitute such a threat.[59] Others contend that a direct threat to international peace is too high a threshold because it would preclude action on too many humanitarian crises and that the time has come to recognize humanitarian concern as a ground for intervention. This ideal would require the development of normative standards as well as institutional arrangements, operational principles, and strategies.

With respect to legal standards, debate persists on whether or not existing law provides adequate bases for a comprehensive system of international protection and assistance of the needy within the context of sovereignty. This controversy is both descriptive and prescriptive. To demand international protection and assistance is to assume the existence of a legal justification. Between human rights law and humanitarian law, adequate basis for international protection and assistance exists. But the mere fact that there is need for improvement in the protection and assistance system implies some shortcoming that may be a problem of implementation but may also be owing to gaps in the law.[60] In either case, restatement of the law to clarify the legal bases and introduce any reforms necessary would be appropriate.[61]

Since the political will to act is often critical in providing the needed protection and assistance and in contributing to the setting of standards, the formulation of guiding principles may be as important, if not more so, as the promulgation of legally binding standards. Indeed, an array of proposals has been made in this connection. Some concern the grounds for intervention while others focus on the interveners and the manner of their intervention.[62]

In conceptualizing grounds and methods of intervention, human rights issues should be closely associated with humanitarian concerns and protection with assistance to form a composite whole that is compelling. Nevertheless, there is justified concern, exploitable by vulnerable governments, that powers with the capacity to intervene may hide behind the smoke screen of humanitarianism to pursue the narrow objectives of specific states. In order to circumscribe illegitimate justifications or abuse of humanitarianism for ulterior purposes, the United Nations should have the leadership responsibility for determining the existence of humanitarian crises that threaten international peace and security or otherwise justify international action. Recent events have, however, demonstrated that the role of the major Western powers acting unilaterally, multilaterally, or within the framework of the United Nations, though often susceptible to accusations of strategic motives, has become increasingly pivotal. Indeed, although their motives continue to be questioned, the problem is increasingly one of their unwillingness to become involved or lack of adequate preparedness for such involvement.

Perhaps the most important aspect of the involvement of Western industrial democracies in foreign conflicts is that they are often moved to act by the gravity of the tragedies involved. This makes their involvement an asset in addressing and thereby arresting the tragedy. It is also a limitation, however, because it misses opportunities to engage in preventive actions at an earlier stage. Even in humanitarian intervention, lack of preparedness for an appropriate, timely response and withdrawal is generally acknowledged as a major drawback, which in fact could "reinforce violent disintegration."[63]

Nevertheless, it is argued that there is strong presumption that the interests of Western countries "are very powerfully engaged and that they will eventually be driven to uphold [them]" and promote them through humanitarian intervention in crises. "Industrial democracies," it is argued, "cannot operate without defending standards of human rights and political procedures that are being egregiously violated." Indeed, "they cannot themselves prosper in an irreversibly internationalized economy if large contiguous populations descend into endemic violence and economic depression."[64]

As intervention is a significant intrusion from outside, and despite the obvious fact that there will always be elements in the country who will welcome such intervention, especially among the disadvantaged groups to whom it promises tangible benefits, resistance on the grounds of national sovereignty or pride is also predictable. In this sense, sovereignty becomes more than a state monopoly and is transformed into a notion of nationalistic or cultural pride, which is popularly shared by the people. This was dramatically demonstrated in Somalia where, after an initially positive response to Operation Restore Hope, some important groups turned against the international presence, eventually forcing the evacuation of the UN troops. The same dynamic appeared to be true in Rwanda, where the Tutsi-dominated government that seized power after the genocidal conflict of April–May 1994 became restless with the presence of the international community. It perceived the international presence as more concerned with monitoring the government's human rights performance than with providing resources in support of the government. In Burundi, although the Hutu majority needs protection from the international community against the Tutsi-dominated army, the Tutsi population was bitterly opposed to international military involvement.

Because foreign presence is often humiliating, the justification for and manner of intervention must be respectful of local sentiments and reliably persuasive, if not beyond reproach. "The difference between an intervention that succeeds and one that is destroyed by immune reaction would depend on the degree of spontaneous acceptance or rejection by the local population."[65] But, as Somalia demonstrated, initial acceptance is not enough. Continued prudence in managing the situation with deference and social skills is necessary to a long-term success of such a mission. The principles used and the objectives toward which it is targeted must transcend and yet remain mindful of political and cultural boundaries or traditions and concomitant nationalist sentiments. In other words, an intervention must enjoy an effective degree of local and global legitimacy. "The rationale that could conceivably carry such a burden presumably involves human rights so fundamental that they are not derived from any particular political or economic ideology."[66] Adopting guiding principles or a code of conduct stipulating these principles would not only provide the international community with standards for legitimate action, but could also facilitate conformity and preventive predisposition on the part of governments.[67]

Once principles have been decided upon, the strategy for preventive or corrective involvement in conflict should include gathering and analyzing information and otherwise monitoring situations with the view to establishing an early warning system. Through that system, the international community could be alerted and eventually mobilized to act, once violations of the agreed standards have exceeded the tolerable limits.

The quest for a system of response to conflict and attendant tragedies was outlined by the UN secretary general when he responded to the surging demands on the Security Council to be a central instrument for the prevention and resolution of conflicts. He wrote that the aims of the United Nations must be as follows:

To seek to identify at the earliest possible stage situations that could produce conflict, and to try through diplomacy to remove the sources of danger before violence results;

Where conflict erupts, to engage in peacemaking aimed at resolving the issues that have led to conflict;

Through peace-keeping, to work to preserve peace, however fragile, where fighting has been halted and to assist in implementing agreements achieved by the peacemakers;

To stand ready to assist in peace-building in its differing contexts: rebuilding the institutions and infrastructures of nations torn by civil war and strife; and building bonds of peaceful mutual benefit among nations formerly at war;

And in the largest sense, to address the deepest causes of conflict: economic despair, social injustice and political oppression. It is possible to discern an increasingly common moral perception that spans the world's nations and peoples, and which is finding expression in international laws, many owing their genesis to the work of this Organization.[68]

What is envisaged can be conceptualized as a three-phase strategy that would include monitoring the developments to draw early attention to impending crises, interceding in time to avert the crisis through diplomatic initiatives, and mobilizing international action when necessary.[69] The first step would aim at detecting and identifying the problem through various mechanisms for information collection, evaluation, reporting, and early warning. If sufficient basis for concern is established, the appropriate mechanism should be invoked to take preventive diplomatic measures to avert the crisis. Initially, such initiatives might be taken within the framework of regional arrangements, for example, the Organization of African Unity. In the context of the United Nations such preventive initiatives would naturally fall on the secretary general acting personally or through special representatives. If diplomatic initiatives do not succeed, and depending on the human suffering involved, the secretary general may decide to mobilize international response, ranging from further diplomatic measures to forced humanitarian intervention sanctioned by the Security Council. Such intervention is called for not only to provide emergency relief but also to facilitate the search for an enduring solution to the causes of the conflict.

Responsible Sovereignty in Perspective

In confronting the challenges of reconciling sovereignty with responsibility, certain principles are becoming increasingly obvious as policy guidelines. First, sovereignty carries with it responsibilities for the population. It is from acceptance of this responsibility that the legitimacy of a government derives. The relationship between the controlling authority and the populace should ideally ensure the highest standards of human dignity, but at a minimum it should guarantee basic health services, food, shelter, physical security, and other essentials.

Second, in many countries in which armed conflicts and communal violence cause massive internal displacement, the country is so divided on fundamental issues that legitimacy, and indeed sovereignty, are sharply contested. Consequently a strong faction always exists to invite or at least welcome external intervention. Under those circumstances, the validity of sovereignty must be judged by reasonable standards of how much of the population is represented, marginalized, or excluded.

Third, living up to the responsibilities of sovereignty implies the existence of a higher authority capable of holding the supposed sovereign accountable. Some form of international system has always existed to ensure that states conform to accepted norms or face consequences, in the form of unilateral, multilateral, or collective action. Equality among sovereign entities has always been a convenient fiction that has never been backed by realities because some powers have always been more dominant than others and therefore have been explicitly or implicitly charged with the responsibilities of enforcing the agreed norms of behavior.

Fourth, the dominant authority or power must assume responsibilities that transcend parochialism or exclusive national interests. That kind of leadership serves the broader interests of the community and the human family beyond the barriers of sovereignty.

No government that will allow hundreds of thousands, and maybe millions, of its citizens to starve to death when food can be made available to them, allow them to be exposed to deadly elements when they could be provided with shelter, or permit them to be indiscriminately tortured, brutalized, and murdered by contending forces can claim sovereignty. A government that allows its citizens to suffer in a vacuum of responsibility for moral leadership cannot claim sovereignty in an effort to keep the outside world from stepping in to offer protection and assistance.

2

Governance

*I*F sovereignty is responsibility, governing is managing conflict. Governors of sovereign states must make decisions to manage the conflict among policy options and groups. "To govern is to choose," said French Premier Pierre Mendès-France. Choosing means exercising the basic responsibility of the state to manage the conflicts of society, those that society does not manage of itself. The body politic—civil society—has its needs, interests, and demands, which it brings to the attention of the governors. In a perfect world, it would be possible to meet them all out of unlimited resources. But the world is not perfect and resources are limited. That limitation causes conflict among competing demands, and then among competing demanders within society. The job of governing is to manage these conflicts. Even when governments and candidates for government get ahead of current demands and put forward a program for their society's future betterment, they are managing conflicts by preempting them. In conducting its relations with other states, a government also manages conflict by winning it, by resolving it to the parties' satisfaction, or by overcoming it through mechanisms of cooperation. "Every decision," writes John P. Powelson, "is a conflict resolved."[1] There is little involved in government except parades that is not conflict management (and even then conflicts arise about marching orders).

This approach to the understanding of government is new, but there is nothing new in it. The many different, standard angles to the study of governance—for example, institutionalization, legitimization, problem solving, nation building, integration, and allocation, to name a few[2]—can all be related to the "exercise of political power to manage a [country's] affairs"[3] through the process of handling conflicting demands. This exercise, well or poorly realized, is designed to retain the

34

allegiance and participation of the demanders in the national political system. Thus understood, state building becomes a matter of establishing the institutions for this task; legitimization becomes a matter of building types of support for those who carry out the task; problem solving becomes a matter of building the power and procedures for providing appropriate answers to the groups' demands; nation building means transferring a sense of belonging from the group to the overarching state unit; integration and allocation means bringing such groups into a national interaction in such a way as to provide and distribute returns to them; and so on.

But an awareness of the common element behind these approaches, and an appreciation of the importance of the organizing focus for the deeper understanding of government's functions and the better evaluation of its performance, are new and are gifts from Africa. Not that any other continent could not have supported the same approach: the importance of the conflict management focus is its universality, to developed and developing polities alike. But the image of Africa as a continent of conflict composed of countries of conflict, although a caricature, draws attention to the need to understand government as the management of conflict. For all the examples of collapsed states and debilitating conflict that the continent provides, there are many more instances of successful management of the same types of conflicts that debilitated some states.[4] It is the many successful cases, in contrast to the few failures and their negative lessons, that force attention to the lessons of conflict management for effective governance.

Africa also reminds us of the current relevance and reality of the literature from two centuries ago on the social contract.[5] Today as earlier, the social contract notion seems basic but fictional, a return to mythical origins to explain a current situation, a political Genesis. But for African polities, the social contract is a part of recent history, a constitutional bargain written on a tabula rasa—written with colonial chalk and a nationalist hand, to be sure, but essentially a start from scratch. All problems and differences were overridden by the independence struggle, whether political or violent, and therefore the new state began with all its conflicts apparently managed. That this too was only mythology merely points to the importance of looking at governance as conflict management.

All is relative, and one can well argue that the slate was not completely clean: the competing colonial and nationalist influences affected something preexistent, that in turn influenced the impression made. In fact, one can even maintain that the colonial and nationalist layers were rather superficial and that underneath, African society led its own life, which had maintained a vigorous existence through colonial rule and nationalist protest.[6] This is not the place to deny that thesis or settle the argument, but rather to insist on a different one: that *politically*, in matters pertaining to state structures and state building, the colonial and nationalist influences predominated. Unlike the Fifth Republic after the Fourth in France, or the U.S. Constitution after the Articles of Confederation, the African constitutional bargain was not a reaction to and correction of a previous indigenous form but a new African creation. As such, it contained a social contract among the various groups and forces in society represented in the political life of the moment, ethnic groups as well as political elites, to continue, prevent, and settle conflicts among them inherited from the past and foreseeable in the future. Some such new constitutional bargains were better made than others, but all were new attempts to set up a political system for conflict management.

What is to be gained by introducing yet another way of conceiving of governance? Simply, posing the function as conflict management allows better answers to such basic questions as, How is governance practiced when it is practiced well? Why is it practiced badly? How can its practice be improved? When a well-routinized, solidly institutionalized, constitutionally based polity is functioning smoothly, the problems of administration or the philosophical underpinnings of policy debates may be on the top of the agenda. But in developing polities, where these conditions do not obtain, inattention to the basic element of conflict management prevents progress and may well produce the phenomena of state collapse and authoritarian reconstitution—the violent swings of the political pendulum—that prevent institutionalization and development from ever taking place. Even in well-established polities, inattention to the conflict management dimension can lead local grievances and policy debates to tear apart a seemingly stable system, as in Egypt or Peru.

Conflicts to be Managed

Whether it acts as a neutral arbiter or rulemaker or as a partisan steersman or policymaker, government is hired to manage conflicts.

These may be actual conflicts between scrapping constituents or potential conflicts among contradictory issues. They may elicit reactive efforts to calm the contest or preemptive policies to reduce future problems. In all cases, the conflicts are calls for the attention, resources, and energies of government, and whether government wants to defuse intergroup disputes or advance policies to solve problems, it is managing conflict.

Conflicts can be either normative or distributive, that is, about what is right or what is allocated, what is believed or what is possessed (or both). Differences in beliefs may or may not be conflictual, depending on whether the believer believes that the belief must be imposed on others. Muslims and Christians can inhabit Nigeria (or anywhere else) in close proximity to each other without any impact on cooperation as long as they are tolerant of one another's presence, beliefs, and actions; however, when the same groups come to believe that each owns the society or polity—either because God has told them they do (or should) or because they are a majority (but not a totality), conflict is the product of their beliefs. Again, such conflicts may be less than violent or total; they may lead to pressure groups' demanding competing allocations of scarce resources or of exclusive behaviors (such as weekend holidays). A higher being is not the only source of conflicting beliefs: free traders and protectionists will be in conflict with each other because their beliefs are mutually exclusive and are designed to affect public action that affects both of them.

Identity is a particular kind of belief about who one is. Identity as such is not inherently conflictual, as the preceding chapter has noted. Most people in most situations can be themselves without impinging on another's identity and hence without raising conflicts. Identity labels may be attached to distributional issues, which have a greater tendency to be inherently conflictual, but then they simply fall under the category of different groups' demands for competing allocations. Interregional and interethnic conflicts in Nigeria leading up to the Biafran war of 1967-70 or the sporadic Tuareg dissidence, 1990-92, in Algeria, Mali and Niger since independence, or the long Ethiopian history of conflict between the Amhara and the surrounding ethnic groups over who should rule or benefit from ruling, or the more recent clan conflicts within Somalia between Marehan and Mijertein (and many others) under Siad Barre and then after 1990 between Mohamed Farah Aidid's Habr Gidir and Ali's Mahdi's Abgal, both of the Hawiye clan, are examples. So too are the more benign conflicts among groups and regions in Côte d'Ivoire and Ghana.

Identity issues may also involve positions as well as resources, an aspect usually considered separately from (other) economic goods and services. If demands for certain positions cannot be accommodated by other groups' demands for the same posts or percentages of posts, then these too become conflictual and are treated as any other. The complicated regional allocations of seats on party tickets in Nigeria, the Baurilé-Bété balance in the Ivoirian government and the Akan-Ewe balance in Ghana, and the conflict over positions between the African National Congress (ANC) and the Zulu Inkatha Freedom Party (IFP) in South Africa are examples. Numerically proportionate allocations may not be enough to satisfy other claims to possession based on history, equity, social ranking, or compensation.[7] In these instances, it is not identity that is at stake but other items claimed by identity groups.

But some claims of identity can also be realized only at the expense of others, so that being oneself means reducing the other. These are pure identity conflicts of a distributive nature, in which identity becomes a zero-sum proposition, independent of (but determining) the ethnic dimension of conflicts over resources or positions. Such a zero-sum identity issue is at the basis of the evolving ethnoreligious conflict within the Sudan and also of the apartheid system (also sanctioned by religion) in South Africa. Sometimes the line is thin: Is the 1993 spiral of reciprocal massacres between Tutsi and Hutu in Burundi a matter of positions, notably who holds the presidency or who controls government more broadly, or is it a matter of the inherent necessity of the Tutsi to institutionalize superiority over the Hutu, or even of the Hutu majority to institutionalize rulership over the minority, which is Tutsi? In any case, the conflict and the need for its management are evident.

Similarly, differences in allocations may or may not be conflictual, depending on whether the haves and have-nots accept their respective status; unless one side gets its due at the expense of the other or considers that it is not getting its due because of the other, there is no conflict. Conflicts based on identity and those concerned with economic welfare both involve distributions, although the distributional or zero-sum nature of the latter is more intuitively obvious than that of the former. Economics deals with scarce resources, and African states suffer among the most in the third world from exceptional scarcity of resources. Any policy involving allocations from the budget or regulation of activity involves distributions to one party at the expense of another and therefore conflict. The conflicts among the groups making demands on the government and among the demands that they make must be handled in some way by those in authority.[8]

A special case of distributional issues, as already suggested, concerns the distribution of power and authority. In a condition of normal politics, when conflicts and issues are brought before the government for resolution, the government is considered legitimate in its constitution. As conflict and dissatisfaction increase, groups begin to challenge not only the substantive decision of outcomes and distribution of resources but also the procedures of decisionmaking, including the distribution of power among the decisionmakers. Representational issues take over, to the point at which demanding parties begin to require a place among the deciders in order to get a fair (or favorable) decision. Distribution of power and positions then becomes a subject of conflict in addition to the original substantive issue. Procedural conflicts are not necessarily an indicator of crisis in conflict management. In democratic systems, they are a standard way of managing conflicts, as groups band together to put forward candidates who will represent their demands. In authoritarian systems, however, when groups lose confidence in the conflict managers because their demands are not being met, they move on to support or organize a replacement of the governors by others more favorable to their concerns.

Normative and distributional conflicts are not disembodied philosophical discussions. They become political—that is, they involve power—when the issue becomes formulated as a demand by an identifiable and self-identifying group of people. Until that point, the issues are interesting but not the stuff of politics and not the subject of conflict to be managed. Groups without demands are no more sufficient to the conflict process than are abstract debates; there are lots of groups that are not vehicles for demands, notably activity and identity groups such as churches, professional associations, and sports and cultural clubs, whose members cohere in order to do something together or to share a common sense of who they are without imposing any demands on anyone outside their own circle. Only when these groups impose their issues on others as demands do they initiate conflicts to be managed. It is the mobilizing relation between the demand and the group that is most important. Thus spontaneous groups without prior organization such as a street demonstration are nonetheless as much a demand-bearing group as a well-articulated organization such as a labor union, as long as both cohere about a particular demand.

Such political groups also have a double support function in addition to their demand-bearing nature. As vehicles of demands to be brought to the attention of the government, creating conflicts that the government is expected to manage, these groups also need to support the government in the function of its tasks. The system cannot function properly if only demands are advanced, without supports from the groups of society for the institutions and processes of management. Similarly, groups make their contribution to society through the performance of their own activities, activities which in turn underlie the demands that they pass on. If labor unions do not produce labor, or the military does not produce defense, or the journalists newspapers, or civil rights groups a better public understanding of civil rights, and so on, but only pile demands on the government in relation to these subjects, they are not supplying their proper share of the activities of society. The demands of groups must be balanced by their supports for the society and the polity in which they operate if these systems are to function properly.

Obviously, conflict does not imply violent conflict any more than governance is inherently good governance. Violence may be a means of pursuing conflicts, but it is an ultimate means. It is the end of a progression, which begins in politics and only rarely reaches its final expression in violence, and it is only understandable as such; without being situated in a progression that covers all forms of conflict, violence is inexplicable.[9] Conflict and its management are normal and unavoidable in human relations, and they constitute the essence and the necessitating condition of politics. Too much conflict, unresolved conflict that prevents action and solutions, and violent conflict are all undesirable situations requiring management. But unless conflict is understood as beginning with normal demands of the components of society that clash with other normal demands and unless governance is understood as beginning with the normal handling of these demands that begins before their expression comes to violence, violent conflict will come as a surprise and neither policymakers nor policy analysts will be doing their job.

The conflicts that destroyed the state in Uganda, Chad, Somalia,

Ethiopia, Rwanda, and Liberia, and severely limited it in Nigeria, Sudan, Burundi, South Africa, Angola, and Mozambique reached that catastrophic level of violence because they were badly managed when still in their political stage. It is therefore at the previolence level that examining the conflict management process as the essence of governance is most instructive. At this stage the responsibilities of sovereignty are most evident, for proper and effective handling of political conflicts prevent them from turning violent. Management does not imply total acceptance or full satisfaction or caving in before the demands of the group. Indeed, the unlikelihood of full satisfaction is an implication of conflict and conflict management, since full agreement to one group's demands would increase the chances of rejecting those of another group. Generally, at the political stage, demand-bearing groups are much more likely to settle for less than the whole loaf than at the violent stage. Nor is there any basis for a moral judgment of conflict management, as defined, other than its success in preventing violence. There are obvious problems in such value neutrality, but it shifts the burden of judgment from the observer, who may have his own demand-based biases, to the groups themselves. Although refusal to resort to violence may not be a criterion of satisfaction and success at conflict management, willingness to resort to violence is certainly a criterion of dissatisfaction and failure.

In internal governance, even more than in international politics, the management rather than the resolution of conflict is the maximum attainable goal. Conflicts among demands and demanders are rarely eliminated; at best they are only reduced, satisfied, downgraded, contained, and so on, until the demanders get new ammunition, new evidence, new pressure, new followers, or new issues and demands that break up their ranks and overshadow their earlier appeals. In developing countries, demands tend to be rather constant over long periods; even when well managed, old demands tend to remain or reemerge, another reason for conscious institutionalization as a strategy. There has been relatively little issue realignment, and few new demands and demanders have entered into new conflicts for the governors' attention in Africa.[10] Here and there an issue dies (for a while); Somali unity or irredentism is an example. Now and then an issue is settled (at least in its historic form); the Eritrean question is a case in point. Once in a while a new issue appears; AIDS and the environment are examples. Sometimes issues that seemed settled return, as in the demand for self-determination in Somaliland and in Zanzibar. Demand-bearing groups may multiply, but the nature of the demands goes on.

Ways of Management—How to Tame Conflict

Conflict management can be analyzed in two different ways, through strategies and through institutions. Strategies used to handle conflicts can be directed toward demands or toward groups. Demands can be handled by government as the agent of the sovereign state through an array of strategies to deal with allocative conflicts. These strategies may be termed reconciliation, adjudication, competition, augmentation, submergence, and suppression (RACASS). Demands can be reconciled with one another so that the conflict among them is reduced. Thus demands for self-determination can be harmonized with state insistence on sovereignty through provisions for regional autonomy. This is a solution that has been attempted in varying degrees in Eritrea, southern Sudan, Zanzibar, northern Somali(land), Western Cameroon, the states of Nigeria, and now the regions of South Africa; where it has not been effective, it is more often because governments did not keep their word in implementing the solution than because regional groups did not keep theirs. Demands can also be adjudicated, whereby the decision assigns a right and a wrong and awards a total allocation to one party. Thus groups may be satisfied by simply having their day in court even though their demand is rejected in favor of another group's (or vice versa). Courts have played a crucial role on occasion in the management of conflict in Africa, even in some of the more corrupt states such as Nigeria, Kenya, and South Africa during the transition from minority to majority rule, and they have reinforced their legitimacy as a conflict management institution by showing integrity of judgment and independence from other branches of government. Executive allocation may also be necessary to resolve conflict in a similar way, such as the granting of large land rights to the Zulu nation in 1994 by President F. W. deKlerk as the price for IFP participation in the South African elections.[11] Demands can also be subject to competition, so that distributional decisions apportioning the disputed item among the parties are made after open debate by the informed members of society. Thus political parties in Zambia in 1991 and in South Africa in 1993 battled politically over different conceptions and solutions regarding their countries' economic and socio-political problems at crucial junctures and resolved them through the voice of the electorate.[12] Where parties were not effective, ad hoc and professional groups of society acted in the same way to compete decisively with the plan of General Ignatius Kutu Acheampong for union (that is, no-party) government in Ghana in 1978.[13] Conflicts can also be resolved by increasing resources to be allocated, so that the conflict is eliminated by the fact that both parties can now enjoy all or a larger portion of their demands. Thus the dramatic increase in oil revenues in Nigeria from the mid-1970s to the mid-1980s permitted the military government to resolve conflicts among local groups by increasing the number of states and then to resolve conflicts with civil society by handing over government to civilians; the fall of oil prices brought an end to management by augmentation and a return of the military to government. Finally, demands can be submerged under other overarching or distracting goals that manage the conflict by paving it over, or they can be simply suppressed so that their expression disappears from view without necessarily being satisfied. Thus wars or other national causes can be used to divert attention from internal conflicts, and police powers can be used to suppress conflicting demands. The Mali-Burkina Faso six-day war in December 1985 and the various acronymic campaigns in Ghana and Nigeria are examples of the first, none of them successful for long, and the Sudanese government's campaign of repression against southern grievances or various instances of the banning of labor, ethnic, and student demands elsewhere are examples of the second.

To contrast the different approaches, labor demands have often been reconciled by a partial allocation that splits the costs among labor, management, and consumer; sometimes they have been subject to a comprehensive judgment that decrees the demands fully justified or totally unjustified; and on the occasion of high oil revenues, some African states have been able to eliminate labor unrest by drawing on their petroleum windfall. In the 1983 constitutional dispensation in South Africa, the conflicting demands of the black majority and the white minority were handled through an attempt at reconciliation outside the tricameral parliament in a series of inventive but inadequate offers by President P. W. Botha, covered by strategies of submergence under the goal of meeting the "total onslaught" of communism, adjudication in favor of the minority's demands, and attempted suppression of the majority demands. Neither the composite strategy nor any of its parts succeeded in managing the conflict; it was only exacerbated, as Ohlson and Stedman's volume in this series indicates.[14] The negotiations a decade later toward a one person, one vote constitution, preceded by the removal of adjudication and suppression strategies against the majority demands, were based on a reconciliation strategy, but their effectiveness in even the middle run depends on new strategies of competition and augmented resources, without which procedural demands simply cannot be reconciled. Similar combinations of strategies characterized the failed policies of the Mengistu Haile Mariam regime in Ethiopia in the 1980s and the still-pending policies of the regime of Meles Zenawi of Ethiopia in the 1990s.

Incomplete results would suggest that reconciliation is a better policy than suppression, that strategies of shifting focus either procedurally, by adjudication, or substantively, by submergence, tend to be only short-term diversions, and that allocation perceived as fair and justified often depends on augmented resources for its effectiveness. Reconciliation of demands allows the groups to increase their support functions for the improvement of political and the expansion of social processes, as social pacts and labor-management agreements illustrate. Adjudication and submergence tend only to have the perverse effect of exacerbating demands, as the efforts of the General Sani Abacha regime in Nigeria after 1994 to control civic, labor, and regional protests have indicated. But unfortunately, increased economic growth, or at least a constant supply of economic resources undepleted by corruption, appears to be a necessary requirement for the effective handling of demands and management of conflict; austerity unending is no condition for reducing conflicts, satisfying demands, or generating supports. Instead, declining resources merely foster reduced supports, heightened conflict, and misappropriation of the resources that remain.

Groups, as opposed to demands, can be handled by government through other strategies, including cooptation, repression, authorization, institutionalization, and negotiation (CRAIN). The measure of the sovereign state's responsible action is its responsiveness to the groups in its own society, which bring their demands to it in the course of normal politics. Groups can be coopted into the allocation structures of the state so that they become part of the solution as well a part of the problem. Elections and the procedural aspects of normal politics allow for such cooptation, but responsive authoritarian regimes can also incorporate societal groups within their coalition. There are more examples of the latter than of the former in Africa, since authoritarian and single-party regimes tend to include their own representatives of various social groups within a great coalition, although often their very inclusion delegitimizes the representatives. Repression means destruction of the groups themselves, in the hopes that silencing the voice will eliminate the grievance. Sudanese repression of the various southern groups for forty years and Ethiopian repression of the Eritreans for thirty years have not had the desired effect, nor has the occasional banning of labor and student groups in other countries. The opposite strategy is to authorize the formation of demand-bearing groups to speak out on their issues, although such a measure is only half a response. Ethiopia has authorized the Oromo People's Democratic Organization (OPDO), a branch of the Ethiopian People's Revolutionary Democratic Front (EPRDF), the state single party, to speak for the Oromo population but has repressed the Oromo Liberation Front (OLF), a more representative spokesperson. Finally, states can negotiate with demand-bearing groups for settlement of their grievances. Niger negotiated with Targui representatives in 1994, and Sudan negotiated with the Anya-nya in 1972 in an effort to manage the Tuareg and southern Sudanese conflicts, respectively, and the National Party (NP) and ANC (and other groups) negotiated a new political system in South Africa in the early 1990s. On a less dramatic level, but one that preempts conflict escalation, governments negotiate widely with their labor and student unions, although they often follow a pattern of "stonewall, then cave in," that only encourages escalation.

As in the case of strategies toward demands, strategies toward groups are usually adopted in mixtures. The Ethiopian strategy of repression of national groups in the 1980s was mixed in the 1987 constitution with some attempts at cooptation; the successor EPRDF policy has involved some negotiation and a broader attempt to resolve the national problem through institutionalization of approved ethnic demand-bearing groups and repression of others. Similarly, the Nigerian policy toward the national question under the first republic in the early 1960s was one of cooptation and repression of demand-bearing groups and individuals; as it has moved through three republics and six military regimes, it has achieved some success in handling the conflicting groups through complex forms of institutionalization under a federal system.

These strategies meld into each other, and possibilities change according to their circumstances. Yet a few lessons are apparent. One is the inescapable conclusion from repeated experiences that demands and their groups are best dealt with early, when they are the subject of normal politics within a legitimate political system and when their conflicts are manageable, rather than later, when the demands have become less negotiable and the groups more committed to the violent end of conflict. Had basic demands of the population in Mozambique been met or even managed by the Frente de Libertação de Moçambique (FRELIMO) government, the Resistência Nacional Moçambicana (RENAMO) would never have had a chance. Had the Casamançais peasants, the Targui nomads, or the Sekondi-Takoradi railway workers been addressed by the governments of Senegal, Mali, and Ghana, respectively, the civil unrest they created would not have taken place. Again, had the federations that gave Eritrea special status within Ethiopia or the southeast state special status within Nigeria or the southern provinces special status within Sudan not been abolished, in 1962, 1966, or 1983, respectively, the national conflicts within those countries could have been more easily managed, if not actually resolved in the longer run.

Positive illustrations are harder to find, since the successful management of such political conflicts would be supported counterfactually by violence that did not take place. Yet the thirty-year history of independent Côte d'Ivoire or Tanzania shows how a combination of reconciliation and augmentation, cooptation and negotiation, kept rising and pluralizing demands and groups on the level of normal politics and away from the temptations of escalation into violence.[15]

Early management means adoption of positive strategies for dealing with conflict, rather than ignoring and repressing. Such strategies involve a combination of authorization, institutionalization, and negotiation and cooptation. The three decades African states have lived since independence have seen an impressive amount of societal differentiation and pluralization, despite the slow progress in economic development.[16] The emergence of different interests is as important an element of modernization as the advancement of economic growth, leading to the formation of demand-bearing groups and, in the absence of economic growth, to increased societal conflict. Early management sets up a virtuous cycle, where groups learn that their demands are being taken seriously, their efforts treated legitimately, and good-faith attempts being made to deal with them—indeed, coopt them into the dealing process—despite limitations on resources. This type of atmosphere is self-reinforcing, and it is more important than the actual success in satisfying groups' demands. Unfortunately, it is lacking in much of Africa.

Early management comes down to handling conflicts, demands, and grievances within the routines and processes of normal politics. Normal politics refers to an ongoing flow of demands presented by groups of society before their peers who act on behalf of the state to meet the demands and resolve the conflicts both among them and between them and the available means. Both the "upward" act of demand presentation and the "downward" act of managing conflicts are normal aspects of the political process.[17] Self-constituting parts of society have a right and duty freely to form groups for the expression of their demands, and government has a right and duty to manage the conflicts among them and with "nature" (resources), when they do not manage these conflicts themselves. Under normal politics, the array of potentially effective measures is wider than under higher levels of confrontation, above all because government disposes of a greater degree of authority in influencing the way in which allocations are viewed or beliefs shaped. The first part of this equation—the formation and activation of representative groups—is characteristically missing in Africa, so that the second part—the governmental response—is atrophied and limited to repressive measures.

More than that, the effectiveness of particular conflict management measures depends to a large extent on the level of conflict to which they are applied. Conflict level dictates the availability of strategies. When normal political levels of conflict management are deemed unsatisfying by the demand-bearing groups, conflict escalates toward a second level, of more violent expression. Here groups begin to position themselves for violence, devoting greater attention and resources to the consolidation of their control over their client population and to the means of conducting the conflict rather than dealing with the issues themselves.[18] Their efforts turn inward, to assert their position of unique spokesmen for their client population, and outward, to contest the right of the government to speak for them. This in turn has an effect on the capabilities and resources that the government can devote to the substance of conflict management. Strategies for handling demands and even groups therefore become more limited.

This second level of conflict is uniquely unsuited for the resolution of the very grievances and demands that gave rise to the escalating violence. After their attempts at normal politics in a federation with Ethiopia had been aborted by the emperor, the Eritrean nationalists, divided between the Eritrean Liberation Front (ELF) and the Eritrean People's Liberation Front (EPLF) and their subfactions, spent the thirty years of their struggle in the second or consolidation phase of their conflict, unprepared to negotiate their grievances.[19] Spurred by an ideological program of neglect and repression by the government in Mozambique, RENAMO spent the decade of the 1980s in the consolidation phase up to its first party congress in 1989, when it finally was ready to begin negotiating an eventual agreement in 1990–92.[20]

Violent conflict constitutes a third level, often confounded with the second, where strategies are at their most limited. Suppression, submergence, and, only exceptionally, reconciliation, are all that are available. Typically, the procedures of conducting conflict at this level overcome the means of substantive management, and handling the groups takes precedence over managing their demands. That is a major reason why it is so difficult to move to a fourth—reconstruction or deescalation—level. There, an effort at healing requires a shift to demand-management strategies and an expansion of group-management strategies beyond simply repression. At this level, too, resources are needed to bring demand-bearing groups back into loyal participation in the political system, beyond merely dealing with their demands. Thus, in reconstruction, more resources are required for a return to normal politics than were needed when politics stayed at the first level, another reason why it is advisable to handle demands early, before they pose a double drain on the scarce resources of the country.

Institutionalization, through periodic political contests and established organizational forms, is the most effective way of dealing with persistent ongoing conflicts.[21] Institutionalization is the regularization of strategies, and concerns both the state and the groups and the process of interaction between them. That process, in turn, covers both the presentation of demands and the management of conflicts, and the selection and accountability of those in government. Institutionalization is not a static matter of building and filling bureaucratic boxes but a dynamic process of maintaining a well-running machine. It requires creative tension and dynamic balance between a strong state and active demand-bearing groups, where overdevelopment on either side would produce autocracy or anarchy. Africa errs on the former side, not on the latter, but, paradoxically, when the former topples under its own weight, the latter ensues.[22]

It was the state's attempt to repress and control the emerging groups—eventually rallying around their ethnic identities—in society, while pulling into its own narrow dimensions, that caused the state to implode and collapse in Mengistu's Ethiopia and Siad Barre's Somalia. In Ethiopia, ethnic liberation fronts were then regrouped under the control of the new single party, the EPRDF, raising specters of the same problem all over again. In Somalia, alienation and disaffection with the experience of the takeover of the state by one clan has destroyed the chance of any effective state control over ethnic solidarity groups and caused outbursts of violent conflict and anarchy where group jurisdictions overlap. In Nigeria, the very size of the state gives an element of protection to the many groups of civil society that continue to thrive, though in conflict with the state's efforts to escape demands and control from below and to impose its control from above. Here the two components of institutionalization exist; what is lacking is the institutionalized interaction of accountability and responsiveness needed to complete the proper functioning of state and society.[23]

Agents of Management—Who Governs?

Discussion has focused thus far on the state as the agent of conflict management, with government hired to serve as allocator, judge, and policeman over a jostling crowd of petitioning groups. Authorities and petitioners relate to one another across the bar as in a court; groups' access and standing are decided by the state, and government ensconced in authority hands down its decisions to their requests. Governors have their own interests as conflict managers, and they also relate to the interests of different client groups. There are variations on this model, and they make a difference.

At one extreme is a completely authoritarian government, alone in its world with its own interests and without any groups around it, deciding among issues as it judges their urgency. It applies rigid rules to which society must conform and represses those who do not. Such a situation is unlikely to last very long in its pure form, and it is usually brought about in the first place by a crisis in governance, a need to suppress demand-bearing groups, eliminate disorder, and restore government authority. Mengistu's Ethiopia after the Ogaden war of 1977–78 may be a rare example. Perpetuation of the system beyond a moment of emergency is likely to raise more opposition than it overcomes and end up either in clandestine bargaining or in civil war. But the tendency is to perpetuate, and so the state finds itself confronted with emerging groups that contest its heavy hand. It took more than a decade after the Ogaden war for the Mengistu and Siad Barre regimes on either side of the Ogaden border to fall, and they clung to office mercilessly, destroying society around them. Conflict was imposed, not managed.[24]

At the other extreme is an acephalous society that manages its own conflicts and handles its own demands. The state is merely the name of the territory or the mythical family, charged at best with external relations or external defense. Internal conflicts are handled by coalitions, alliances, and a balance of power mechanism. This is the model of a segmentary society drawn by anthropological studies of Africa and elsewhere.[25] In its image it still has great explanatory power. It may never have existed anywhere in its ideal form, but it does capture the reality in pieces of contemporary African countries—Zaire, which Amnesty International declared in virtual collapse as a state in September 1993; Ethiopia in the late 1980s; Somalia in the early 1990s. Yet it is the limiting, ideal type of a society that manages conflict without the need for a state.

Two other, more realistic variations of state-society relations exist in demand handling and conflict managing. In one, the state penetrates society and society the state, with the characteristic mode of relations being that of bargaining.[26] Whatever the formal procedures of making, implementing and enforcing laws, demand-bearing groups of society are no longer mere petitioners but active agents in these processes. The most resolutely political participants in these processes are political parties, which have a crucial role to play in institutionalized procedures tying state and society together.[27] But other associational groups have regular and ad hoc roles to play in the same process and play an important role in anchoring parties in society (counterbalancing the attempts of the state to coopt the parties) as well as in tying state and parties together. The ad hoc role of professional groups during the Acheampong regime in Ghana is a particularly good, if atypical, example.

Legislatures, ministries, and courts function but with support, participation, and assistance of public groups. In the legislative process, these groups lobby, campaign, and testify; in the implementation process, they guide, consult, and empower; and in the enforcement process, they buttress norms and supplement activities. They provide support for the legitimate political process of conflict management performed by the government and contribute their own activities to a functionally growing society. Periodic elections allow society to pass its judgment in an institutionalized conflict management process among the competing demands of its groups and register changes in the public agenda. Much of this picture, including the electoral component, reflects the rich associational life that grew up in Africa along with the nationalist movements, in the early years of independent government, and again in the emerging currents of pluralism in the 1980s.[28] It also reflects the participatory democracy of the North Atlantic countries (where the institutionalized conflict management of regular elections does play an important role).

In the other variation, the state is no longer the manager but the focus of conflict. It manages conflict only by occasionally becoming the unifying opponent of demand-bearing groups, who momentarily bury their divisions to unite in fighting government. Repression and acceptance of demands, confrontation, and cooptation of groups are the alternate strategies used by the state. Except when these relations crystalize into an intense face-off, the groups cannot take over the state, and the state can only temporarily repress or coopt the groups: the two entities live locked in combat. This was the condition of Africa in the period of nationalist protest, and it was the heritage of the anticolonial struggle that set the pattern for future state-society relations after independence. The confrontation of the colonial period turned into a focused combat that ended with the overthrow and withdrawal of the colonial state, but the spirit of the antistate confrontation continued into the 1970s and 1980s even after society had taken over. The democracy movement of the early 1990s, three decades later, appeared to constitute the same sort of phenomenon, in which society once again took over the state. Unfortunately attitudes and relations appear to be settling back into the same confrontational pattern—in Zambia, Ethiopia, Senegal, Zaire, Niger, Benin, Nigeria, Kenya, Ghana, and Congo, among others.

African states at the end of the twentieth century face the choice among these four models of conflict management as their pattern of governance. In an era when the substance of the demands tends to be unchanged from the time of independence, their structure has slipped back into a preindependence pattern. Government is not hired to resolve the conflicts among demand-bearing groups, in cooperation with society; government has become the focus of conflict, and as a result there is no autonomous agency to manage it. Even in the best of cases, a growing number of groups throw their demands at government but withhold their support. The cause goes back to the early years of independence. Besides the many demands of nationalism, which have been amply discussed, nationalist populations rose against colonial rule in a distributional revolt. They found economic growth to be improving, particularly in the world economic boom of the postwar and then Korean War period of the late 1940s and 1950s, but their share was decreasing. Expectations raised by increased supplies of economic goods, followed by the success of the anticolonialist movement in the 1960s, were mobilizing weapons for the leaders of the nationalist assault on colonial rule but a real burden for these same leaders when they came to power in independent governments and had to meet those expectations. They discouraged the expression of demands by controlling their followers in single party regimes, and when these proved inadequate to the task and were overthrown, their military successors were even less interested in hearing popular demands. Normal politics, the expression of demands on the government and the exercise of responsibility by the government, was abolished and bureaucratic politics became the only replacement.

Three decades later, where democracy movements have taken over government, they have soon become captives of the same mold and have taken on the same role as the butt of conflict rather than its manager. In Namibia, independent only in 1990, the mold was not yet set, but in Benin, Mali, and Niger, and in Zambia and Tanzania, efforts at democratization are still dogged by their past. This is partly because the strategies of reconciliation and augmentation are sorely limited by a lack of resources and partly because the mold is so well established by now, by history and by habit. The development that has been achieved has produced a greater pluralization of demand-bearing groups, but they immediately take up an adversarial role, because that is what they and their perceived adversary, the government, are used to. The groups are long on demands but short on support. Incumbents, on the other hand, are accustomed to seeing their position as one of uncertain duration. They can provide for their own material needs in a "one-time feeding frenzy," existing in an ethos of "time at the trough."[29] Neither group nor government knows how to act toward the other in the situation, and the pattern is perpetuated.

There may be one positive aspect to this development. Freed of reliance on government for governance, society becomes its own conflict manager in parts of Africa. It acts like a frontier society or like a human body rather than a physician.[30] When the state breaks down, the informal economy continues to function, if not thrive. Even when the state continues to function but as the adversary, local institutions and organizations of civil society take up the task of managing their own conflicts. Although this response may lead to a stronger society, it does little to prepare people for a responsible state or for governance that will be able to handle the conflicts of an increasingly complex society.

Nothing in this model of normal governance as conflict management suggests that civil society cannot manage its own conflicts. It does, to a large extent, and if it did not, even the strongest state would be overwhelmed. But a large, if variable, segment of society's demands cannot be reconciled without a mediator, or met without an allocator, or enforced without a policeman—all functions that require government, as the social contract theorists readily recognized. The important role of society in regulating its own conflicts needs to be recognized, but so does the absolute need for government,[31] which is where this chapter in the discussion of sovereign responsibility has begun.

Good Governance—
African and International Roles

How then can this trend be reversed, and good governance—the proper functioning of a system of conflict management—be installed? Unfortunately it is late to activate the lesson of early attention to conflicts; many countries of the region now have a tradition of seemingly permanent cleavages and conflicts, and even a culture of violence, as part of their formative history.[32] In general, this history needs to be overcome by a new tradition of conscious problem solving and conflict management on the part of government and of continuous opportunities for demand-bearing groups to make their needs known. This means replacing the fast-feeding frenzy or the time-at-the-trough ethos of short-term exclusionary satisfactions that is now the shared expectation of incumbency by both the public and the politicians. Some suggestions on how to make this change, and the problems associated with it, come from the strategies of institutionalization and augmentation.

Institutionalization means that representatives of demand-bearing groups are guaranteed open channels to present their demands and shared responsibility to support the conflict management process of governance, and that conflicts among such groups are submitted to regular occasions for management through elections. An institutionalized conflict management structure involves five items:[33] firm and flexible rules of the game as embodied in a program constitution,[34] separation of powers to provide checks on efficiency and integrity, free formation and operation of political parties and other associations as demand-bearing groups, regular competitive elections freely and fairly conducted under a neutral administration, and responsible, decentralized government to provide a large measure of local self-determination.

New constitutions are needed as realistic guidelines for the functioning of the official conflict-management mechanism. They must specify the broad principles of capability, accountability, and responsibility that allow government to function and that tie it to its population. Separation of powers needs to be specified, with provision for an independent judiciary to defend entrenched principles of governance; a bill of rights must be composed for the people and a meaningful role enunciated for a regularly elected legislature. Constitutions need to be normative and empowering, constraining governors to follow rules and enabling government to play its roles.

The democratization movement has given some African states the chance to develop multiparty systems, which are not—for the moment—seen as preludes to the single party monopolization of power, as was the case at the time of independence. Morocco, Senegal, Mali, Niger, Côte d'Ivoire, Kenya, Benin, Togo, Ghana, Nigeria, Central

African Republic, Congo, Zambia, and Namibia have taken up effective political pluralism to the point where alternatives to the dominant party have or have already had a real possibility of taking their turn at government. Algeria and South Africa are special cases of the same principle. Even in Guinea, Botswana, Mozambique, and Tunisia, safety-valve parties have a chance at free expression if not of assuming power. Even in the absence of alternance in office, sometimes wrongly held to be the only effective test of democracy, opposition parties play a very positive role in managing conflicts by making their voices heard, employing alternative elites, bringing up alternative ideas, and making politics public.

But even where party pluralism has begun, old habits threaten its continuity. Bandwagoning, where newly elected representatives cross the aisle after the elections to join the party in power, has dogged Zambia and Tunisia in the 1990s as it destroyed the multiparty system in Somalia in the 1960s.[35] The opposite habit, of uncompromising opposition to the point of governmental paralysis, has nearly stopped democratization in Mali, Niger, and Benin; this tendency among parties is doubled by a tendency of the newly separated branches of legislative and executive power to seek to block each other, fighting for control of the third branch—the judiciary—in an unstable balance of power contest. Again, the roles of loyal opposition and checks and balances need to be learned on the job (as experience in 1995 in both Benin and Niger has shown to be possible).

Government only becomes real to people as their possession when they are able to take part in self-rule on topics of local importance. This need is significant when ethnic and regional identities and concerns are the basis of demands and conflicts. Government structures need to include greater regional autonomy and a greater articulation of local and national government institutions to provide a bottom-up rather than top-down hierarchy.[36] It is a little hard to understand why the emperor abolished the federation with Eritrea, why local channels for transmission of popular demands and government responses were not established in the Casamance,[37] why local councils with local participation were not created to train citizens and take the load off central government in Liberia,[38] or why the civic associations have not been used further as a place where civil society and state met in South Africa,[39] among many other similar examples. The obvious answer is that the governors feared a loss of control and eventually a threat to their own positions, including their own prebends, but the obvious answer is not convincing, especially in the light of the consequences of such neglect.

There is no doubt but that regional autonomy and federalism (when there is a sufficient balance among numerous units) are the appropriate answers to problems of self-determination. A proliferation of mini-states is in the interest neither of the smaller amputees nor of the larger body politic, no matter which unit holds special resources. Secession may become necessary as a threat (and a threat is effective only if it is real) to make governments live up to the responsibility for all their people that sovereignty implies. When identity issues have not yet reached a level requiring regional autonomy, other strategies of power sharing and regional competition, as the Ivorian case illustrates, are effective ways of combining identity and allocation responsibly.

Beyond government capabilities, the problem of resources is equally crucial but more complicated. Increases in resources depend in part on the increased capacity of the government to extract resources from society (which in turn depends partially on increased productivity), but also on external terms of trade, beyond the control of African governments. Whatever the difficulties in the latter, the former requires a government that is seen as the leader of its people, inspiring them to greater efforts by its own example and by structural incentives. This means the reverse of the past situation, where government example pointed to the privatization of public resources and the creation of incentives against production. The social contracts of independence were doubly deleterious: they lowered expectations in rural society, thus lowering productivity, and they raised them in urban society, thus setting the stage for continual labor pressures on government and eventually for time-at-the-trough takeovers.

Structural adjustment policies are aimed at reversing this imbalance (without tipping it in the opposite direction of urban unproductivity). Without a corresponding increase in productivity and revised terms of trade that reward such efforts, however, such adjustments merely reaffirm the static and conflictual nature of allocation. Allocation then will continue to be a zero-sum exercise, absolutely and relative to expectations. That inherently conflictual nature can be diminished only by increased resources and lowered expectations (either sectorially or generally). Both are important for Africa in the 1990s, and both are part of the current structural adjustment programs, an aspect that has sometimes been overlooked.

Polities are often debilitated, development stymied, and governance impeded by inexperience in posing and handling demands. Because of fear of the challenge of demands and their threat both to governors' perquisites and to their ability to satisfy expectations with scarce resources, governors actively discourage demands and repress conflict. Knowing that their demands are not welcome, groups withhold support and rapidly escalate their pressure, without leaving much time for response or sharing the sense of responsibility that the situation requires. Government reacts, confirming the groups' expectations. The result is a learning and confirming process—either repression, which teaches the groups about the real adversarial nature of government, or sudden concession, which teaches the group that all this pressure was necessary and that government's initial refusal was merely a ploy to be overcome. Ghanaian and Nigerian interaction between labor groups and government since the 1970s provides a sorry illustration of this repeated pattern.[40] The Senegalese government's efforts to explain the structural adjustment plan to its constituents is a contrary example.[41] Governments need to work out with their societies the patterns of responsive behavior in protest and allocation.

What are the implications of conflict management for an interdependent world? Can the outside world help? The first, but not final, answer is that foreigners cannot do the job. Sovereignty is its own practice, and responsibility begins at home. Governance is self-governance, just as democracy is self-rule. Any assumption by others of these functions reduces their integrity. That very basic, almost definitional trust strengthens, not weakens, the basic message of this work, that sovereign states have a supreme duty to manage their own conflicts, and if they did not perform that duty, the absolute need for its performance gives others the right to intervene. The damaged state restores its sovereignty by reasserting its capability to resolve its own conflicts.

But there is a deeper answer, filled with further complications. In deciding what kind of help can be given to African states as they build their capabilities, one needs to consider not only what kind of capabilities are needed but also how such building of the new (and unbuilding of the old) can be assisted. There are only four ways of creating a new system of political behavior—conscience, training, incentives, and structures. The first refers to innate values held by actors, charismatic leaders with a calling who somewhere in their heredity and environment have picked up a sense of a working system. Such leaders are necessary, but waiting for them to appear is a frustrating experience. Léopold Sédar Senghor of Senegal, Félix Houphouët-Boigny of Côte d'Ivoire, Amilcar Cabral of Guinea-Bissau, Seretse Khama of Botswana, Julius Nyerere of Tanzania, Nelson Mandela of South Africa, and Olusegun Obasanjo of Nigeria have made their mark in their time, but they are necessarily rare. Their work can be generalized by their peers through the adoption of norms of governance by the club of African heads of state, the Organization of African Unity (OAU). Indeed, this is one of the principal proposals of the far-reaching proposal launched by Obasanjo himself at Kampala in 1991, in calling for a Conference on Security, Stability, Development and Cooperation in Africa (CSSDCA), where the second "calabash," stability, refers to norms and practices of governance.[42] It is encouraging that such a proposal should come from within Africa itself, even though there has been no rush to adopt it.

The second means of creating a new political system refers to deliberate education sessions to shortcut the lessons of experience and reorient the paths of behavior. Training is usually a long-term remedy too, although it can come through an inspiring speech or an awakening encounter as well as a long-term session.[43] External agencies can provide training experiences, and they already come in such forms as World Bank conferences, U.S. international visitors programs, and others. They need to be carefully and explicitly planned and executed for they are precious moments. Unfortunately, the higher level the learner, the more immediate the results (if successful) but the less amenable the subject to training. As the experience of Mikhail Gorbachev's brain trust or of the Dartmouth Conferences or of the Arab-Israeli encounter groups show, such reorienting efforts are a long-term effort.

The third means, incentives, refers to more immediate and less personal means of redirecting behavior. Incentives are the basis of the whole World Bank program of structural adjustment and are becoming part of its efforts at encouraging accountability, openness, and predictability in governance. They have aroused an equal and opposite reaction in many African quarters against foreign interference in established habits that needs to be considered, not because it is right but because it impedes the effectiveness of the reforms. Ghana under Jerry Rawlings is often cited as a prime example of responsiveness to incentives to restructure the economy; unfortunately the same government has made less progress in implementing the three virtues of good governance.[44] The use of incentives to encourage effective conflict management is a more delicate challenge than is economic restructuring. Economic incentives need not be specific rewards and bribes for good behavior, however. A more important element of incentive is a general reward system for increased productivity. For more than three decades, Africans have complained—and rightly so—that the more they produce, the less they receive per unit, so terms of trade become a disincentive—a negative learning device—for improved effort. It is little wonder that Africans complain about intrusive effects of the international financial institutions in their economies. Since economics is not just a matter of static price setting but a dynamic interplay of learning and producing, Africans need to be given incentives for economic activity that manages conflict by increasing distributable resources.

Fourth, even a successful policy response may be only as lasting as the incentives if they are not the product of dynamic structures and mechanisms that perpetuate the values and practices of conflict management in the same way that the preceding African systems of governance perpetuated the reverse. To some extent these can be written into constitutions and built into institutions but only if the dynamic underpinnings of politics and society are supportive of the new structures. This path, after all, was tried once before in the social contract that permitted independence, and it was undone by its own ingredients. The success of the charismatic nationalist leaders in galvanizing the nationalist movement made them irreplaceable, creating the problem of succession that was the greatest single structural problem of the new African polities. The success of the nationalist movement in mobilizing demands to take over government made it necessary to demobilize demands once it came to power.

New structures have to be established that break the old and set up the new patterns, in a situation where the reformers are inexperienced and the sons of the old are pervasive. As in the Soviet Union and then Russia, the reformers may be able to implement yearnings for a new way, but once they have set it up, the unemployed politicians of the old order have all the skills and resources to take over the new machines, changing only their ties to prevent instant recognition. The sovereign national conference (CNS) invented in Benin and used through much of French-speaking Africa, is an admirably suited device for the nation to assume sovereignty, gather together a comprehensive assembly of civil society, renounce the old ways, and establish new orders.[45] But the new order is a fragile creation and both the conference and the constitution can be subverted and eventually hijacked by former incumbents.[46] The challenge is to help African political analysts and practitioners devise ways of making competitive elections, separation of powers, the rule of law, and decisionmaking transparency appropriate to their needs.

Finally, interstate structures can also be focused on conflict management activities in the furtherance of domestic efforts at governance. International relations has long been seen as a study of conflict, both on the regional and the global level, to the neglect of the overriding activity devoted to the prevention, reduction, and resolution of conflicts. Subregional and regional neighbors, acting individually and in international organizations, mediate one another's disputes, but they also cooperate to manage potential sources of conflict—borders, migration, trade, environment, and development.[47] Global efforts at conflict management in the post–cold war era range from far-reaching new ventures in the legislation of worldwide regimes in law, development, and environment to uncertain attempts at stopping famine and genocide and cobbling together collapsed states.[48] It is not too little to expect of the world community that the shared challenges of domestic conflict management be the subject of cooperation and coordination rather than of beggar-thy-neighbor policies and international conflict.

3

Identity

ONE OF the major challenges to national sovereignty in the African context is the management of identities based on race, ethnicity, culture, language, and religion. Given the fact that most African countries were carved out in a manner that separated some groups and brought together other groups, diversity of identity is a pervading reality of the African state. Nor is this diversity only a function of the more easily identifiable racial, ethnic, "tribal," or religious differences. As Somalia has so dramatically demonstrated, even differences among clans, and, indeed, lineages or families, in a society that is otherwise homogeneous can be most violent and threatening to the survival of the state and society. If ethnic conflict, whether broadly or narrowly defined, is an increasing phenomenon in the world today, especially after the cold war, and if governance is conflict management, then managing or resolving identity conflicts must be high on the agenda of responsible sovereignty. This is particularly the case considering that identity cleavages, if not bridged creatively and equitably, can generate violent conflicts that can be zero-sum and severely threatening to the integrity and, therefore, the sovereignty of a state.

Addressing the identity factor in conflict and the prospects for its resolution in the African context requires focusing on four interrelated aspects: the nature of identity; identity as a source of conflict; the ways in which diversities of identities are being managed by individual countries; and the implications of both the conceptual analyses of identity and country experiences for conflict resolution, including the role of external actors in mediating identity conflicts.

Anatomy of Identity

Among the most common bases of identity that generate conflict and threaten the survival of a nation are race, ethnicity, culture, language, and religion. Territory as a concept of identification usually overlaps with one or more of these factors and is, therefore, a complementary or an affirmative factor. Self-identification and identification by others imply elements of subjectivity and objectivity; the relative emphasis to be placed on these dimensions for analytical and policy purposes is a complex issue.

There are two sets of discrepancies which might arise. One has to do with the degree to which the subjective factors of self-identification match the objective elements of the claimed identity. Under normal circumstances, this is a personal matter that should not concern others. The other set of discrepancies has to do with the degree to which exclusive individual or group identities are reflected or represented in the definition of the collective national identity framework. The discrepancy between the exclusive identities and the collective national identity makes the issue of identity, in both its subjectivities and objectivities, a matter of public policy and, therefore, scrutiny. To the extent that the issue impinges on the interests of other citizens, identity enters the public domain and ceases to be purely personal or exclusive to a group.

Several themes need to be highlighted on identity as a factor in conflict. First, it is recognized that identity is basically a subjective concept; it is what people perceive themselves to be that principally establishes what they are. Second, an important element of such subjective identification is genetically related; in many instances this associates the concept with ethnicity or race. Third, recognizing identity (including its genetic or racial component) as subjective does not mean that it cannot be challenged by objective facts or criteria; one's personal identification may be in sharp conflict with what one actually is according to established standards. And fourth, as a policy implication, if an exclusive identity conflicts with the requirements of national unity in a framework of diverse identity, then a need arises either to remove the divisive elements and redefine the national identity framework to be all-inclusive, or to design a system of coexistence among the diverse groups through constitutional arrangements that accommodate at least the more significant diversities, or, as a third option, to allow the diverse parts to go their separate ways.

Ethnicity usually implies that the group is, in large part, biologically self-perpetuating; shares fundamental values, realized in overt unity in cultural forms; makes up a field of communication and interaction; and has a membership that identifies itself, and is identified by others, as constituting a category distinguishable from others of the same order. These elements of the definition support "the traditional proposition that a race = a culture = a language and that a society = a unit which rejects or discriminates against others."[1]

While these criteria are accepted as objective indicators, the general tendency among scholars is to recognize self-identification with a particular group as the crucial determinant of identity. As Crawford Young puts it, "in the final analysis, identity is a subjective, individual phenomenon; it is shaped through a constantly recurrent question to ego, 'Who am I?' with its corollary, 'Who is he?' Generalized to the collectivity, these become 'Who are we?' and 'Who are they?'"[2] According to Nelson Kasfir, ethnicity "encompasses all forms of identity that have at their root the notion of a common ancestor-race as well as tribe."[3] Kasfir goes further to link religion and region with ancestor-race and ethnicity. Although he concedes that the choice "depends on the particular situation, not merely on the individual's preference," he concludes with an emphasis on personal choice: "Though objective ethnic characteristics (race, language, culture, place of birth) usually provide the possible limits, subjective perception of either the identifier or the identified—whether objectively accurate or not—may turn out to be decisive for that social situation."[4]

Young adds the qualification that "subjective identity itself is affected by the labels applied by others." These labels may become internalized and accepted as part of the subjective sense of self. The main point, however, is that "although identity is subjective, multiple, and situationally fluid, it is not infinitely elastic. Cultural properties of the individual do constrain the possible range of choice of social identities. Physical appearance is the most indelible attribute; where skin pigmentation serves to segment communities, only a handful of persons at the color margins may be permitted any choice of identity on racial lines."[5]

Even as a theoretical problem, without considering any public policy issues, it is intriguing to look at both how people identify themselves and the degree to which that identification tallies with the objective facts. The quest for clarification of these issues becomes even more pressing when they touch on the public interest, the extent to which the shared arena reflects, or at least accommodates, the component identities, and the degree of discrimination, if any, that is involved. It is the discrepancy between these two sets of categories—the subjective and the objective, the exclusive and the collective—in a pluralistic state that provides grounds for conflict. Correlatively, narrowing the gap between the subjective identification and the objective indicators, and between the local and the national, can become a significant strategy for the management or resolution of conflict.

The discrepancy between subjectivity and objectivity is more manifest in ethnicity, based normally on attributes such as language, territory, political unit, or common value systems. Race, the breeding ground for racism, the "stepchild of prejudice," is based "on conspicuous physical differentiation . . . which facilitate[s] the stereotyping process."[6] Apartheid South Africa is an example of a racially stereotyping model, although even there, particularly among certain categories of the "coloreds," borderline cases would still raise issues of subjectivity and objectivity. Sudan is an example of a context in which applying racial or ethnic standards is particularly problematic. The Sudanese, who are commonly referred to as Arabs, are primarily Africans who speak Arabic, are Muslims, are culturally Arabized, and have some elements of Arab racial characteristics, such as they are. The Northern Sudanese claim to Arab race can only be valid for a negligible few. And yet it is one of the factors in the overwhelming identification of the North and the country as a whole with Arabism, and one of the major reasons for the conflict with the South and between the government and the non-Arab elements in the North.

Ethiopia is another country where the issue of identity is controversial both in the narrow sense of what an individual or group identity means in subjective and objective terms, and the extent to which the national framework is identified with the dominant group rather than accommodating all identities. Historically the Amhara have played a role similar to that played by those who claim to be Arabs in the Sudan. The only difference, but a major one, is that except for the royal lineage of the emperor, which attached importance to ancestral origins and genealogy, the Amhara placed more importance on their culture than on ancestry or genealogy as the source of their identity, which then became synonymous with the national Ethiopian identity. Yet although Amhara culture was used as the basis of nationwide assimilation, which in itself is contestable, Amhara descent still gave claim to a preeminent status over other Ethiopians.

In most African countries, however, identities are based on distinctions within a broad racial or ethnic categorization as Africans, and although nonetheless grounds for tension and conflict, as Burundi, Rwanda, Somalia, and a host of other countries testify, do not pose the same issues of race and ethnicity as the apartheid South African, Ethiopian, or Sudanese models. Consequently the discrepancies between subjectivity and objectivity, or between the exclusive (local) and the inclusive (national) identities, though still applicable, are less striking. Ultimately race, ethnicity, tribe, and even clan are various means of expressing the same notion of exclusive, as opposed to inclusive, identity.

Burundi and Rwanda are good illustrations of situations where subjective assumptions of who is a Tutsi or a Hutu, racially classified as Nilo-Hamitic and Bantu-Negroid respectively, continue to defy the realities of considerable intermarriage and fusion between the two groups, complemented by residential mixing. Being a Tutsi or a Hutu, although "racially" based identifications, became flexibly molded to reflect material status determined largely by cattle wealth. Individuals were, therefore, able to cross the dividing line on the basis of economic and concomitant social status. As a result of that intermingling, while there are Tutsis and Hutus who meet the stereotypical criteria of ethnic identity, many would challenge the standard models.[7]

Although the issue of the discrepancy between what people think they are and what they are in fact, as well as how that discrepancy affects the collective structures or frameworks, may be more noticeable with respect to ethnicity, it also applies to the supposedly more circumscribed "tribal" identities and even to clans, lineages, and families, largely because there is usually more intermarriage and mixing than people realize or care to admit. Whatever the level of the identity crisis, the conflicts generated become most acute in the context of the national power struggle. To the extent that these conflicts result from inequitable allocations made on the basis of these fictions of identity, or create structures or common frameworks that then discriminate through the stratification of these assumed identities, too many interests become involved for the matter to be left as the private affair of the individual or the group whose identity is in question. Seen from this perspective, the issue of identity is by no means only a matter of concern to a few countries. Quite the contrary, it is safe to say that most, if not all, countries suffer from some form of identity crisis based on the two sets of discrepancies, between the subjective and the objective, and the exclusive and the collective.

Conflict of Identities

The point has been made that it is not the mere differences of identities but the incompatibilities of their objectives or interests that generate conflicts. Incompatibilities can relate either to such tangible issues as the distribution of power, wealth, and other assets, or to the intangible and more elusive issues of the definition of the nation in ways that affect the relative position of the various identities in nationalistic, cultural, or moral and spiritual terms. As has also been noted, it is not the self-perceptions of the individuals and the groups concerned that are in question, but what those self-perceptions mean in terms of the common framework of the state and its impact on the status of the groups concerned.

Identity conflicts in the pluralistic context of the state become particularly acute when one of the parties involved insists that the contradictions be eliminated by forcing the other to give up their contradictory beliefs, values, interests, goals, and the like, or when each of the contending parties insists that their beliefs be accepted as superordinate.

The disadvantaged party is likely to enter into a retaliatory conflict only if it believes that there is value to be gained, or less to be lost, in engaging in the conflict. The role of the elite, intermediaries, cultural mediators, or those who have been widely termed "political entrepreneurs" who mobilize group sentiment, organization, and action on ethnoregional, religious, or other factional terms, has been emphasized as pivotal. The implicit counterpart of these preconditions is action by the dominant elite to undermine the dissident movement by denying it the conditions necessary for its success in challenging the status quo. But while this may impede the progress of the dissident group, it may not altogether succeed in frustrating the movement and may well deepen animosities and sharpen the incompatibilities behind the conflict.

Most, if not all, cultural groups in their relative isolation are ethnocentric and idealize their identities and correlative values. Conflict ensues in pluralistic contexts only when interactive groups perceive their identities and interests as incompatible. Since these perceptions are essentially functions of cultural conditioning, cultural values, or perceptions about them, the differences and incompatibilities associated with them may create misunderstandings, prejudices, and behavior that becomes inherently offensive. Unless the pluralistic context has forced a group to recognize its comparative disadvantages, the perceptions involved often have a subjective parity in that each of the interactive groups sees itself as superior and, therefore, cannot negotiate subordination or its threat.

Ethnic relations in African countries must be viewed contextually and historically with special reference to three phases—the precolonial, colonial, and independent periods. Each of these contexts has policy implications in terms of the shaping and sharing of power, wealth, and other values.

During the precolonial period, when in many areas the concept of state in the European sense had not yet been instituted, communities coexisted and interacted horizontally on the basis of relative parity and mutual accommodation in the common interest. The fact that their separate identities and intercommunal relations had survived the test of time was adequate testimony to both the relative balance of power and their mutual interest in peaceful, or at least functional, coexistence.

The formation of the centralized state system that became responsible for the distribution of power and resources shifted the focus away from local arrangements. Although the colonial government and its agents were seen as relatively neutral and, therefore, sources of impartial justice, they often favored certain groups and regions over others. This introduced into the equations of power at all levels elements of stratification that had not existed in precolonial times. The tensions which this stratification generated were, nevertheless, contained by both an emphasis on law and order and the relative neutrality of the state.

Independence nearly always implied greater identification of certain groups and regions with the central government than others, and that implied even greater disparity in the shaping and sharing of power and national resources. Because the process became geared toward the center as the ultimate source of power, wealth, services, employment, and development opportunities, as the structure of identity penetrated down to the local level, it commensurately empowered those who shared elements with the wielders of national power, while marginalizing and alienating those who did not. The local balance of power that had sustained mutuality of interest in coexistence was consequently disturbed. And for those groups at the local level that felt themselves advantaged and strengthened by these changes, the tendency to ally with the central authorities against their disadvantaged and weakened neighbors increased. Tensions and even violent conflicts ensued as a result. As a prominent African observed recently,

> Perhaps the most important challenge facing African countries today lies here—how to transform the ethnic diversities, inherited from colonial boundaries, into nation states. There is, in effect, an acute crisis of identity. The political identity of an African is rather like a three-tier edifice. At the top of the structure is an over-arching sense of continental identity which all Africans share. Thus they can all say without any hesitation: "We are Africans." At the base of the edifice lies a sense of ethnic identity; this is a powerful force that enables most Africans to proclaim with complete confidence: "We are Kikuyu"; "We are Yoruba"; or "We are Baganda." The crisis arises in the middle of the edifice, that is to say at the national level. Those who can truly affirm with feeling and conviction that "We are Ugandans" or "We are Ethiopians" are still far too few. Oh yes, there is much lip service given to this! But deep, deep down, sentiments and actual practice betray a different reality.
>
> The result of all this is that the sense of national identity remains the least developed of all the levels of political identity within the African personality. This problem has assumed tragic proportions in recent times because of the policies of some African leaders who, instead of correcting the legacies of colonialism, have adopted the same stratagem of divide-and-rule, that is to say manipulating ethnic loyalties in order to gain or retain power.[8]

During the cold war internal conflicts were both aggravated and contained by the involvement of the superpowers on both sides. The end of the cold war removed this external dimension, leaving the struggle between the central government and dissident groups with minimal input from outside. Since the state is usually the main beneficiary of the international system, the loss of strategic alliances has led to its weakening which, at least in part, accounts for the massive breakdown of law and order, and even the total or partial collapse of states.

Under these conditions, the conflict becomes a zero-sum contest for the identity of the nation that determines the quality and level of participation of different groups in the political, economic, social, and cultural life of the country. As one observer has noted, "if ethnic groups or classes or political parties can capture the machinery of state, they can use the identity of the state to justify their domination and exploitation of the population."[9] The larger the gap between the characteristics or attributes considered representative of the national identity and the characteristics or attributes of a subordinated group, the more the discrimination and threat of marginalization, if not extinction, felt by members of the disadvantaged groups, and the higher the level of resentment and animosity toward the dominant group. Indeed, the ability of the group members to participate effectively in the public life of the country correlates directly with the dimensions of the gap between the characteristics or attributes of the national and the group identities. Depending on the degree of parity or disparity, the resulting discrimination may trigger a separatist movement or a contest for the redefinition and restructuring of the national framework so that it is more accommodating of the groups that are excluded or grossly discriminated against. Since this would imply a major change in the status quo, it is often resisted by the dominant group.

In a stratified, conflictual identity structure with major gaps between the preferred national identity and the excluded or marginalized groups, the pyramidal segmentation, as opposed to a crosscutting social organization, creates a higher level of ethnocentrism and destructive intergroup confrontation which, in turn, fosters solidarity with the largest group in the configuration of the conflict. In many instances this means that conflicts within the component groups tend to be submerged. The configuration of the groups, the nature of their demands, and the intensity of the conflict are all concomitantly determined and affected.

This analysis logically leads to two policy choices. Either the subjective element of identity is recognized and given legitimacy as a basis for nationhood, whether or not it is supported by objective facts; in which case, nations should be fashioned along those identity lines through decentralization, power sharing, or self-determination that might lead to partition. Or it is questioned and invalidated on objective grounds to give room for a more accurate and all-embracing concept of a unifying national identity.

Perspectives from the Case Studies

Despite the pervasiveness of identity conflicts in Africa, African elites maintain an ambivalent attitude toward the issue of ethnicity. The problem, generally described in pejorative terms as tribalism, is usually pushed under the rug, either denied or lightly dismissed as a colonial legacy, false consciousness, or the result of manipulation by political entrepreneurs. In reality, however, African governments have responded to the challenge in a variety of ways that range from pragmatic management to blind neglect and catastrophic mismanagement. The particular form of ethnic policies that a country adopts may, in large measure, be dictated by the characteristics of its identity configuration. With significant exceptions, African countries have succeeded relatively well in managing their identity crises.

The fact remains, however, that much of this relative success is the result of ad hoc pragmatic management, rather than a well-considered strategic approach to a problem that is generic to the continent. Indeed, the issue of management of the diversity of identity, especially those based on tribal and ethnic differences, remains one of the weakest points in Africa's systems of governance.

Perspectives from the regional case studies covered in the Brookings Institution's project on conflict resolution in Africa reveal a considerable variety in the ways in which identity has generated conflicts and the manner in which these conflicts have been resolved or managed. The studies indicate at least four possible models, based on the scale of the identity conflicts involved and the appropriate methods for preventing, managing, and resolving them. The first, at the lower end of the scale of conflict, is the integrated model, in which the degree of diversity of identities and the disparities involved in the allocation and distribution patterns does not pose a major problem for governance. The second is the managed diversity model, applied to situations of compound or complex pluralism in which differences based on ethnicity or religion are serious enough to threaten the cohesiveness and stability of the system but are, nonetheless, managed with a degree of success and, therefore, do not seriously challenge the existence and legitimacy of the state. The third is the ambivalent accommodation model, applied to those situations in which the conflict of identities is severe and requires exceptional forms of management, through various degrees of decentralization and power sharing. The fourth, the acute identity crisis model, comprises the most serious situations that involve cleavages so severe and conflicts so intense that the very framework of a unitary state is called into question, and the available resources are so meager and strained that the state cannot maintain effective security and stability in the country. Alternative options must, therefore, include partition where territorial configurations permit.

The Integration Model

The integration model comprises those countries in which there is a high degree of homogeneity or in which diversity is relatively slight and inconsequential. Botswana has many of the characteristics of this model because it reflects an exemplary degree of cohesiveness, democracy, stability, and sustained growth. As Somalia is one of the most homogeneous countries in Africa, it also belongs to this category, but the level of violence and social disintegration makes it an anomaly.

BOTSWANA. Although Botswana has its own share of the ethnic diversities that characterize most African states, it enjoys a large degree of cultural unity. The country was settled some two thousand years ago by peoples who engaged in hunting, farming, and animal husbandry. Between the seventeenth and nineteenth centuries the territory was principally occupied by the Tswana people alongside several other minor groups. While ethnicity remains a significant feature of contemporary Botswanan politics, it has been significantly contained by the sensitivity of the Tswana to the minority groups. A study conducted by the University of Botswana's Democracy Project under the sponsorship of the National Democratic Institute for International Affairs noted that the Tswana are reluctant to impose cultural and political hegemony on others. Even though the ruling Botswana Democratic Party (BDP) could carry a parliamentary majority almost exclusively because of the monolithic support it would receive from the largest subethnic group and an alliance with one other group, the party has chosen to accommodate all groups alike, leaning over backward to favor less politically friendly groups by providing them with government services and resources. Furthermore, "the decentralized political structure of Botswana ensures considerable autonomy for the eight subethnic groups of the Tswana people, thereby ensuring accommodation, a desirable approach to diversity."[10]

The authors of the southern African Brookings case study have presented a laudatory picture of Botswana as an exception in the region, with the highest growth rate in the world sustained over twenty years and a liberal democracy established through democratic elections.[11] It is said to rank extremely low in terms of conflict, and high in institutional capacity for conflict prevention, management, and resolution.

Apart from its rich endowment of natural resources, one factor in the successful governance of Botswana is the effective way in which its leadership has integrated tradition into the modernization process, building on indigenous institutions and values. The Botswana legislature includes a fifteen-member House of Chiefs whose role is that of wise men who counsel the nation.

SOMALIA. Although Botswana is given as a case of a relatively harmonious society, Somalia shows that homogeneity does not guarantee peace and stability. Somalia is considered one of the most homogeneous countries in Africa from the point of view of ethnicity, language, culture, and religion, which has fostered an aspiration for a "Greater Somalia" that threatened neighboring colonial borders. And yet, viewed from the perspective of the segmentary lineage system that organizes society on the bases of clans, lineages, and families, it is a diversified society with inherent competitiveness among groups and individuals. While this diversity was regulated by traditional norms, it was manipulated and exploited by the military dictator Siad Barre, and subsequently by the militia leaders in the ensuing conflict between the clan-based insurgent movements that overthrew him.

The role of identity in Somalia is informed by the interaction of the dynamics of the clan system, regionalism as determined by colonial borders, and the crisis of ethnicity across international borders. While there have been disparities among various groups and regions in the political, economic, and social processes of the country, and some identity groups have benefited more than others because of the degree of their representation at the political center, the crisis of identity has not arisen primarily because the country has been defined in discriminatory ethnic or cultural terms. The conflict among the various clans and regions is more a competition for power and resources than a contest for the identity of the nation.

Both the segmentation and unification of Somali society have historically been shaped by the interplay of "pastoral nomadism, migratory movements, coastal urbanization," and Islam.[12] For centuries before the colonial period, particularly in the hinterland, where an estimated 80 percent of the population resided, clan-based political systems practiced what has been termed pastoral democracy. Instead of resorting to the anarchic warlordism that has characterized the past decade, clan leaders sought recourse in the *heer* kinship system, a type of social contract or unwritten constitution that transcended blood and lineage ties.

Despite the acuteness of the conflict in Somalia, it essentially falls into the integrated model (possibly with the exception of the North-South divide), provided that its own internal diversities and distinctive attributes are recognized and utilized. Reconstructing the collapsed state and society, many now argue, will require making use, or at least taking account, of the traditional values and institutions of the clan system. Part of the collapse of the Somali state has to do with a dysfunction in the reciprocal relationship between state and society that predates the colonial period, resulting from the intrusion of broader regional market forces into the isolated agrarian economy within which the *heer* system had evolved and functioned. In the process, the cattle-based pastoral economy was eroded under the onslaught of a money economy that involved a market extending beyond the cultural borders of Somali society. Correlatively, constructive elements in traditional culture were also disregarded, especially those pertaining to the two dimensions of kinship—lineage ties and the *heer* system that fostered concepts of reciprocal kinship ties beyond the bond of blood.[13]

The Managed Diversity Model

The next level of complexity and complications is that of managed ethnic pluralism. This is the situation in most African countries, represented by the Brookings case studies of the West African countries,

Kenya, and the other southern African countries (exclusive of South Africa). According to this model, ethnic pluralism is recognized as significant, but containable through an effective system of distribution that does not question the integrity and legitimacy of the state. In these situations there is no significant gap between the way in which the nation is defined and the self-perceptions of the component groups. The main problem thus becomes the degree to which ethnic groups are represented in the political process, the institutions of central government, and the distribution of national wealth, resources, services, and development projects.

The demands which have been made by ethnically oriented groups in the countries in this category have generally been for the allocation of power and resources within the context of state legitimacy and have, therefore, largely been negotiable. The West Africa case study reveals that "for a large extent, the demands made by domestic and international interest groups upon the West African state . . . consist largely of claims for distributable goods and therefore can be accommodated within the political system. . . . The result is to enhance the possibilities for constructive social interaction—and effective governance over time."[14]

The West African experience highlights the critical role which group intermediaries play in channeling the felt dissatisfactions of the public to state authorities. Unless presented by the state representatives, group grievances are likely to remain unrecognized and unaddressed. What makes the difference is the ability of the elite representatives or intermediaries to marshal symbolic and substantive resources in a way that threatens the state authorities with consequences if the grievances are not meaningfully addressed. When the state is significantly representative of the group dynamics, the corporate significance of this intermediation is likely to be commensurately reduced. But where there is a conspicuous gap between the state and a particular identity group, the role of the intermediary becomes crucial. Apparently, in the West African environment "the elite broker or 'political entrepreneur' is well equipped for the task of channeling collective demands to those controlling state resources."[15]

GHANA. Ghana's success in submerging ethnic and religious identity to a significant degree despite the persistent use of ethnicity as a basis for making demands (albeit mostly within the range of negotiation) may in part be the result of its unique colonial legacy, and in part the outcome of the policies adopted at independence. Despite some innocuous references to north and south, Ghana (formerly the Gold Coast) appears to have been spared the extremely divisive policies which British colonialism adopted in the Sudan and Nigeria. During the independence movement, while several political parties represented major ethnic groups, among them the Ewe and the Asanti in the south and the Guan and Gurma groups in the north, the leading political party, the Convention People's Party (CPP) of Kwame Nkrumah, which led the country to independence, was not ethnically based. The ethnically based political parties were, for the most part, relegated to the opposition.

One of the first moves that Nkrumah made against the opposition parties was to pass the Avoidance of Discrimination Act, banning political parties, organizations, and societies organized on regional, religious, or ethnic lines. Nkrumah also moved inexorably toward the one party system and a modified Marxist socialism that he tried to justify with reference to indigenous African political and economic culture. Whatever the merits or demerits of Nkrumah's political philosophy, it provided Ghana with an ideological framework that contributed toward the relative submergence of ethnicity as a political base of power.[16]

Nkrumah's stance against ethnicity and its regional correlations has been followed, varying in forms and degrees, by subsequent leaders in Ghana. The relative weight of ethnic groups in the government has varied with the successive regimes but, for the most part, their demands have been reasonable and negotiable, and have focused on competition for positions in the central government or allocation of resources, without questioning the legitimacy of the state.[17]

CÔTE D'IVOIRE. Management of pluralism seems to have been quite effective at maintaining relative peace and stability in Côte d'Ivoire, although possibly using an unsustainable level of resources. Indeed, of all the West African countries Côte d'Ivoire has perhaps been the most successful in preempting ethnic conflict, largely through a system of allocative co-optation, the essence of President Houphouët-Boigny's consensus leadership. It is particularly ironic that ethnicity seems to have been at the center of the colonial perception of Côte d'Ivoire and its policies of statecraft and development planning. Having been thus central to the perception, planning, and execution of policies, and to the initial response with which they were met, it should not be surprising that ethnicity has remained central to governance but has concomitantly been contained through the consensus strategy.

"Ethnicity" is considered "the content of the essential building blocks of political stability which are social and cultural rather than economic, so that economic changes have occurred through social motivations," in Côte d'Ivoire.[18] What is particularly remarkable is the manner in which the ethnic constructs of the colonial state were initially politicized and developed into the nationalist movement that threw the foreign rulers out of the country. With independence, the national leadership inherited a situation in which ethnicity had become a necessary building block for constructing and maintaining the unity, cohesiveness, and stability of the nation. Given the state's central role in the allocation of resources, the competition to ensure a place in political and decisionmaking circles became constructively intense. While the rule of the game was "acknowledgment," not public display, of ethnic politics, Houphouët-Boigny structured the branch and sub-branch levels of his ruling party along ethnic lines. Rather than challenge ethnically based fears, he accepted them as a reality and sought to disarm major ethnic challengers by carefully distributing material benefits to the most influential representatives of ethnoregional groups, thereby co-opting them into his government on a proportional basis. His cabinet included all the major ethnic groups, roughly in proportion to their positions in the national assembly. Even when the scale shifted in favor of subregional identity, educational achievement, and, above all, fidelity, loyalty, and attachment to the ideals of the party and its leader, Houphouët-Boigny, ethnic identity remained an important factor in the recruitment to high positions in the government and the party.[19]

Ethnicity is still recognized as an element of contemporary politics in Côte d'Ivoire, but it is argued that relations among ethnic groups do not reflect the bitterness of those in neighboring countries, and that the management of political conflicts has proved relatively stable over the years. Ethnicity is an important fact of life that politicians prudently take into consideration as they organize their political parties, form their governing organizations, and enter into reciprocal relations with ethnic and subregional representation. Given the fact that the politics of identity based on ethnicity, regionalism, religion, and aspects of culture will remain a feature of African politics for the foreseeable future, the success story of the Ivorian management of legitimate ethnically based demands is an important lesson for the continent.

KENYA. Kenya's case falls into the same category of diversity management as the West African examples but with significant differences. From the ethnic perspective, Kenya's problems emanate from its internal configurations and their regional affinities with those in the neighboring countries, especially Somalia. Generally speaking, Kenya is a case of relative success with a potential for explosion, reflecting a downward slide from the high point of Jomo Kenyatta's presidency at independence to President Daniel arap Moi's increasing crisis of governance and his struggle to remain in power. Through this evolution, ethnic politics has allegedly degenerated from being a reality that was pragmatically managed through the hegemonic exchange process, the popularity of Kenyatta as the "father of the nation," and the dominance of his political party, the Kenyan African National Union, to become an increasing threat to the unity of the nation under the controversial leadership of Moi. This threat was used by Moi to resist multiparty democracy and continues to be used as a justification for his authoritarian rule, on the argument that a multiparty system would trigger ethnic hostilities and undermine the unity of the country. It was only after intense and sustained pressures from the international donor community that he eventually succumbed to multiparty democracy.

Meanwhile, Moi is reported to have pursued a two-track policy. On the one hand, he permitted opposition groups to organize as a concession to donor demands. On the other, his government and its supporters engaged in harassing the opposition and interfering with their political activity. Both the police and members of the president's ethnic group instigated ethnic clashes aimed at terrorizing the Kikuyu in the Rift Valley. Moi seemed intent on fulfilling his own prophecy that multiparty competition would create communal strife, and was prepared to incite it if necessary.

Ethnic fighting in Kenya's richest farm region caused thousands to flee their homes and led to the arrest of opposition members, further casting doubt on the future of multiparty democracy. In the worst ethnic violence since independence, more than 1,000 people were reported killed, and an estimated 150,000 to 200,000 made homeless, in the year and a half 1992–93 as violence tore through the Rift Valley region, which constitutes 40 percent of Kenya's territory. After a lull of several months the fighting flared up again, causing considerable internal displacement in the area.

This violence represents the outcome that Daniel arap Moi had warned against in his resistance to multiparty democracy, but it also supports suspicions that the government has been involved, and for calculated reasons. According to one line of argument, "while diplomats and human rights officials say they believe the Kenyan Government is responsible for promoting the violence, they are perplexed as to what it hopes to achieve . . . courting further violence and civil war by fueling ethnic hatreds," but according to another, "the government is reverting back to its whole routine that it is abused by the world."[20]

NIGERIA. The Nigerian variation of the management of diversity model is, in effect, illustrative of the range of responses to the inequities or disparities of the distributive or allocative structures and processes. Of the countries of West Africa, Nigeria is among the most divided along ethnic and religious lines, the main divisions molded by the colonial rulers into a North-South dichotomy somewhat comparable to that which prevailed in the Sudan. The states that came together under British rule had already been interacting through commercial relations and influencing each other's languages and religious cultures, while remaining mutually independent as political entities.

The process of amalgamating groups into new administrative units eventually resulted in the creation of regional identities, some of which are ethnically based, with the North-South dualism persisting as an overarching framework for procedural and substantive demands. In this context, the pivotal role of the political entrepreneurs has been particularly significant in Nigerian ethnic politics. Prominent personalities in modern Nigerian history have played pivotal roles in creating ethnic group associations and mobilizing their peoples politically to champion ethnoregional interests in the struggle for central government power and resources.

The dualism of the North-South demands made by representative elites is poignantly illustrated by two contrasting statements from southern and northern leaders. The first was issued by the Eastern

Regional Government in 1964, referring to its northern NPC coalition partners:

> Take a look at what they have done with the little power we surren-
> dered to them to preserve a unity which does not exist: Kainji Dam
> Project—about N150 million of *our money* when completed—all in
> the North; Bornu Railway Extension—about N75 million of *our
> money* when completed—all in the North; spending over N50 million
> on the Northern Nigerian Army in the name of the Federal Republic;
> military training and ammunition factories and installations are
> based in the North, thereby using *your money* to train Northerners
> to fight Southerners; building of a road to link the dam site and the
> Sokoto cement works—N7 million when completed—all in the
> North; total on all these four projects about N262 million. Now they
> have refused to allow the building of an iron and steel industry in
> the East and paid experts to produce a distorted report.[21]

Northern complaints (voiced in another context) were equally specific and forceful:

> You are advanced educationally, because when the Europeans
> came, you were the people that they first made contact with. . . .
> We recognize the fact. You're more educated. Especially the Yoru-
> bas. They're all over. The civil service, they're all over. The Ibos
> had their setback during the civil war and which also helped them
> because they tried to learn a lot of technologies which is now paying
> off. Up here (north), we have nothing, apart from the population.
> And therefore you find that the Ibos have the economy and the
> technology, and the Yorubas the education and also the economy
> because of the virtue of the port in Lagos. . . . Therefore what are
> we left with? My people . . . today when I say *north*, I mean those
> parts of the country that don't have the education you're talking
> about. We only rely on the population we have . . . sitting under
> the trees, having nothing to do.[22]

These two perspectives reflect what is perhaps the secret of Nigerian success thus far in managing the contrasting North-South identities and their competing demands, which is essentially embodied in a
balance between the weight of economics and that of politics. Even

with the traumatic episode of the Biafran civil war, Nigeria can be said to have transformed the nonnegotiable secessionist demands of the Ibos into the negotiable demands for allocations and distribution that constitute the "federal character." The substantive content of the federal character essentially means that all the regions, and therefore, the various identities through their states, are reflected in the prism of the national identity, which thus becomes all-encompassing, with little or no gap between the whole and the particulars. The relevant constitutional principle provides that "the composition of the Government of the Federation or any of its agencies and the conduct of its affairs shall be carried out in such manner as to reflect the federal character of Nigeria and the need to promote national unity, and also to command national loyalty thereby ensuring that there shall be no predominance of persons from a few States or from a few ethnic or other sectional groups in that government or in any of its agencies."[23] This clause has been interpreted as emphasizing the need to accommodate the ethnic groups that constitute Nigeria. And because the federal character is based on the state system, the number of states proliferated.

The controversy over the 1993 presidential election results and the eventual return of the military to power confirm the apprehension that the situation in Nigeria is far from stable. And yet the issue of ethnicity as a threat to nationhood appears still to be reasonably well contained, albeit with continuing fragility and potential flare-ups.

Ambivalent Accommodation Model

What was an extreme but exceptional episode in the Nigerian experience is the normal state of affairs in the third model, which represents countries where racial, ethnic, religious, or cultural divisions are so severe that they require special arrangements to be mutually accommodating in an ambivalent form of unity in diversity. This was initially the case in Zimbabwe and Namibia, and recently in South Africa (although the latter will be discussed in the context of the zero-sum conflict of the apartheid system). Other examples of this model might be Burundi and Rwanda, even though both also have aspects of a zero-sum conflict. Sudan, too, is a candidate, although current developments place it in the worst-case scenario.

ETHIOPIA. Perhaps the best illustration of the ambivalent accommodation of diversity or pluralism is the present system in Ethiopia.

With the exception of Eritrea, whose struggle was conceptualized as a resistance to colonial control by Ethiopia, most of the insurgencies that have proliferated in Ethiopia over the past three decades have been based on ethnicity. Armed struggle in Ethiopia has been characterized as a rejection of the hegemonic state, seen as a symbol and expression of domination by the northern Abyssinian people, of whom the Amhara are the preeminent group.

Ethiopian national identity prior to the 1974 revolution was associated with the continuity of the monarchic line, providing the symbol of pride for the nation. But the significance of genealogical connection to an original ancestry, although exalted for the monarchy, does not appear to be widely held in Ethiopia. Unlike the case of the Sudan, where those who claim Arab-Islamic descent try to trace their genealogy, albeit fictionally or mythologically, to a founding ancestor in Arabia, and in the case of preeminent lineages, to the tribe and even the family of the prophet Mohammed, only the monarchy in Ethiopia appeared to employ that legitimizing mythology.

And yet Amhara identity historically provided the framework for upward mobility. As a result, Ethiopians tended to assimilate themselves to Amhara culture without the need to trace their identity through Amhara genealogies. This is perhaps one of the major distinguishing factors between the dominant role of Arab-Islamic identity in the Sudan, which is genealogically based, and Amhara identity, which was culturally based and supposedly did not require blood credentials. Nonetheless, despite the pull of the Amhara culture as a framework for national assimilation, the stratification of identities implied in the system was inherently objectionable to members of the subordinated groups, especially because it involved more than sentiments of belonging; it was a question of the demand for equitable participation in the shaping and sharing of power and national wealth by all Ethiopians, both as individuals and as members of identifiable groups.

Amhara domination, from the perspective of those who invoke it, seems to have three dimensions. One dimension connotes the official imposition of the Amharic language and culture on the country, along with the designation of Orthodox Christianity, the religion of most of the Abyssinian highlanders, as the official religion. The second implies control of the political and economic institutions and processes. The third is a more embracing condemnation of the "colonial subjugation" of the other identity groups.

The Eritrean demand for self-determination goes beyond these arguments and alleges a special colonial relationship, emanating from its particular historical context and experience. While the argument of Amhara domination is also advanced, the situation is distinguished by the fact that Eritrea was ruled by the Italians and the British for some sixty-five years before it federated with Ethiopia in 1951 by a United Nations mandate. It then was fully annexed by Emperor Haile Selassie in 1962, following a highly controversial vote by the Eritrean national assembly that was allegedly marked by intimidation and fraud.

In 1991 the new Ethiopian government recognized the right of the people of Eritrea to decide by referendum whether they would like to be separated from, or united with, Ethiopia and accepted their choice of independence. The government has also embarked on an experiment which, whether it succeeds or fails, is bound to have significant implications for the role of ethnicity in nation building in Africa. The charter establishing the transitional government provides that every "nation," "nationality," or "people" will be allowed to determine its borders, administer its own affairs within its territory, and "exercise its right to self-determination of independence."[24] Those principles of ethnic autonomy and self-determination have now been enshrined in article 39 of the 1994 Constitution of the Federal Democratic Republic of Ethiopia.

These federal-type innovations are generating concern within and outside Ethiopia. It is feared that reorganizing the country along ethnic lines might increase ethnic awareness and tension. And there is the old African concern that the recognition of ethnicity could open Pandora's box and lead to the disintegration and dismemberment of the states as they are presently known. On the other hand, disregarding legitimate demands by ethnic groups for equitable participation in the political, economic, social, and cultural life of the country has also been a source of tension and conflict, and cannot be a viable option in nation building. At least the Ethiopian experiment has raised awareness of the need to address this dilemma.

The experience of Ethiopia, both with Eritrea and internally, suggests that a seemingly nonnegotiable alternative may prove to be the most cost-effective way of ending a chronically destructive conflict. Although the Eritrean demand for independence from Ethiopia was perceived as an unachievable challenge in view of the dogmatic commitment of the Organization of African Unity (OAU) to the preservation of colonial borders (introduced by Emperor Haile Selassie to guard against Eritrean independence), the de facto situation of military victory by the Eritrean People's Liberation Front (EPLF) in Eritrea and the cooperation of the equally victorious Ethiopian People's Revolutionary Democratic Front (EPRDF) in Ethiopia dramatically altered the situation in 1991. This is bound to influence future responses to conflicts of a similar nature. Even more important, there is a strong argument, especially in the post–cold war international community, that when conflict has devastated a country for many years and has led to extreme human suffering, the dislocation of innocent masses, and the destruction of material resources, and there is no end in sight, radical solutions to save lives and move forward with the more positive challenge of reconstructing and developing the country in whatever configuration are more creative and constructive ways of managing the conflict than continuing with an internecine war.

DJIBOUTI. A case that can be classified as ambivalent accommodation, but that also cuts across the integrated and the managed diversity models is that of Djibouti, whose composition and conflicts of identity make the country figuratively, and almost literally, a "reflecting pool" of the region. Not only are ethnic identities in Ethiopia and Somalia also represented in Djibouti, but even more important, the conflicts in those countries have generated confrontations and have begun to influence the domestic issues of governance and their ethnic dimensions.

Djibouti's population is primarily made up of two major ethnic groups, the Isaaks and the Afars, the majority of whom live in Ethiopia. About four-fifths of the Afars live in Ethiopia and Eritrea, while three-fifths of the Isaaks live in Ethiopia and about one-fifth live in Somalia, leaving only a fifth of each population in Djibouti. In addition, the population of Djibouti comprises other Somali and Ethiopian ethnic groups as well as Arabs and French. This configuration reveals the historical process that has brought together various peoples from the core populations of the region since its earliest times, and that significantly distinguishes the country from the rest of Africa in terms of physiological, linguistic, and cultural affinities.

With a background of manipulation of ethnic conflicts for colonial divide-and-rule policy, and being particularly vulnerable on account of its ethnic composition, Djibouti adopted at independence a program of coalition among component identities that would ensure the support of all groups. The state sought to achieve this through several strategies: the enactment of what is called "tribal and ethnic dosage" in the sharing of power between the different groups in the highest institutions of the states; the maintenance of peace within national frontiers at all costs; and scrupulous observance of neutrality in conflicts within and between the neighboring countries.

It should be mentioned in this context that Djibouti's independence was achieved through a turbulent process in which both Ethiopia and Somalia played ambiguous roles; both countries had ambitions over Djibouti because of their ethnic affinities and economic interdependencies. In the end, with the Organization of African Unity and France, as the colonial power, both vigorously committed to the independence of Djibouti, Ethiopia and Somalia had no alternative but to endorse it. Yet the bonds of their relationships were such that the Ogaden war between Ethiopia and Somalia and the internal wars in both countries would eventually involve Djibouti through heightened local tensions and the influx of refugees. As Ali Moussa Iye explains, "Economic recession in Djibouti, domestic political repression, and the worsening situation in Ethiopia and Eritrea, reignited the resentment of the Afars as they began to question the socio-political consensus. They accused the Djiboutian state of favoring the Somalis in general and the Isaaks in particular to the detriment of their community."[25] Their rebellion was allegedly a struggle for justice, democracy, and equality for all the different communities in Djibouti.

This, then, became the crux of the Djiboutian conflict that, while caused by ethnic factors, postulated nonethnic objectives. Accordingly, the solutions which have since been advanced to resolve the conflict have addressed the larger issues of a nonethnic nature, such as democracy, respect for human rights, and policies of socioeconomic development, while at the same time recognizing that the root cause of the conflict lies in ethnic demands.

Empirically, Djibouti has managed its ethnic problems through consensus by means of the policy of tribal and ethnic dosage, which is essentially not much different from the practice in other African countries. Normatively, Iye makes a case for integration into a wider regional framework. Since the country is a "reflecting pool" of the ethnic groups in the neighboring countries whose conflicts have been imposed on it and internalized by the Djiboutians, the appropriate strategy of conflict resolution for Djibouti, in his view, is not to try to delink from these countries but rather to foster a wider context of confederal regionalism. Djibouti is obviously too small to be fragmented further on ethnic bases. The confederal solution, on the other hand, would reconcile two seemingly contradictory aspects of the problem: satisfy the identity needs of the nationalities and ethnicities concerned, and involve all the states of the region with vital and interconnected interests. Iye argues, "Regionally, the current situation of anarchy . . . is leading to a broader reassessment of political strategies for conflict resolution." He writes that "considering the multiple links existing between the various nationalities in the region, these states could collectively agree on means of enhancing the rights of minority groups within their borders so that secession and irredentism are preempted."[26] There is no evidence on how much this normative perspective is shared within Djibouti or how receptive other countries in the region are to the idea of a regional federation.

Although the confederal solution suggested by Iye for Djibouti may seem rather impractical in the short run, given the contradictory trend toward fragmentation and localized nationalism, it could prove to be a means of reconciling the enlargement and narrowing of identities. Certainly, the southern African experience suggests that enhancing security, stability, and socioeconomic development in a region demands addressing the basic sources of conflict in the region: domestic spillover, economic asymmetry, and military asymmetry.[27] Ultimately, the security of groups within a country, however identified, means peace, security, stability, and development for the region as a whole.

Acute Identity Crisis Model

The last category of conflict, zero-sum situations, comprises acute identity crises where there is no collective sense of identification, no shared values, and no common vision for the nation. Having to coexist in the framework of the nation-state is perceived as an imposition by the colonial forces, now perpetuated by the dominant group whose identity defines the national character. Such a definition might be explicit, as in apartheid South Africa, where race and ethnicity were factors in allocating or denying the rights of citizenship, or in the Sudan, where the identification of the country as Arab and Islamic carries inherent stratification and discrimination on racial, ethnic, and religious grounds.

SOUTH AFRICA. The consolidation of identities on a racial basis in South Africa evolved as a result of interactive factors, among them the pull of economic opportunities caused by the discovery of vast riches in the region, which coincided with intense industrial competition among the European powers; the contact and interaction between the Europeans and the Africans resulting from the massive inflow of migrants from Europe; the perceived incompatibilities of interests demarcated along racial lines; and the shift in global norms that triggered the process of decolonization and international pressures for the elimination of racial discrimination. Boer identity, which in the apartheid system developed into an all-embracing white identity, was the product of this hostile confrontation. As Thomas Ohlson and Stephen Stedman observe, the Boers' experience of war, their bitter enmity with the British, and their impoverishment, combined with the establishment of organizations such as the Broederbond in 1918 produced a coherent and compelling mythology and group identity.[28]

The changing international climate after World War II that triggered the wave toward equality and decolonization, combined with the rapid economic growth which attracted masses of blacks into the industrial workplace in the cities and away from agricultural labor, threatened the racist colonial and settler regimes in the region. A shortage of labor led to sharp increases in the wages of the blacks, which reinforced the black trade union movement. The rise in the economic strength of an African urban, organized, industrial work force contributed to the political strength of the African National Congress (ANC) and the Communist Party, which organized the black population to demand basic political, economic, and social rights. The superiority that the Afrikaners claimed over black Africans challenged black economic gains, despite racist legislation. The Afrikaners, who were in a position inferior to English-speaking South Africans, feared that English-dominated business would concede to African demands for reform. A unified Afrikaner stance was needed not only to stand up against internal demands for change, but to roll back black gains and equalize Afrikaner status with that of English South Africans.[29]

Apartheid developed as the Nationalist Party, which represented Afrikaner extremism, won a plurality of seats in the 1948 elections and enacted stringent laws and policies to regulate relations between the races in South Africa. The objectives of this categorical separation of the races were:

(1) to create a completely segregated society, in keeping with the precepts of Afrikaner politicoreligious doctrine, and in so doing preserve Afrikaner identity; (2) to secure white political supremacy and its resulting economic privileges from potential internal and external threats (the former represented primarily by the black majority and the latter by an international community increasingly inhospitable to notions of racial rule); and (3) to move the Afrikaner community into a position of social and economic parity with the English-speaking community, which had dominated the modern economy and urban sector since the dawn of capitalist economic development in South Africa.[30]

As recent developments in South Africa indicate, this program could not be sustained within a one state system.

And yet, precisely because of the magnitude of the national crisis of identity, South Africa cannot be viewed as a simple case of governance such as the rest of the countries in its region or the West Africa model. The South African conflict remains the most challenging on the continent, despite the extraordinary transformation that has taken place with the end of apartheid. Even assuming the transformation of the zero-sum conflict of identities that characterized the apartheid regime and defining the challenge as one of the distributive management of political power and national wealth, any narrowing of the gap between the whites and the blacks will almost inevitably involve exaggerated demands by the blacks and painful concessions by the whites. This is why it is difficult not to agree with Ohlson and Stedman when they recommend a midway course between what is likely and what is preferable.[31]

SUDAN. A country whose zero-sum conflict approximates that of South Africa under the apartheid system in the gravity of its racial and ethnic cleavages is the Sudan. Crisis of national identity is not purely a matter of personal or group self-identification but rather how the national identity framework is defined, and how that definition affects the status of individuals and groups. On those bases, of all the countries in Africa Sudan has the most acute crisis of national identity. With a vast territory of nearly one million square miles, a rudimentary infrastructure, a relatively small population of just over twenty million inhabitants distributed among nearly six hundred tribes with some

four hundred languages and dialects and a variety of religious traditions that include Islam, indigenous religious beliefs, and Christianity
in order of descending proportion, Sudan is more an international
entity and an elite conception than it is reflective of communal sentiments. As one observer has remarked, Sudan "is one of the world's
more heterogenous societies."[32]

The identity crisis in the Sudan is particularly acute due to the fact
that the policies of the various governments since independence have
tried to fashion the entire country on the basis of their Arab-Islamic
identity. The South, with a bitter historical memory of slavery and a
colonial legacy of separate development in the modern context, is decidedly resistant to racial, cultural, and religious assimilation into the
Arab-Islamic mold of the North. It is not, however, the integration of
African and Arab elements which the South uncompromisingly resists;
rather, it is the political domination of the South by the North and the
imposition of its racial, cultural, linguistic, and religious elements of
identity on the whole country. Conflict over identity takes the form of
opposition by the non-Muslims and non-Arabs to the adoption of:
Islam as the state religion and the basis of the constitution and public
laws of the Sudan; Arabic as the official and national language of the
Sudan; and Arabism and Islam as determinative factors in national
self-identification and in foreign relations.

Unlike in Nigeria, where the political weight of numbers in the
Muslim North and the economic, educational, and bureaucratic power
of the South balance each other and contribute to the federal character
to their mutual advantage, in the Sudan the North is the beneficiary
of all political, economic, social, and cultural power, and the South is
relegated to the lowest end of the scale. The situation was made even
more divisive when the National Islamic Front, led by Hassan al-
Turabi, the party most committed to the Arab-Islamic agenda and
which had been extending its basis of support into all political, economic, social, and cultural fields of life, allied itself with sympathizers
in the army and overthrew the democratically elected government of
Sadiq al-Mahdi on June 30, 1989, in the name of the "revolution for
national salvation." Since then the government has consolidated its
unwavering pursuit of the Arab-Islamic agenda.

The fundamentalists and the secularists represent the competing
counterparts of parallel identities which have now come into intensive
contact within a unitary state system and are offering alternative vi-

sions for the country. As one observer noted, "what we are witnessing is the clash of two antagonistic cultural outlooks, both of which are experiencing a revival."[33] Given this zero-sum confrontation, Sudan seems destined for partition, unless something most unexpected occurs to reverse the trend.

Identity Issues in Perspective

From a normative perspective, the regional case studies in conflict resolution in Africa reveal a modestly encouraging picture of the management of identity crises. Apart from the extreme racial situation in South Africa, now seemingly resolved, the acute cleavages that threaten to tear apart the countries of the Horn region, and the crises in Burundi and Rwanda, most African countries reflect a satisfactory level of success in addressing identity issues through a pacifying system of distribution and allocation. Nevertheless, virtually all African countries still suffer from national identity crises.

The issue of identity is particularly acute for the continent because it does not only touch on politics, but also on economics, cultural and organizational resources, and the capacity of the continent for a self-generating and sustainable development. Dismissing or ignoring the identities of component groups in a country is not only to deny them their sense of dignity, but also to disregard their unique cultural and environmental experiences, skills, and capabilities for a self-sustaining approach to the challenges of their context. This is a fundamental incapacitation which any group can be expected to resist. Conflicts, even to the extent of devastating civil wars, can be attributed to this crisis in building an equitable pluralistic nation-state.

From a policy perspective, four options seem open to the African state in its management of pluralistic identities. One is to create a national framework with which all can identify without any distinctions based on separate identities. This is more easily achievable in the first type of societal models, characterized by a high degree of homogeneity and integration. What is envisaged under this model is the typical unitary state system. The second is to create a pluralistic framework that would accommodate the more complex models of nationhood that are characterized by the diversity of competing racial, ethnic, cultural, or religious identities. This model calls for a consociational system of power sharing that involves the acceptance of common objectives despite ethnic diversity. In the more serious cases of racially or ethnically divided countries, characterized by ambivalent accommodation, a federal or confederal decentralization may be the answer in those cases where identities are geographically defined. In the zero-sum conflict situations, the answer would be to expand federalism into confederalism, paradoxically trying to reconcile unity with separation. This would be an unprecedented attempt to respond to Africa's desire to preserve existing state borders while also recognizing the practical difficulties involved. Where even this degree of accommodation is not workable in a zero-sum conflict situation, then partitioning the country ought to be accepted, for unity is not an end in itself, but a means of attaining higher objectives in the best interest of the people. Where unity ceases to be an asset and instead becomes a liability for a significant portion of the population, if not the country as a whole, then it will fail to achieve this overriding objective and should be terminated.

In assessing these options, there is always the operational issue of how to bring them about. The decision as to which option to adopt is, in the first place, the sovereign right of a people of the country to make. On the other hand, there is a responsibility for regional and international actors which cannot be abdicated in the name of national sovereignty. By its very nature, sovereignty implies a tension between the demand for internal solutions and the need for corrective remedies from the outside. In other words, the responsibilities of sovereignty require both internal and external accountability, which may be at odds, especially when internal practice departs from the universal standards that the international community is responsible for defending. Given the international system's ambivalence about intervention, this responsibility may be prioritized to obligate the subregional and regional levels, with recourse to the international community through the United Nations as the ultimate resort.

In the original analysis, issues of identity and the crises they generate in nation building are essentially internal to a country and can be subsumed in several factors: the diversities of the racial, ethnic, religious, and cultural groups incorporated into the nation-state; the gap between the symbolic and substantive definition of the national framework and the way groups define themselves or are defined by others; the disparities, inequalities, and gross injustices implied by this gap; and the reaction of those marginalized or disadvantaged by the identity configuration and stratification.

The remedies required emanate from these factors and include: defining national identity to be equitably accommodating to all the contending groups; developing principles of constitutionalism or constitutive management of power that creatively and flexibly balance the dynamics of diversity in unity to promote national consensus and collective purpose; designing a system of distribution or allocation of economic opportunities and resources that is particularly sensitive to the needs of minorities and disadvantaged groups, and inducing them to see unity as a source of security and not a deprivation; and through all these measures, challenging every group to recognize that it has a distinctive contribution to make to the process of nation building by making use of its own cultural values, institutional structures, and a self-propelling sense of purpose within the framework of the nation. This is only possible in a context of equitable pluralism.

It is becoming recognized that the interconnectedness of the conflict situations of neighboring countries means that preventing, managing, or resolving conflicts is a matter of interest and concern not only to the individual countries directly involved, but also to the countries of the region as a whole. This has the paradoxical effect of both provoking a jealous guard of national sovereignty and encouraging regional security arrangements, or at least cooperative efforts, to resolve internal conflicts. This means that realizing the responsibilities of sovereignty and the accountability which it implies are, essentially, also challenges for regional actors or organizations.

As indicated by the experiences of the Economic Community of West African States (ECOWAS) in Liberia, the Southern African Development Community (SADC) in Mozambique and Lesotho, and the Intergovernmental Authority on Drought and Development (IGADD) in Somalia and the Sudan, regional awakening to the common threat of internal conflicts is relatively recent and is still at a nascent stage, but there is no doubt that its importance is becoming increasingly realized, especially in view of the tendency toward isolationism in Europe and the United States, the only powers still capable of intervening effectively for humanitarian reasons or for the causes of peace, security, and stability in other parts of the world. But while regional interests are more conspicuous and easily identifiable, and despite the growing isolationism in countries around the world, accountability for the responsibilities of sovereignty must ultimately fall on the international community, and more specifically, the United Nations. The interventions of international financial institutions in the affairs of sovereign countries to ensure a more efficient management of their economies has now become a truism. International concern with issues of governance, such as democracy and respect for fundamental human rights, has also become widely accepted, despite the lingering resistance of vulnerable regimes. Beyond the issue of protecting minorities, long recognized as a legitimate concern for the international community, the politics and conflicts of identity and their impact on the prospects for peace, stability, development, and nation building must also be recognized as critical items on the agenda of a responsible and accountable sovereignty.

4

Economics

*A*CCORDING TO the normative framework for managing conflict outlined in chapter one, the focus of conflict management is human dignity, deriving from an underlying respect for the fundamental rights and freedoms of the individual. Viewed thus, human dignity encompasses, among other things, the economic well-being or welfare of demand-bearing groups in a society. Moreover, effective management of the conflicting demands of these groups requires good governance.

Distributive economic conflicts must be resolved—whether through market, administrative, or communal methods—producing broadly acceptable outcomes that confine conflict to the "normal" or low level of intensity. In this process, steps relating to efficiency, legitimacy, and other features of the specific modes of distribution play a major role. Just as important are the efforts directed at enlarging the available economic "pie," thereby facilitating the attainment of "win-win" outcomes that are conducive to the containment of conflict.

From a long-term perspective, it is clear that economic policies relating to the distribution of income and wealth, growth, and good governance play a predominant role in the management of conflict. In the short term, policies aimed at ensuring financial stability and at "fine-tuning" the goals and tools of economic management can also have a significant effect on conflict. More specifically, financial stability can facilitate the management of conflict by rendering the outcomes of distributive approaches (notably via market mechanisms, administrative decisions, and communal systems) more transparent and predictable. Moreover, through its beneficial effect on resource mobilization, allocative efficiency, and growth, financial stability does play a positive role in enhancing the pool of available resources, thereby facilitating the reconciliation of conflicting demands.

Where conflict has escalated beyond the normal range, the goals of economic management cannot remain immutably fixed on growth, equity, and stability. Rather, economic management may have to be fine-tuned to respond more effectively to the exigencies of the underlying level of conflict. In particular, where conflict has escalated beyond the normal range, a change in the relative emphasis on individual long-term economic goals (growth, equity, and stability) or in the use of specific policy instruments (for instance, varying the availability of donor support) could help reduce the intensity of conflict.

From an economic perspective, it is important to view conflict in terms that transcend the conflicting exigencies of demand-bearing groups. Economic deprivation, shortages, bureaucratic regulation of transactions, skyrocketing inflation, and other conditions that are commonly associated with gross economic mismanagement undermine personal security and dignity. Because of this, good governance—a prerequisite for effective management of conflict—must include sound economic management.

Long-Term Considerations in Managing Conflict

A durable framework for managing conflict must include policies aimed at promoting a sustainable improvement in the economic welfare of the principal demand-bearing groups. Such policies (summarized in table 4-1) should focus not only on the more aggregate objectives of growth, equity, and stability, but also on considerations relating to the welfare of the individual, both in a personal capacity and in the context of demand-bearing groups. Accordingly, the orientation of economic policy to the challenge of managing conflict requires a simultaneous focus on the neoclassical issues of efficiency and growth as well as on the governance matters concerning distributive justice and basic economic rights and freedoms. While the relevance of the goals and policies summarized in table 4-1 is not unique to African countries, the economic experience of these countries since independence lends special importance to the underlying concerns.

In the case of basic needs, for example, many African countries have experienced a marked deterioration in their economic performance since the mid-1970s. In particular, real per capita incomes declined

TABLE 4-1. *Economic Goals and Policy Focus in Managing Conflict*

Economic goals	Relevant policy fields
1. Satisfying basic needs (food, health, housing, and education)	Economic growth/development policies; income/wealth distribution policies
2. Equitable access to economic opportunities	Economic development policy; manpower development and other policies impinging on the long-term welfare of individuals and the demand-bearing groups
3. "Fair" distribution of wealth and income, domestically, regionally, and globally	Policies for promoting balanced development and equity within national boundaries; external commercial policies; regional and extraregional cooperation policies
4. Protecting individual rights to property and income	Policies concerning the functioning of markets, the legal system, crossover labor movements
5. Individual freedom in exercising economic decisions concerning production and consumption	Regulation of financial and economic markets
6. Financial stability	Macroeconomic policies

substantially as a result of a combination of adverse "external shocks" (deteriorating terms of trade, droughts, and many other factors) and domestic policy failings.[1] By undermining the ability of African countries to provide basic food, health, housing, and education requirements of their peoples, these developments have eroded the security and dignity of the individual and constituted an important source of conflict. A notable manifestation of such conflicts has been the substantial movement of persons, in many cases illegally, across national boundaries in search of a livelihood or gainful employment. Such movements—particularly marked in southern and western Africa— have for the most part proceeded without attracting international headlines but have been accompanied by substantial social and economic hardships for the migrants: expulsions (in Nigeria and Ghana and from former East Germany); politically inspired retrenchment (Mozambican and Malawian workers in South Africa during the era of apartheid and Kenyan and Tanzanian workers following the breakup of the East African community); acrimonious political campaigns against foreigners (in the United Kingdom and France); and racial harassment (Germany, apartheid South Africa, and Sudan).

The African countries' ability to ensure equitable access to economic opportunities has likewise been weakened by the deterioration in their economic performance and the limited opportunities for good education, training, and other means for improving employment prospects and raising labor productivity. For many African countries, the erosion of educational standards and effective manpower training, the general collapse of yield-enhancing extension work in agriculture and the other productive sectors, and the limited access to land and credit facilities have conspired to keep basic living standards low and to deny Africans the opportunity to raise their material welfare. Thus, while the consequences of these policy failings have been endured in silence, they still have the potential for conflict.

For many African countries, the task of safeguarding individual rights to property and to the fruits of one's labor is compounded by legacies of the colonial period and the decades immediately following independence. In the settler-dominated economies (notably in eastern and southern Africa), land was forcibly taken from the native populations during the colonial era. The colonial governments also implemented social and economic policies that conferred special advantages of property ownership (for example, along racial lines in South Africa, Zimbabwe, Mozambique, and Angola) on the expatriate population. Furthermore, in some countries (such as Mozambique) the coming of independence was accompanied by a massive exodus of the expatriate population, with personal property being unwillingly dumped at below-market prices or abandoned entirely.

Adding to the confused picture of property ownership was the widespread confiscation of property and nationalization of banks, plantations, industries, and other so-called commanding heights in the initial decades following independence. Subsequent witch-hunts for large bank accounts and economic saboteurs contributed to the problem. Furthermore, during the postindependence period of one-party systems and autocratic rule, political leaders increasingly assumed power over the ownership of property.

Individual rights to property and incomes in many African countries thus lack transparency, a fact that has profound political and economic implications for the management of conflict. Politically, the dispossessed individuals often are malleable into distinct demand-bearing groups, seeking a restoration of their rights to property and to compensation for lost income. Economically, the erosion of property rights fosters uncertainty, with an attendant decline in savings, investment, and growth compounding the task of managing conflict.

Individuals' basic freedom to exercise economic decisions (as producers and consumers) were particularly threatened in the 1970s and 1980s as the economic and financial situation of many African countries came under pressure from myriad domestic and external factors. In responding to the attendant problems, governments assumed increased control over their economies by resorting to administrative regulation of economic transactions.

Thus, for example, rigid control systems for trade and exchange were commonly used to support inward-looking industrialization and to protect the balance of payments. Tax systems were manipulated first one way and then another to avoid an erosion of budgetary revenue while at the same time pursuing growth, equity, and other goals. Moreover, restrictions on crossborder movements of persons and goods were intensified to cope with external imbalances.

These developments had the combined effect of fostering economic inefficiency and decay and, of course, of severely limiting individual economic freedoms. Indeed, the spectacle of women and children being chased by armed guards because of petty border trading and of queues of sad-looking faces awaiting interrogation by immigration officials were constant reminders that many Africans were being denied their basic freedom. The erosion of basic economic freedoms was also evidenced in other forms, including the rounding up and occasional imprisonment of alleged economic saboteurs; widespread recourse to illegal operations in the underground economies; denial of basic goods and services produced abroad; and frequent interruptions of road traffic and, often, discourteous searches of innocent passengers by gun-toting law enforcement officials.

Unfairness in the distribution of wealth and income is, perhaps more than any of the goals outlined above, an important source of conflict. This stems not only from human envy and the understandable refusal to be marginalized, but also from the fact that economic inequities often derive from a basic unfairness in the relationship between the haves and the have-nots. From the standpoint of managing conflict, fairness in the domestic distribution of wealth might in the first instance be viewed in terms of conventional measures, such as the Gini coefficient.[2] However, these technical measures that are commonly used by economists need to be supplemented by considerations bearing specifically on the management of conflict. In particular, there is a need to consider more explicitly issues relating to distributive concerns of actual or potential demand-bearing groups. The political and social dynamics of these groups, including boundaries that cut across families at different income levels, cannot all be captured easily through the Lorenz curve, the Gini coefficient, or other such tools that economists commonly use to gauge income distribution.

While governments may be able to take more effective steps in addressing domestic inequities—say, through progressive taxation or through equalization of budgetary expenditure—comparable room for maneuver at the regional or the international level is much more limited. At these levels, actions of individual governments need to be complemented by the actions of others. Moreover, such actions could take the form of actively negotiated approaches, but complementary and conciliatory policies, resulting from otherwise benign pursuit of partisan interest, also have an important role to play.

Policy Implications of Different Levels of Conflict

The economic concerns and goals discussed above are of general relevance to the long-term management of conflict. Societies that are more able to address these concerns and goals effectively are likely to have relatively long periods during which conflict is maintained at a normal level, thereby permitting sustained economic development. In other words, sustained success in managing economic conflicts is an integral part of efforts aimed at improving human well-being and dignity.

The "Normal" Level of Conflict

The concept of sustained (and successful) management of economic conflict is no more normative than the notions of sustainable economic growth or a sustainable balance of payments position. Thus, while there might be an understandable tendency for contemporary scholars to see sustainable or normal management of conflict as being associated with normative concepts such as reconciliation, democratic participation, good governance, and market competition, the temporal or historical uniqueness of these concepts should be emphasized. Humankind has had periods of sustained management of conflict—when societies experienced stability, growth, and development—and when reconciliation, democratic participation, good governance, and market competition were not uniformly present or sought after.[3]

Two general points are worth emphasizing. First, policy requirements for managing conflict are not uniform. Each level of conflict is derived from a unique set of political and economic circumstances and, therefore, mirrors a distinct pattern of conflict-generating forces. Viewed thus, similar levels of conflict are different across countries and, for any given country, also over time. Failure to recognize this point could result in the mismanagement of conflict, as conflict-resolving models that may have worked well in specific situations are uncritically applied to others.

Second, even though the forces of conflict could be contained over a relatively long time, they could simply remain dormant or suppressed, only to erupt again at some future date. This is the case, for example, with the land-grabbing that occurred during the colonial period and the property expropriations that accompanied the nationalization of the commanding heights. For many years, the issue of land ownership was not an active or prominent source of conflict, but later it played a dominant role in the struggle for decolonization. Latent unhappiness over past land expropriations also played a role in the nationalizations of large-scale plantations in the first decade of independence. Moreover, in some instances (Zimbabwe, Namibia, and South Africa) land issues complicated the negotiation of majority rule. To the extent that questions relating to land ownership are not addressed fully, conflicts will probably resurface, especially if the economic situation is poorly managed and new demand-bearing groups see access to land as a way out of poverty.[4]

The Level of Escalating Conflict

During periods of escalating conflict, the contending parties start positioning themselves for the possibility of a violent confrontation. The economic objectives of individuals and demand-bearing groups, including governments, also begin to change. The private sector attempts to hedge against potential economic losses through capital flight, speculative activities, and shortened horizons to savings, investment, and productive decisions. For the contentious groups, defense and security considerations assume increased importance. Beleaguered governments start reorienting macroeconomic policy toward a buildup of strategic supplies such as food and petroleum products. Where possible, efforts are made to increase the capacity to produce weapons and other materials that would be needed if a violent confrontation occurred.

In these circumstances, production and allocative decisions are based increasingly on administrative rather than on market approaches. In the external sector, for example, governments are likely to rely more and more on trade and exchange controls as the situation worsens because of capital flight and increasing imports of weapons and other strategic materials.

During this period of escalating conflict—likely to be associated with deteriorating financial and economic performance—pressure for external assistance is likely to intensify. Bilateral support is exploited with the help of ideological or other symbols (socialism or capitalism), exaggerated threat of a particular religious domination, or ethnocentric appeals. By the same token, the support of multilateral institutions is likely to be sought, with friendly countries being relied on to expedite favorable responses.

The donor support secured during the period of escalating conflict, being fungible, is largely diverted to partisan ends. Moreover, attempts to tie the use of the support to nonviolent means are bound to fail. Because of this, the withholding of all donor support (except that aimed at humanitarian ends) is likely to be a better policy.

The Level of Violent Conflict

During the level of violent conflict, economic policy takes on the character of economic warfare. The focus of the contending demand-bearing groups is on inflicting calculated damage on those perceived as the enemy. Special efforts might be aimed at interrupting the enemy's access to essential supplies (food, energy sources, armaments) and strategic infrastructure (notably transportation and communication links). Efforts might also be directed at impairing the opponent's primary sources of income. Violent conflicts are likely to result in declining economic activity, as the displacement of persons and the disruption of social and economic infrastructure militate against the continuation of normal economic life.

Meanwhile, partisan support from multilateral sources (mostly to states) tends to become rare, entailing increased reliance on assistance from bilateral sources. Each contending party seeks to intensify the exploitation of the bilateral sources for support, previously nurtured during the period of escalating conflict.

With the dwindling of support from multilateral sources, the support from the bilateral sources, coupled with the use of their own resources, provides the primary means of supporting the violent confrontation. In due course, the internal resources also decline (at least for some of the contending parties) as economic activity collapses under the weight of continuing violence. Thus the lack of resources could result in a military defeat of one (or more) of the contending parties, thereby facilitating the cessation of violence.

The Period of Reconstruction

Following the cessation of violent confrontation, the ensuing period of reconstruction (sometimes referred to as a "post-chaos" phase within the UN system) is essentially a healing stage. Inability to cope with the aftermaths of the ended violence and to come to grips with the underlying sources of conflict could impede a return to the normal levels of economic conflict.

In many cases the policy agenda for the reconstruction phase will have been set during the stages of escalating and violent confrontation. Sometimes an overriding economic challenge will be to bring relief, notably in the form of food, clothing, and housing, to those whose lives have been ravaged by the violence. There might be a pressing need to deal with displaced persons—through repatriation, resettlement, and reinsertion into normal economic life. The disarmament and demobilization of the warring groups will require attention. A reorientation of the armament industry might be necessary to minimize the dangers of vested interests' reigniting conflict. Moreover, the lifelines for the past violent confrontation—for instance relationships with external suppliers of arms—should be discontinued.

A major policy problem that is likely to be encountered during this phase derives from the fact that the reconstruction and rehabilitation efforts often coincide with situations calling for macroeconomic stabilization and structural reforms. In such circumstances, the urgent aftermaths of violent conflict and the challenges of restoring financial stability and longer-term economic recovery must be addressed simultaneously. In this regard, the balancing of goals and means constitutes a special challenge for governments as well as for the international community.

More specifically, at the international level, there is a worrisome institutional vacuum, stemming from the fact that, with few exceptions, most of the multilateral organizations lack adequate flexibility to cope with the exigencies of a reconstruction phase.[5] Institutions such as the World Bank, the International Monetary Fund, and members of the UN family are operationally geared toward normal levels of conflict. Thus, although these organizations are in principle favorably disposed toward assisting countries in a reconstruction phase, the instruments available to them are fundamentally geared toward promoting macroeconomic stability and long-term growth and development.

This notwithstanding, and in the absence of an international institutional reform to address the specific policy challenges at each level of conflict, there is an overriding need for heightened sensitivity to the requirements of the reconstruction period. In particular, the application of macroeconomic conditionality, notably in regard to fiscal and monetary policy, could reflect increased appreciation of conflict-related factors such as the repatriation of refugees; resettlement of displaced persons; demobilization of armed forces; and the fostering of ethnic balance in the civil service and other areas of employment.

Another relevant issue for the international community is the relatively high level of external support that is likely to be required during the reconstruction phase. Effective accommodation of conflicting demands, including an early demonstration of benefits to all the demand-bearing groups, will in many cases be an important consideration in consolidating the peace process and accelerating the return to a normal management of conflict. In this connection, expanding the resource pool, including through effective mobilization of external support, is an important economic consideration. The commitment of nearly $2 billion to Zimbabwe's peace process immediately following its independence and similar shows of support for Namibia at independence and, more recently, for South Africa on its transition to majority rule, should be seen in this light. By relieving the resource constraints facing the managers of conflict at this critical juncture, demonstrable benefits can be extended to the hitherto disadvantaged parties to the conflict, thereby helping to forestall a relapse into irreconcilable zero-sum demands.[6]

There is, of course, always the danger that enhanced availability of resources in what falsely appears to be a reconstruction phase could be followed by a recurrence of violence. This underscores the need for the international community to proceed cautiously and, preferably, to link the availability of assistance to demonstrable progress in addressing the underlying sources of conflict. The relevance of this point is vividly illustrated by the recent resurgence of macabre violence in Rwanda, following intense lobbying by the Habyarimana government for the resumption of full-scale international support.

The need to mobilize adequate levels of international assistance during the reconstruction phase points to yet another problem relating to the prevailing modalities for pursuing such assistance. More specifically, there would seem to be a need to rationalize the existing avenues for mobilizing donor support, particularly the roundtables of the United Nations Development Program (UNDP), the Special Program of Assistance (SPA) process, and the Paris Club meetings.

The UNDP roundtables seeem to offer a more flexible avenue for meeting some of the urgent needs of the post-chaos period. In contrast, the SPA and the Paris Club processes—closely associated with the Bretton Woods institutions—are oriented toward longer-term concerns in the normal management of conflict. Given the apparently superior effectiveness of the latter processes in garnering donor support, it is not clear whether the tasks of short-term reconstruction and rehabilitation always attract adequate assistance. Viewed more broadly, there seems to be a need for linking the various processes of mobilizing donor support more closely to the challenges of each level of conflict.

Beyond Reconstruction

Together with the more immediate tasks of economic rehabilitation, resettlement, and the related international issues of resource mobilization and institutional adaptation, the consolidation of the peace process will need to be supplemented. In particular, a full reintegration of soldiers into civilian economic life and a complete transformation of the armaments industry will need to be incorporated into the respective country's long-term economic strategy. Governments will need to finesse the institutions for channeling competing demands. Moreover, the state's ability to respond effectively to changing concerns of old and newly emerging demand groups will need to be strengthened. In brief, for societies steering beyond periods of violent conflicts there will be a need for a thorough cleaning up and for charting a new course that will obviate a recurrence of heightened levels of conflict.

Domestic Management of Economic Conflicts

In any economy, the sharing of the available scarce resources among the principal economic groups (among the providers of labor, land, and capital; between the state and the private sector; or between residents and nonresidents) is essentially a zero-sum game—more resources can be allocated to one group only at the expense of another. The sharing of income and wealth is thus a principal source of conflict. In the case of African countries, the management of such conflict has been complicated by three rather distinct forces: (a) unequal distribution of economic activity or resources among the different parts of a country inequities (intranational); (b) ethnic (tribal) and racial inequities; and (c) distributional inequities associated with the transitional phases of economic and political reform.

Intranational Inequities

Intranational conflicts are to a large extent associated with uneven distribution of economic activity and resources; the fluctuating levels of aggregate resources to be allocated; and the relative effectiveness of the different agents (notably central and local governments) responsible for managing economic conflicts.

UNEVEN DISTRIBUTION OF ECONOMIC ACTIVITY AND RE-SOURCES. In a general framework of perfect markets and mobility of labor and capital, an important factor giving rise to intranational inequities is the tendency of industry to polarize around developed areas to take advantage of available infrastructure and of the coexistence of many industries.[7] Such polarization, especially in situations of imperfect labor mobility and limited commercial linkages, gives rise to uneven geographic and sectoral development and attendant regional and social problems. Indeed, the European Community has been intensely concerned with problems of this sort since the 1970s, and efforts aimed at enabling individual member countries to cope with their subnational inequities have gained substantially in importance.[8]

The geographic unevenness of economic activity has been relatively pronounced in the African countries, notwithstanding the generally mixed record of industrial development in the urban areas. The governments of these countries, despite their avowed interest in the early years of independence to promote intranational balance (notably in the context of the then popular multiyear national plans), have generally tended to focus on the promotion of employment and diversified economic growth in the urban regions. The urban areas have thus become the hub of administrative and economic activity. The cities and towns have also become the base for the more vocal elements of the labor force, including the the civil service, military, and unionized labor. Subnational distributive conflicts have therefore tended to take the form of a contest between demand-bearing groups in the urban areas and the state.

Meanwhile, the relative economic performance of the rural areas tended to deteriorate. While real per capita incomes of virtually all groups declined, those of the rural population fell more sharply, reflecting the combined effect of overvalued exchange rates, unremunerative producer pricing, and other policies. Aggravating the general erosion of rural incomes was a major decline in budgetary spending in the rural sector—a factor that complicated the task of those mediating relationships between the political center and the rural populations.

These developments alienated the rural sectors. Cash and export production were neglected as the rural population confined its efforts to subsistence activities. This situation, prevalent in most African countries at least through the mid-1980s, was conducive to intranational conflicts, including secessionist tendencies. This would seem to be particularly so since rural areas with distinct ethnic or tribal concentrations may be more prone to politicize their distributive demands. In hindsight it is indeed surprising that the bulk of the African countries have until now been able to contain rural-urban conflicts and intranational secession pressures. For some countries, the apparent success in maintaining cohesive nation-states is attributable to the progress they have made in forging a sense of national purpose. However, other factors, notably the power of autocratic regimes to stifle rural opposition, and, more recently, the beneficial effects of wide-ranging structural adjustment programs, have also played important roles.

In some African countries, the uneven sharing of depletable natural resources, notably minerals, has had profound implications for the management of intranational conflicts. The discovery or exploitation of such resources does not necessarily result in conflict but could compound its management in situations of latent or poorly managed distributive tensions. Thus in Nigeria ongoing debates on the sharing of oil revenue are rooted in underlying distributive conflicts between the relatively poor North and the more affluent South. In the Sudan the discovery of oil and the attendant distributive concerns contributed significantly to the eventual collapse of the National Reconciliation government and renewed a violent confrontation between the northern and the southern parts of the country.[9] In South Africa, Namibia, and Zimbabwe, acrimonious debates over the sharing of the abundant mineral wealth between the hitherto dispossessed black population and the whites abated only after the establishment of majority rule.[10]

The management of tensions relating to the sharing of depletable natural resources—and, indeed, of all scarce economic resources—is often linked to that of managing conflicts in other areas. In such cases no formula, no matter how efficiently designed, will fully address the problems of sharing resources unless there is an effective framework for handling the political and other concerns of the principal demand-bearing groups. This point has been appropriately underscored in the context of the Sudan and Nigeria.

There can be no fair oil revenue sharing formula in the Sudan without a workable scheme among the relevant groups/regions in the country. Oil is power, and neither it nor any other sources of wealth and power can be fairly shared in the Sudan without first putting in place a fair system of power sharing. The absence of these preconditions makes the sharing formulae from other countries, such as Nigeria, not very useful at this stage. In Nigeria, control of oil has implications for the strategic balance of political forces in the state and that probably explains why the Nigerian revenue sharing schemes have proven disturbingly unstable since the 1960s.[11]

By the same token, the perception, by the principal demand-bearing groups, that a transitory income flow from a depletable mineral resource is being used prudently is just as crucial to the management of conflict. The pervasive belief that mineral receipts have been siphoned off for the enrichment of the political leaders in Zaire and Sierra Leone significantly affected the management of conflict in those countries. Likewise, the rapid depletion of a country's mineral wealth without a matching improvement in the economic situation is bound to complicate the management of conflict.

In other words, a prudent management of mineral wealth, including transparency and good governance, is crucial to the management of conflict. Together with this, any contrived formula, stressing such aspects as basic economic needs, "rental" payments to the geographic area of origin for the resources, and a balanced development of the different parts of the country, must be sufficiently versatile to meet the concerns of the contending demand-bearing groups. The development of such formulas often requires a compromise between economic allocative efficiency and sociopolitical stability.

THE FLUCTUATING LEVEL OF AGGREGATE RESOURCES. The management of distributive tensions can be facilitated by enlarging the pool of resources to be allocated among demand-bearing groups. This consideration is generally borne out by the relative success in managing conflict in the post-independence period through the mid-1970s and the general escalation of conflict since then. In particular, during the 1960s and early 1970s, distributive tensions, both within and between rural and urban areas, were generally masked by a relative abundance of resources deriving from:

—buoyant state revenue, thanks to rapid economic growth, globally, and in most of the countries;

—substantial savings that had been accumulated in the metropoles, including sterling balances resulting from the policies of the agricultural marketing boards;

—buildup of comfortable levels of international reserves accompanying the substitution of national currencies (notably in anglophone countries) for "colonial currencies";

—relatively low price of energy, presaging the era of international oil cartels;

—some scope for inflationary financing (in the contexts of relatively low inflation rates); and

—generous donor assistance, especially from the metropoles.

This apparent abundance of resources in the early years of independence facilitated the forging of conflict-minimizing relationships between rural and urban areas and, more generally, between society and states. States could confer substantial patronage, notably in the form of employment in the urban areas, while at the same time supporting the agricultural smallholder, primary health and education, and other types of social and economic infrastructure in the rural areas. Even intergroup distributive tensions in the urban areas remained remarkably under control at a time when governments were taking steps to rein in unionized labor, the civil servants, the military, and the other important demand-bearing groups.

Following the first oil shock in 1972–73, the resource bases of many African countries came under increasing pressure, partly as a result of factors that were beyond the control of the authorities. Perhaps the most important of such factors were severe droughts in the Sahel and elsewhere; the onset of a trend of declining terms of trade; the second oil shock in 1979–81; the escalation in international debt and interest rates; liberation wars (Zimbabwe, Angola, and Mozambique) and regional destabilization by South Africa. The adverse effect of these developments on the resource bases of most African countries persisted (at least through the mid-1980s), notwithstanding the efforts of the affected countries to mobilize external finance and to initiate macroeconomic and structural reforms.

The shrinking resource base in the later period substantially compounded the difficulties of managing conflict generally and, more specifically, between the urban and rural populations. Recourse to force and intensified government regulation tended—at least in the decade ending in the mid-1980s—to assume a more prominent role than conciliation or the use of market-dependent mechanisms in the resolution of economic conflict. Government suppression of organized labor, students, and other demand-bearing groups tended to increase, thereby fostering resentment; and basic economic freedoms, including transactions in the commodities, labor, and capital markets, were subjected to tighter regulation.

Against this background, it is understandable that since the mid-1980s many African countries have espoused macroeconomic and structural reforms aimed at accelerating economic growth. The adoption of growth-oriented policies, which attracted strong donor support, was a significant step toward effective management of economic conflicts. The liberalization of financial and economic markets, including the pursuit of realistic producer pricing and exchange rate policies, has enabled African countries to start addressing the distributive concerns of the rural population and to respect the economic rights and freedoms of the individual.

AGENTS OF CONFLICT MANAGEMENT. From the standpoint of effective management of conflict, a grossly neglected area of economic policy has been the sharing of budgetary resources and responsibilities among the different levels of government. At the same time, institutional capacity at the local government level has been allowed to remain extremely poor, with minimal attention from the central governments and the donor community.

Economic policy has been largely urban-oriented, reflecting the polarization of economic and political power in the urban areas. Fiscal reforms are confined to the finances of the central government. International technical assistance to strengthen revenue administration, expenditure control, and budgeting has likewise targeted the central government. Similarly, the renewed emphasis on efforts to bolster institutional capacity has tended to focus on economic management and government administration at the central government level.

In contrast, local government finances in most African countries are in a shambles, and local administrative authorities have inadequate resources to carry out their assigned responsibilities. For all practical purposes, the support of budgetary processes and institutional development at the local government level is at present a no-man's-land, even for the multitudes of organizations under the UN system.

From the standpoint of managing conflict, this situation would not have been worrisome if the central governments were in a position to carry out all the governmental functions. This is, of course, not the case. In Africa as elsewhere, services consumed at the grass-roots level—primary education, health, community roads, and local law and order—can be produced most efficiently at the local government level.

Moreover, as broadly based political participation gathers momentum in more African countries and subnational identity groups gain in prominence, institutional deficits in local government could well be a matter for increased concern. Local governments without a resilient institutional capacity could not provide effective avenues for channeling resource claims vis-à-vis the center. Without such avenues, democratic political participation could easily degenerate into zero-sum claims, with imminent danger of the fragmentation of the national political-economic system.

Anemic local governments could also seriously compromise economic reform processes by not being in a position to absorb the numerous urbanites who will be cut back from the civil service, military, and public enterprises. Inability to meet the basic needs of these politicized returnees could easily turn them into champions of irreconcilable demands based on ethnic, tribal, and other forms of subnational identity, thereby resulting in a substantial escalation of conflict.

The above considerations underscore the need to strengthen substantially the budgetary processes and institutional capacity of local governments in Africa. This would require decisive action. First, there should be a clearly defined devolution of responsibilities to each level of government—local, state, and central—based on ability to carry out effectively the attendant functions. Second, such an assignment of responsibilities, according to the so-called principle of subsidiarity, should be supported by well-defined and stable sources of funds. To the extent possible, the lower levels of government should generate their own resources from quasi-automatic or intragovernmental transfers—stable and clearly identified bases. Third, the management of local government affairs, including finances, should be supported strongly, including personnel training and the development of suitable systems.

Ethnic and Racial Inequities

Similar tensions have arisen on a much broader scale from differences on issues such as the control of strategic economic activity (ownership of banks, wholesale businesses, land, and industry); access to technology; and occupation of important positions in government. The distributional issues that must be faced in this regard concern the short-term sharing of available resources and opportunities and the long-term economic prospects of the various ethnic and racial groups in the respective countries.

With the attainment of political independence, the first generation of leaders and technocrats had an opportunity to replace the colonial administrators. This, coupled with the hasty departure of expatriate investors (Mozambique) and the dumping of foreign-owned businesses and properties, helped to provide a distributive relief (interracially) in the period immediately following independence. Nevertheless, a concern remained that the majority of the African population was confined to low-productivity agriculture and other traditional activities affording meager incomes. In contrast, modern economic activity in the urban areas continued to be dominated by foreigners, including nationals of the colonizing countries, Lebanese in western Africa, and people of Asian extraction in eastern Africa. To help remedy this racial inequity in the sharing of economic power, many African countries embarked on widespread nationalization and confiscation of properties, especially in the late 1960s and early 1970s.

The success of these policies in bridging the interracial economic gaps has been at best limited. Some Africans were exposed to the challenges of running modern businesses, and featherbedding allowed unsustainably large numbers of middle-rank employees to gain rudimentary business experience. In a number of countries (Kenya, Zimbabwe, and Nigeria) Africans in the private sector now own and manage respectable financial institutions, medium-sized farms, modern dairy and chicken projects, and respectable hotel, tour, and transport services.

Nevertheless, there is broad agreement that the initial nationalizations and confiscations and the subsequent state-engineered efforts at industrialization have not significantly improved the relative economic position of the African population. Moreover, as more and more African governments embark on a restructuring and privatization of public enterprises, the prospect of the foreigner's being restored to the commanding economic heights is, at least for a considerable number of countries, a distinct possibility.

This policy reversal, resulting in the reinstatement of a predominant role for the foreigner is, arguably, advisable on economic grounds. However, such a reversal could have profound implications for the management of conflict in Africa. First, the underlying rationale for reducing racial economic imbalances, or the raison d'être of the earlier nationalization efforts, may not have changed. Second, the policy shift is in many cases occurring at a time when large numbers of politicized employees are being cut from the public enterprises, the civil service, and the military. These employees, who will have to find alternative employment in traditional agriculture and the informal sector, will probably provide a fertile breeding ground for organizers of zero-sum demands, exploiting ethnic, racial, and other forms of identity. Third, there is still a lingering uncertainty concerning the claims of the original owners of properties and industries that were nationalized. Reprivatization, resulting in the taking over of these properties and industries by new owners, could significantly compound the issue of property rights. Finally, in the present context of fierce and challenging global competition, there remains a question as to how African countries should significantly entrust the industrial transformation of their labor forces to private hands.

The effective management of conflict in many African countries will thus need to be supported by policies that are specifically aimed at eliminating ethnic and racial economic imbalances. The details of such policies will no doubt vary from country to country, but some themes will probably be common: creation of interethnic and interracial ventures; reinforced human development efforts for the hitherto underprivileged populations; and sound investment and fiscal policies aimed at creating an enabling environment for private investment and at ensuring a more equitable sharing of benefits.

To succeed, such policies will have to be anchored in a framework of good governance, including a transparent legal system that protects the rights of all and that addresses lingering issues from past nationalizations. Successful policies in this regard will require an effective framework for managing conflict, a framework in which issues of ethnicity and racialism are explicitly and fully addressed.

Transitional Inequities

Major economic and political reforms often entail changes that could significantly affect the demand-bearing groups, especially in the initial phase of the reform. While virtually all such changes need to be addressed in any successful management of conflict, some of them—exchange rate adjustment, retrenchment of employment, reduction of food subsidies and winner-take-all types of political competition, for example—easily degenerate into the escalation of conflict. This is often the case in the urban areas where well-organized groups, such as unionized labor, the students, the military, the civil service, and other competing political groups, are able actively to mobilize support for their interests.

On the economic side, policies aimed at minimizing the effect of reform-related escalation of conflict have had to tread a delicate (and not always successful) path between compensating for the effect of the reform and spreading out or moderating the pace of reform. Action on these fronts may not, however—even if buttressed by adequate financial support from the international community—be enough to avert escalation of conflict. A basic fairness in sharing the burden of adjust-ment, domestic ownership of the reform process, and credibility that the reorientation of policies will bring a lasting improvement in the economic situation might be just as necessary in avoiding conflict. Furthermore—as recently illustrated by the case of Lesotho—the read-iness of military personnel to use the gun in preventing the erosion of their economic position remains a major problem in many African countries. This must be a central issue in the rethinking of Africa's economic development strategy.

On the political side, a major factor contributing to the escalation of conflict, especially in the present context of democratically oriented reforms, is the winner-take-all approach to political competition. An effective management of conflicts of this kind would—as argued in other sections of this volume—require enhanced reliance on more broadly based schemes for the sharing of political power. Pending the development of such schemes, African countries espousing winner-take-all approaches to political reform will need to create more level playing fields for the competing parties, thereby strengthening the fairness and legitimacy of the electoral process. In this regard, an important consideration is the amount of resources available to each political party in preparing for the elections.

For many African countries, such resources will be limited because of the generally low level of incomes and, in the case of the emerging political parties, because of their small membership. Incumbent polit-ical parties are, however, able to exploit the many advantages of being in office, including personal and official relationships cultivated pre-viously. This fosters the perception that unequal access to economic resources could be an important factor in the electoral outcomes, thereby undermining the legitimacy of political reform—an important factor in the management of conflicts.

There is as yet no generally agreed approach to the handling of this kind of resource problem in Africa. In some countries (South Africa, Tanzania, and Burundi), budgetary provisions were made for the par-ties participating in the elections, but the amount allocated was se-verely limited because of budgetary problems. Accordingly, the polit-ical parties have had to look elsewhere for help, including official (or quasi-official) and private sources abroad and contributions from rel-atively affluent individuals in the respective countries.

For the most part, official support has been measured, the preference being for support of mass voter education and related civic activities, the setting up of electoral machinery, and other methods that underpin the overall democratic process without conferring partisan advantages on the individual parties. Financial assistance (from private as well as official sources) for the special use of individual parties has generally been handled confidentially. It is reasonable to expect that political parties acceding to power on the strength of such assistance would remain beholden to their patrons and, accordingly, endeavor to return some favors. From the standpoint of the management of conflict, this is a very worrisome aspect of the unfolding process of democratic reform in Africa. While some return of favors might be expected even in the more mature democracies, in African countries this phenomenon is particularly troublesome since parties could remain beholden to a few large supporters capable of controlling governments to further individual ends.

The foregoing considerations underscore the need for economic policies that would promote fairness in democratic political competition. Such policies should include a stronger and more even-handed support through central government budgets, guided, perhaps, by ground rules that limit the proliferation of competing political parties. There would also seem to be a need for constitutionally based codes of conduct that are aimed at limiting incumbent parties' use, for partisan ends, of general budgetary appropriations and other public resources.

Regional Management of Economic Conflicts

In the preceding section, economic aspects impinging on the management of conflict have been examined largely from a domestic perspective. Other economic issues weighing heavily on the management of conflict are essentially regional in character. Most of these regional issues tend to vary according to the level of conflict (table 4-2).

Normal Level of Conflict

In the periods when the forces of conflict are being managed successfully, attendant efforts on the regional side will entail, among other things, an effective management of the processes of regional economic cooperation and integration. In this regard, and in the African context, perhaps the most challenging issues are those relating to approaches to cooperation; unequal sharing of the fruits of enhanced cooperation;

TABLE 4-2. *Regional Issues in the Management of Conflict*

Level of conflict	Major policy preoccupations[a]	Specific regional concerns
Normal level of conflict	Using regional economic cooperation and integration to attain the long-term goals of conflict management	Reducing the conflicts inherent in —the choice of strategies and organizational frameworks for regional cooperation —economic polarization —unsustainable crossborder labor movements —production of regional goods —sharing of natural resources
Level of escalating conflict	Different parties to a conflict endeavor to have regional economic allies	—Factional arming and provisioning of parties to conflicts —supporting conciliatory efforts aimed at forestalling escalation into violent confrontation
Level of violent conflict	Ensuring the availability of adequate economic resources for purposes of the confrontation, including —repair, replacement, or expanded supply of arms —provisioning of food, medications, and other essential materials	—Coping with problems of refugees —reducing the supply of materials that fuel conflict —supporting peacekeeping and peace-observing activities —supporting peace-brokering activities
Reconstruction phase	—Ability to show material benefit, actual or prospective, to the demand-bearing constituency; —maintaining the potential to revert to violent conflict	—Supporting postchaos activities, notably repatriation of refugees, resettlement of displaced persons, military demobilization, and infrastructural rehabilitation —military conversion —supporting sustained peacekeeping and peace-observing activities

a. Viewed from the standpoint of the state and other domestic demand-bearing groups.

problems relating to migrants; and special questions relating to the development and exploitation of natural resources, as well as the more general problems of the environment.

APPROACHES TO REGIONAL COOPERATION. African efforts at regional economic cooperation have thus far proceeded along three conceptually distinct paths.

First, there have been numerous and only partially successful efforts at negative integration, focusing on the reduction of tariff and nontariff barriers at the border. For the most part, such efforts follow the Vinerian conceptual framework, according to which countries move progressively from simple preferential trading and customs union arrangements, to higher forms of integration, involving the free movement of goods and factors of production.[12]

Second, there have been efforts focusing on functional cooperation in specific sectors. Such cooperation—very common in the colonial period—has been extended to new concerns after independence, including South Africa's destabilization; increasingly severe droughts in the Sahel and elsewhere; and exploitation of water resources.

Third, there have been positive integration efforts directed at a broader coordination of policies with a view to strengthening overall economic performance. Such efforts have, for instance, included monetary cooperation (among South Africa, Lesotho, Swaziland, and Namibia, and in French-speaking Western and Central Africa); attempts at monetary harmonization among the countries of the Common Market for Eastern and Southern Africa; more recent initiatives to coordinate certain budgetary and exchange control aspects among Kenya, Tanzania and Uganda; and the crossborder initiative (CBI)—being sponsored by the World Bank, the International Monetary Fund, the Commission of the European Union and the African Development Bank—with the aim of promoting crossborder trade, investment, and payments among some countries in eastern and southern Africa.

Another important force, albeit indirect, contributing to positive integration in Africa derives from ongoing country-specific liberalization of goods and factor markets. Such liberalization fosters a linking, through market-determined signals, of the various economies, thereby prompting an invisible coordination of economic policies.

The pursuit of regional cooperation along these varied approaches has raised practical problems that remain to be addressed if conflicts are to be contained. Regional cooperation among the African countries has been pursued through hundreds of organizations, many of which are poorly funded and generally unable to fulfill their mandates. Future attempts to come to grips with this problem—by closing or merging some of them—will have to confront the fact that most of the organizations have strong partisan support, including from the host country, as well as from their intellectual mentors and donors.

Thus, for example, it would seem that pan-African organizations, notably the secretariat of the Organization of African Unity and the Economic Commission for Africa, have been—in keeping with the Lagos Plan of Action—strong supporters of regionally based, Vinerian approaches to integration. On balance, these organizations have been uncomfortable with the flexible approach (so-called variable geometry) of the CBI, according to which any grouping of countries willing to move at a faster pace toward deepening the integration of their respective economies can do so, notwithstanding the countries' membership in a larger integrative grouping. In contrast, donors have in general been wary of unwieldy and top-heavy integration organizations and have been inclined to support more narrowly and clearly focused organizations, such as the Southern African Development and Coordination Conference (SADCC) during the period of apartheid.

Any revised organizational framework for regional cooperation in Africa will need to be based on a sound analysis of the possibilities of negative and positive integration and of the potential gains from complementary initiatives, such as the CBI, relying on more flexible approaches to intercountry cooperation. In addition to coping with some of the problems highlighted above, such a framework should provide for voluntary membership in the eventual organizations; endeavor to meet the concerns of the donor community; and include practical mechanisms for addressing distributive concerns. In the final analysis, African governments will have to assume responsibility for the restructuring of approaches to, and the organizational framework for, regional cooperation on the continent.

BALANCED SHARING OF THE BENEFITS OF COOPERATION. In the period ahead—perhaps much more than in the past—the sharing of the costs and benefits of regional economic cooperation and integration will call for enhanced attention to managing conflicts among the African countries. This is partly the result of the "invisible" consequences that are bound to be associated with the increased interlinkage, through market-determined signals of the African economies, resulting from continuing liberalization reforms; the reintegration of South Africa's relatively sophisticated economy into the regional economy;[13] the implementation of initiatives, such as the CBI, without a prominent distributive dimension; and the relatively mild possibilities for equitable sharing of costs and benefits under the existing arrangements for regional cooperation.

In this kind of environment, the effects of economic polarization are increasingly being reflected in problem industries that are unable to compete because of intensifying intraregional competition. Another worrisome effect is the potential diversion of official financial assistance and foreign private capital inflows from the poorer to the more affluent countries (notably South Africa). Given the pressing resource needs and the commonly shared quest for the industrial transformation of African economies, these concerns relating to economic polarization must be addressed forcefully to avert an escalation of conflict at the regional level.

Among the more familiar mechanisms for coping with problems of polarization, two of them are least likely to succeed in the present circumstances. These are a programmed allocation of industries among the countries; and some form of compensatory financing from a regionally managed revenue pool (such as the historically contentious one for the Southern African Customs Union countries). In Africa, as in many other parts of the world, the political resolve needed to ensure the success of these specific mechanisms will remain elusive for some time. Accordingly, more practical avenues for addressing the polarization concerns will need to be explored; such avenues could perhaps include:

—selective and temporary tariff protection, to allow time for orderly restructuring or winding down of problem industries;

—reinforced (but proper) use of antidumping duties;[14]

—concerted efforts to equalize opportunity through coordination and rationalization of fiscal, investment, and commercial incentives;

—subregional, preferential trading schemes discriminating in favor of less-developed regional partners;

—reinforced, even if modestly, compensatory features of existing arrangements for regional integration and cooperation; and

—strategic coupling of regional integration and functional cooperation schemes, with the latter being used more flexibly to channel resources, including donor assistance, to the advantage of the less-developed countries.

LABOR MIGRATION. Sustained and large flows of labor across national boundaries in Africa have been and will probably remain an important source of conflict. The conflicts in this area derive partly from the host countries' inability to continue to offer employment to numerous immigrants while their own population needs jobs. In such cases (for example, in the situation prevailing in Ghana and Nigeria in the early 1980s) the host countries expelled immigrant labor from nearby countries without adequate notice. Such actions have tended to create major problems for the affected migrants, including the abandonment or dumping of personal property and the loss of social security benefits. It remains to be seen whether South Africa's relatively large number of migrants will be spared a repeat of this ordeal.

Conflicts associated with the expulsion of immigrants have sometimes been of a political nature, as governments sought to pursue broader foreign policy goals by using the immigrants as pawns. Thus, for example, following the collapse of the East African Economic Community, the respective member countries expelled each other's nationals in retribution. Moreover, during the period of apartheid and the attendant regional destabilization, South Africa used the expulsion of immigrants, actual or threatened, as a tool for making the smaller countries acquiesce to its policies.

From the standpoint of managing conflict, there is yet another type of problem associated with the crossborder movement of labor, namely that of skilled manpower. For this particular type of labor, the recipient or host countries—notably the more advanced regional partners—have been the beneficiaries of free human capital, while the attendant brain drain in the poorer countries has tended to affect adversely their economic performance and institutional capacity.

The approaches for coping with the problems of migrant labor vary according to the underlying economic and political considerations and the nature (skilled or unskilled) of such labor. Whatever their motivation (economic or political), abrupt expulsions of migrant labor inflict undue suffering and erode the basic economic rights of individuals, particularly their rights to property and income. Even if they are successful in attaining their immediate aims, expulsions that are determined solely by the host country are a poor approach to the resolution of conflicts that essentially involve three demand-bearing groups—the migrants, their country of origin, and the host country.

In managing the conflicts associated with migrant labor, there would seem to be a need, especially in southern Africa and other regions with large migrant populations, for broadly based consultative machinery representing the main demand-bearing groups.[15] Where the underlying source of conflict is economic (say, pressure to maximize employment opportunities for nationals), a satisfactory resolution should involve a win-win or positive-sum outcome for all groups. In particular, the host countries' legitimate concerns of employment creation must be recognized without compromising the basic rights of the migrants or minimizing the sending countries' problems of reabsorbing, on short notice, a relatively large number of returning immigrants.

Where the actions against migrant labor are politically motivated, a satisfactory solution will clearly require effective management of the underlying political conflicts. In such cases, there would seem to be a need for regional or continental codes of conduct, proscribing recourse to expulsions or other acts against migrant labor as means for pursuing political goals.

Problems relating to the crossborder movement of skilled persons would require an essentially different approach. In particular, the countries experiencing the brain drain should as far as possible eschew steps aimed at denying persons the right to emigrate. Instead, emphasis should be placed on creating positive inducements for the would-be emigrants to stay. These countries should also seek to benefit from their skilled nationals' working abroad. In this context, African countries would need to recognize that institutional capacity building requires that superior skills, techniques, and know-how be embodied in their nationals and that for many years to come the more advanced countries in Africa and elsewhere will have a comparative advantage in this area.[16]

REGIONAL ACTIVITIES AND THE SHARING OF NATURAL RESOURCES. Activities that are essentially regional in nature—intraregional transportation and communication; control of plagues and epidemics that do not heed national borders; and control of airborne and similar types of pollution—create yet another type of conflict at the regional level.

An important source of conflict in this area is the perception that the costs and benefits associated with the related activities might not be fairly shared among the regional partners. Another source of conflict highlighted in the southern African case studies derives from the effects of the uneven development of the regional partner countries in the sharing of common infrastructure, notably the rail and road transport network. More specifically, there is a widely shared concern that in the post-apartheid period enhanced intraregional competition, particularly in the transportation sector, will tilt the balance of advantage in South Africa's favor.

The resolution of conflicts relating to regionally oriented activities would also require a consultative machinery for the concerned regional partners. This might take the form of formal organizations, such as the Inter-African Phytosanitary Council, the East African Wild Life Society, or the CILLS (Comité Permanent Interétats de la Lutte Contre la Sechresse dans le Sahel).[17] Alternatively, the consultation or coordination of policies in particular areas of interest could be effected through less formal arrangements, including ad hoc technical and policy meetings. Moreover, the implementation of related policies and measures might in some cases have to be approached flexibly, along the lines of the Cross-Border Initiative, for instance, with any groups of willing countries being encouraged to go ahead. Pending the adoption of more formal arrangements for cooperation in southern Africa, such informal approaches to the management of conflict could play an important role.

At the regional level, conflicts in the sharing of natural resources (such as minerals and bodies of water straddling national borders) have a strong potential for escalating. This is partly attributable to the zero-sum nature of the distributive concerns and to the absence of reliable mechanisms for effecting an equitable redistribution of the associated benefits among the regional partners. Underlying political tensions also tend to compound such conflicts, either by providing a veneer for conflict escalation or by imposing an additional hurdle in the search for solution. Thus the strenuous political relationship during the period of apartheid seems to have provided cover for South Africa's overfishing in Namibian waters. Moreover, military confrontations oriented toward the broader political concerns masked conflicts over mineral wealth at the Chad-Libyan and Somali-Ethiopian borders. A successful resolution of regional economic conflicts relating to the sharing of natural resources must be based on durable political cooperation. Together with this, there have to be mechanisms—formal or informal—for coordinating policies concerning the exploitation of such resources and for sharing the attendant benefits. In this context, it would seem that the proliferation of organizations focusing on the exploitation of major rivers (including the Mano, Senegal, Gambia, Liptake-Gourma, Niger, Nile, Kagera, and Ruvuma) and lakes (Chad and the Great Lakes) may have played an important role in managing conflict. However, given the above-noted weaknesses of such organizations, there would seem to be a need for experimenting with more cost-effective and, perhaps, informal frameworks for coordinating matters relating to the exploitation of regional natural resources. Moreover, the coverage of such frameworks should be extended to tourist, environmental, and other areas where crossborder conflicts could arise.

Levels of Escalating and Violent Conflict

From a regional perspective, the most important feature during the periods of escalating and violent conflict is that individual demand-bearing groups will primarily be exploiting their regional relationships for partisan ends. More specifically, the focus might be on issues such as military preparedness; access to strategic products; and diplomatic or military alliances. An important consideration relating to these types of relationships is the opportunity for regional partners such as South Africa and Nigeria to benefit from the commercial supply of arms and other strategic products (of course, in competition with non-African countries). Though understandable, the exploitation of such opportunities could significantly undermine these countries' (that is, South Africa and Nigeria) ability to play an effective role in mediating conflicts in other African countries.[18] In other words, these countries could experience setbacks similar to those that France faced in its intervention in Rwanda (in mid-1994) as a result of its previous partisan links to the Habyarimana regime.

Such drawbacks notwithstanding, these regional leaders should be able to lend the advantages of their economic strength and to join the efforts of other African countries in this critical phase of conflict management. A collective front, underpinned by the economic strength of the regional partners, would need to be directed at: enabling the regions to detect trends leading to escalation of conflict; coping with the problems of refugees; mounting effective peacekeeping and peace-observing missions; supporting activities relating to reconciliation and the negotiation of peace agreements; and limiting, to the extent possible, the amassing of lethal power in the hands of the various parties to conflict.

At present, African countries do not have a conflict management machinery encompassing all these aspects. Of the organizations that have played important regional or subregional roles in the critical phases of escalating and violent conflict—notably, the Organization of African Unity (OAU) and the Economic Community of West African States (ECOWAS)—the focus has thus far been on mediation, peace observing, and peace keeping. In this context, it would seem, particularly in the light of past experiences with conflict management in Chad, Western Sahara, and Liberia, that the roles of the OAU and ECOWAS have been severely restrained by insufficient funds. Thus, for example, the OAU has not until now been able to mount peacekeeping activities of any significance. In contrast, peacekeeping operations—supported mainly by Nigeria—have been fielded in Chad and, more recently, in Liberia, in the context of the intervention by the ECOWAS Monitoring Group (ECOMOG).[19]

Pending a thorough review of the institutional framework for co-operation in Africa, it would be ill advised to embark on the establishment of new organizations for managing conflict on the continent. Indeed, the experience of ECOMOG suggests that regional and subregional security concerns in other parts of Africa could be integrated into existing arrangements for regional cooperation or integration. In particular, it would seem that using subregional groupings, rather than continent-wide organizations such as the OAU, could confer the advantages of enhanced solidarity and timely action. It remains to be seen whether security frameworks of this type could work without a proactive role of the hegemonic power, comparable to that played by Nigeria in mounting ECOMOG. Even with the active involvement of subregional powers, few countries today can afford the economic costs of a protracted management of conflict outside their borders. Accordingly, African countries will have to evolve mechanisms for ensuring a more balanced sharing of the cost of intraregional management of conflict.

The Reconstruction Phase

The regional challenges of managing conflict in this phase are similar to those in the periods of escalating and violent conflict, notably, the concerns for refugees; supporting initiatives directed at ending hostilities; and active roles in peacekeeping and peace-monitoring operations. Moreover, following violent confrontations, the involved demand-bearing groups are likely to be highly suspicious of each other. Under such circumstances, the regional partners' ability to play a positive role in supporting the transition from violence to the normal management of conflict will clearly require a heightened awareness of the implications of their own roles. Thus imprudent actions, such as a hasty return of the refugees, or sustained supply of arms to individual factions to the conflict could easily trigger renewed violence.

Effective management of conflict in this phase will also require that the regional partners address certain legacies of the preceding phases of conflict management. One such legacy will be the residual arms and, for some regional partners, excess capacity in industries that were producing weapons and other essential materials for the ended violent confrontation. Thus, for example, the crossborder flow of guns from Mozambique to South Africa appears to have contributed to the escalation of violence in South Africa, especially during the period leading up to the elections in April 1994.[20] Moreover, as South Africa proceeds through its reconstruction period, efforts are being made to reorient its armaments industry toward markets in the region and elsewhere.

At the regional level, there would seem to be some scope for addressing these kinds of problems. Cash-for-guns programs, possibly supported by the donor community, could withdraw some guns from circulation. The few African countries that have armaments industries could also make a conscious effort to convert them to the production of goods that will not exacerbate conflicts in the region. In order to be effective, such efforts would, however, need to be supplemented by corresponding initiatives at the international level.

International Management of Economic Conflict

Thus far the discussion has focused on the economic aspects of managing conflict largely from a domestic and regional perspective. From an international or extraregional standpoint, the relevant economic issues in the management of conflict are largely determined by the economic and financial flows between African countries and the international community, including, in particular, their implications for the demand-bearing groups; and the terms and conditions associated with these flows, especially insofar as they are the result of a deliberate policy aimed at influencing the management of conflict. In this regard, perhaps the most important areas of attention should include donor assistance from multilateral and bilateral sources and attendant policies concerning governance and other issues that are particularly relevant to the management of conflict.[21]

By increasing the pool of available resources, donor assistance facilitates the management of domestic and regional economic conflicts. On the domestic front, increased resources enable the states, as the managers of conflict, to meet, at least partly, the concerns of the various demand-bearing groups, thereby avoiding extreme denials that could escalate into conflict. At the regional level, likewise, an enhanced availability of resources, such as those provided in the context of SADCC, improves the prospects for positive-sum regional cooperation, an important condition for avoiding distributive conflicts.

However, enhanced availability of resources will not always play a positive role, especially during periods of escalating or violent conflicts. In these periods, supplementary resources from the donor community are often diverted toward partisan ends, thereby defeating the broader aims of avoiding intensified conflict. A related challenge confronting donors is how to detect temporary interruptions in the escalation of conflict, for example, in the period immediately following the signing of the Nkomati Accord or the Arusha Peace Agreement for Rwanda. Donor resources supplied in good faith in these periods could, presumably, have exacerbated the ensuing hostilities. Indeed, in those cases where donors might not be able to withhold assistance— because of standing commitments or owing to irresistible national pressures to protect export markets—there could be room for a more conscious use of conditionality in influencing the management of conflict.

Donor assistance is likely to play a more positive role when conflicts are being managed effectively and the policy focus is on the longer-term considerations of conflict management. In such circumstances, the pursuit of the broader economic goals of development, equitable growth, and financial stability provides effective leverage for managing conflict. Indeed, it would seem that most of the multilateral institutions today address issues of conflict management largely on the assumption that conflicts are being managed effectively. Partly because of this, distributive concerns, including the incidence of policies on specific demand-bearing groups, are often not addressed explicitly. There would therefore seem to be a need for reorienting structural and macroeconomic policies toward the goals of conflict management.

The objectives of donor assistance are also more likely to coincide with those of African states during the reconstruction phase when the focus of economic policy will be on the resettlement of displaced persons, repatriation of refugees, demobilization of combatants, and economic rehabilitation. In this connection, it is worth emphasizing, once more, that the multilateral institutions that play a major role in the flow of resources to Africa are largely geared to supporting structural and macroeconomic reforms rather than to dealing with the aftermaths of violent confrontations. There is, therefore, a need to review this institutional infrastructure to strengthen the ability of the international system to cope with the aftermaths of violent confrontation.

The importance of adequate availability of resources during the reconstruction phase can hardly be overemphasized. In this period, the leadership of the various demand-bearing groups will need to demonstrate to their constituencies that the agreed formulas for ending hostilities and for addressing underlying (distributive) grievances are credible. Thus by adding to the pool of available resources, positive-sum distributive steps could be taken in favor of the principal groups, thereby helping to consolidate the peace process.

The timing and amount of donor assistance does play an important role in the management of conflict. Thus an important challenge for the international community is how to ensure that such assistance is fine-tuned to the specific levels of conflict. As argued earlier, more diversified institutions, possibly including organizations specializing in the reconstruction tasks, could contribute to meeting this challenge. The conditionality of donor assistance must also be reexamined with a view to strengthening its contribution to the management of conflict. The focus of the conditionality and the tools or approaches through which it is applied deserve attention.

From the standpoint of managing conflict, donor assistance would perhaps play a more effective role if the attendant conditionality were focused more directly on the goals of improved governance. For this purpose, governance should be defined broadly to encompass state and society as well as the economic requirements for effective management of conflict. Consistent with this definition, an OECD meeting that was held in Namibia in 1993 stressed the following requirements for good governance: government legitimacy deriving from popular consensus; accountability, transparency, and competency in policy formulation and implementation; the rule of law; and the respect of basic human rights. Within this relatively comprehensive view of governance, Carol Lancaster has singled out elements that are more pertinent to the economic side. These include:

—"transparent budgeting in central and local government agencies" and public enterprise projects;

—"open and competitive bidding" on large public projects;

—"consistency between major public expenditure decisions and plans and commitments" in lending instruments such as the IMF's Policy Framework Paper or the World Bank's Public Expenditure Review Loans; and

—"fair, timely and consistent implementation of laws and regulations affecting trade, investment, and other economic activities."[22]

The managing director of the International Monetary Fund, responding to a question as to whether the IMF can—through the Enhanced Structural Adjustment Facility (ESAF)—address problems of poor governance among the member countries, underscored the economic dimension of governance:

The ESAF does indirectly address poor governance to the extent that it concerns the economic dimension of governance. Many programs have incorporated improvements in accounting, budgeting, and control of public expenditure, to among several things reduce the potential for corruption. Programs also generally emphasize lowering unproductive spending, including excessive military spending, as a key element in achieving sustainable and high-quality fiscal adjustment. The first steps have been greater transparency in the budgetary accounting, including military spending. But each time we contribute to greater accountability, to more transparency (in public accounts, budgets, and so on), and to reducing the size of the state and administrative interventions, we limit the occasions for corruption. Of course, I have no illusions about how much more needs to be done, but we are happy each time we contribute to the reform of government, making it smaller and more efficient.[23]

The recent efforts by donors to influence the economic aspects of good governance constitute a welcome step toward effective management of conflict. There remains, nonetheless, a clear need to extend these efforts to the distributive variables noted above and to specific challenges of each level of conflict. Moreover, enhanced coordination of conditionality, including joint attempts by donors to reduce assistance that could exacerbate violence, would seem to be necessary.

Together with the focus on the economic aspects of good governance, the conditional assistance of the donor community could also be directed at influencing the noneconomic, governance aspects in the management of conflict, including broadly based power sharing; democratic participation; and the identity issues outlined in chapter three. In this, there would seem to be a need for enhanced clarity concerning the intended goals of good governance or state-society relationships. Thus, for example, in seeking to foster democratic participation, it may be necessary to focus not only on holding elections but also on other important considerations such as the fairness and sustainability of the outcomes.

In reorienting donor assistance to the broader goals of governance, it will be necessary to examine the most effective avenue for handling related conditionality. Thus far, the donor community has sought to attach the conditionality to established lending instruments, notably those of international organizations such as the IMF and the World Bank. This is to some extent worrisome. The instruments of these organizations have been developed over the years with specific goals of supporting macroeconomic and economic structural reform. Moreover, the attendant conditionality is, though controversial, effectively directed at facilitating the attainment of these goals. Were this conditionality to be reoriented to the broader aims of managing conflict, including the noneconomic aspects of governance, the lending instruments of these multilateral organizations would tend to lack a sense of direction, thereby compromising their effectiveness. Accordingly, it would seem that the conditional assistance of organizations such as the World Bank and the Fund should, to the extent possible, focus only on the economic aspects of governance and conflict management. Conditionality relating to the noneconomic aspects could, perhaps, be most effectively handled at the level of government-to-government assistance.

Conclusion

Sound economic management, including the pursuit of equitable growth and financial stability, is an integral part of effective management of conflict. In order to meet the concerns of demand-bearing groups, the neoclassical economic focus on questions of allocative efficiency and welfare maximization has to be supplemented by governance and microdistributive considerations bearing on basic economic rights and freedoms, human dignity, and the material well-being of individuals and demand-bearing groups. Special attention must be paid to basic needs of the individual; to foster equitable access to economic opportunities and fairness in the distribution of wealth and income; to protect individual rights to property and incomes; and to safeguard the freedom of individuals in making decisions relating to production, investment and consumption.

Economic policies should also be geared to meeting the particular challenges that arise at specific levels of conflict. Thus, while the pursuit of the broader goals of growth, equity, and stability is to be expected during the periods of the normal level of conflict, in periods of escalating or violent conflicts the focus of economic policy should be on reducing the intensity of conflict. By the same token, during the reconstruction phase economic policy should focus on the aftermaths of the ended conflict (including such issues as economic rehabilitation, resettlement of displaced persons, and disarmament) while simultaneously aiming at the restoration of financial stability and the resumption of longer-term growth. This requires a careful balancing of economic goals and means and a well-coordinated strategy for mobilizing the required resources.

The interaction of normal market forces, government policies, and natural resource endowments gives rise to various problems that complicate the domestic management of conflict. These include the uneven geographic spread of economic activity and inequities in the sharing of resources; racial and ethnic inequities; and transitional problems that normally accompany the processes of economic and political reform. An effective management of conflict requires that governments come to grips with the tensions that are inherent in these situations.

Also helpful in this regard are macroeconomic and structural policies that are aimed at expanding the aggregate level of economic resources; a more effective enlistment of local governments in managing conflicts; and the establishment of a stable political, social, and legal environment to help underpin the required economic policies.

At the regional level, an effective management of conflict requires economic policies directed at coping with the tensions that are inherent in the ongoing processes of regional integration and cooperation. For African countries, such tensions emanate from the spreading acceptance of market-oriented economic systems, the reintegration of South Africa into the region; the multiplicity of approaches to regional integration and cooperation; and the proliferation of institutions of regional integration and cooperation. There are also tensions stemming from perceived inequities in the sharing of the costs and benefits of cooperation and from crossborder labor movements. In order to address these tensions, there is an overriding need for rationalizing the existing institutions and for more innovative mechanisms and institutional approaches to regional cooperation and integration in Africa.

In Africa, international influence on the management of conflict is transmitted mainly through donor assistance and the attendant conditionality. The adaptation of this conditionality to the special challenges of each level of conflict and to the economic and noneconomic requirements of good governance could provide an important tool for managing conflict.

However, the operations of most multilateral institutions are primarily geared toward the normal level of conflict. Accordingly, there is a worrisome institutional vacuum in coping with the special challenges of escalating or violent conflicts and with reconstruction phases. Because of this vacuum, the machinery for garnering required resources in the reconstruction phase and the coordination of donor efforts during the periods of escalating and violent conflicts are at present grossly deficient. This is a problem that merits the urgent attention of the international community.

5

Regional Dynamics

*A*FRICAN conflicts have their roots in the contentious processes of state and nation building, the complex challenges of dignity and justice, governance, identity, and the competition for scarce resources, as analyzed in the previous chapters. Nearly all of the conflicts that have ravaged Africa have their sources in such domestic issues and actors. As noted, responsible sovereignty most fundamentally applies to this level of management.

Each conflict, however, also takes place in a regional context that significantly shapes the dynamics of the struggles, the resources that competing parties bring to bear in pursuit of their objectives, and, therefore, the prospects for managing, transforming, or resolving specific conflicts. Furthermore, conflicts have significant regional repercussions, as instability in one state generates spillover and demonstration effects in neighboring states. Sovereignty as responsibility also implies a regional obligation to "pool sovereignty" and take actions to better manage conflicts, and thereby accept accountability for conditions in the neighborhood.

In some cases the regional environment has assisted in managing a conflict, demonstrating responsible sovereignty on a wider level. Neighbors can help to create a balance of power among parties that encourages negotiations and can mediate or offer guarantees for peace agreements. Responsible regional organizations can facilitate cooperation, regularize relations, build confidence, and develop norms that help to manage conflict. In other regions, however, the setting has amplified or complicated conflict, making management more difficult. Neighboring states often impose a complicating layer of interstate rivalry by providing support to insurgents, regional organizations are weak, the security dilemma leads to conflict escalation, and established regional norms favor one or the other party and thereby discourage compromise. In most cases of African conflict, responsibility and accountability have been even less present at the regional level than at the level of the state.

The regional level of analysis links the internal dynamics of groups struggling for justice, participation, political power, and resources (that is usually the focus of comparative politics) and the diplomacy and warfare that occurs between states (that is usually the subject of international relations). The structures of various regional systems in Africa generate their own imperatives for policymakers and shape the range of choices available. These systems, therefore, play a role in establishing the pattern of relations and the dynamics of conflict management. Specific conflicts develop regional implications along a number of overlapping but analytically distinct dimensions. Regional organizations influence how conflicts are managed by promoting norms and rules that condition state behavior. Such norms have been successful in limiting border conflict in Africa, but largely ineffective regarding internal conflicts. Changing the structure or functions of the regional context may promote conflict management and more responsible sovereignty at the international level.

Regional Security Systems

The continent of Africa may be divided into a number of different regions, depending on the variable or issue area under consideration. Early writers on regional subsystems defined them on the basis of geographic proximity, intensity and regularity of interaction, and recognition of the region as a distinctive area. Some have analyzed the entire African continent as a subordinate subsystem within the international system. Kenneth Grundy categorizes Africa into five regions with respect to major features of political and economic life: the nature of the struggle for independence; organizational and ideological differences associated with patterns of rule; regime performance relative to developmental indicators; the role of the armed forces in politics; and patterns of regional cooperative functional organizations.[1]

This chapter looks at regional security systems, or regional conflict formations. Security complexes, as defined by Barry Buzan, are groups of states whose "primary security concerns link together sufficiently closely that their national securities cannot realistically be considered

apart from one another."[2] Each subsystem or regional conflict formation has a dynamic of its own and therefore affects the pattern of
conflict in particular ways.[3] Overlapping levels of conflict make the
exact boundaries between security systems vague: many states and
conflicts are implicated in more than one regional system. Furthermore, the definition of regions changes over time as the salience of
security issues shifts to new concerns and geographic areas.[4]

The character of specific regions in Africa varies along a continuum
from anarchic, Hobbesian systems marred by endemic conflict to regions with a fair measure of institutionalized cooperation and stability.[5] The former illustrate that the same problems that lead states to
renege on the responsibilities of sovereignty domestically also plague
relationships among states, while the latter demonstrate the potential
for regional structures to promote accountability and conflict management. Some regions have created organizations that institutionalize
their interactions, and some have developed a conscious sense of common identity. Other regions, however, lack these characteristics. The
critical variable in defining a region from a conflict management perspective is the degree to which the actors within a regional system are
unable to ignore other components with regard to issues of security.
Interlinked conflicts and the implications of these linkages for conflict
management, not regional organizations or common identities, create
regional security systems.

Regions generally are organized around certain states that have the
power and position potentially to play the role of the hegemon or act
as a pole around which the security or insecurity of other states re-
volves. The "core state" in each regional constellation possesses key
assets in the form of geographical position, military, economic, political, and diplomatic resources, and recognition as a regional leader. A
large and powerful state inevitably compels its neighbors to shape
their security policies, and to conceive of conflict management, with
reference to itself. This core state may be perceived by its neighbors
as a source of security and protection, leading weaker and more vulnerable states to seek close relations with their protector, a process
described as "bandwagoning."[6] Alternatively, the core state may be
viewed as a threatening power; the region, therefore, is organized on
the basis of an alliance of the insecure neighbors to contain this potentially predominant force. In addition, the disintegration of a core
state may threaten to swamp smaller neighboring states with the en-

suing ripple effects.[7] Whether as protector or threat, actors in a regional system cannot ignore the core state without putting their security at risk.

Southern Africa before 1990, for example, was structured on the principle of small, vulnerable neighbors organizing themselves in common opposition to the threat from apartheid South Africa. In other cases, the core state has used its resources to create organizations for cooperation that are perceived as benefiting the entire region. In West Africa, for example, Nigeria has played this role by providing the economic leadership for the Economic Community of West Africa States (ECOWAS) and the military leadership in the peacekeeping force sponsored by the Organization of African Unity (OAU) in Chad and the ECOWAS Monitoring Group (ECOMOG) intervention in Liberia.[8]

The Southern and West African regional systems have institutional components (the Southern African Development Community [SADC, formerly the Southern African Development Coordination Conference, SADCC] and ECOWAS) that help, but do not by themselves define, the regions. Other regions lack strong organizations but still provide the terrain in which conflicts are engaged and confronted. Sometimes the core state is under siege by its own internal problems and cannot assert its role in organizing the region. Ethiopia's internal conflicts prevented it from playing a hegemonic role in the 1970s and 1980s.[9] Kenya and Tanzania competed to play the primary role in East Africa, leading, in part, to the collapse of the East African Community in 1977. The Horn and East African systems, therefore, are anarchic and lack strong organization or clear leaders. They are still regional security systems, however, because conflict in one member state inherently has consequences for the other regional actors.

Finally, some regions are simply too ambiguous and diverse to coalesce into clear systems. The only state with the size and geographic position to serve as the organizer of Central Africa is Zaire, but the state has lacked the coherence to play that role. Kinshasa's authority rarely filled its recognized borders and was simply unable to generate sufficient gravitational force to pull others into its orbit. As a result, several states that might have formed part of a Central African system have tended either to look elsewhere for benefits or been forced to focus on another region that was a source of insecurity. Cameroon, for example, generally swings between the West African and the more chaotic Central African systems. East African states stepped forward in 1993 and 1994 to attempt to facilitate peaceful transitions in Burundi and Rwanda, in part pulling these two volatile states into the East African security complex. Angola was compelled to relate to the Southern African structure, due to its border with Namibia and the linkages between its internal security and forces to the south. Chad's security concerns have been linked more substantially to Libya, due to Tripoli's hegemonic designs on its southern neighbor.[10] The ability of a state to opt out of a given regional system suggests the weakness of that system. Tanzania, for example, redefined itself as a Southern African state by focusing its attention on its position within the Front Line States and SADCC following the collapse of the East African Community.

Under the bipolar international system of the cold war, regional systems tended to be analyzed as subordinate systems, whose structure was shaped significantly by the actions of the superpowers.[11] Analysts such as Buzan have speculated that the ending of the cold war might make regional dynamics more salient to world politics as the great powers withdraw and allow regional hegemons or regional balances to follow their own dynamics.[12] Richard Rosecrance, however, has suggested that a new "concert of powers" may continue to shape and constrain the development of regional systems.[13] The role of regional security systems relative to the larger international system continued to evolve in the early 1990s. However, the importance of the regional environment for the course of conflicts and the responsible respect for sovereignty will continue.

The Regional Systems

The structure of each region is distinct and has a specific role in shaping how conflicts evolve and how conflict management is practiced. As noted, some African regions (Southern, West) have institutions that help establish norms and regularize relations. Others (Horn, East, Central) currently lack strong organization, and relations, therefore, are more generally conducted on a bilateral basis. In regions without a strong core state or strong institutions, internal relations tend to be more anarchic. Because self-help remains the principal means to achieve security, it is not surprising that many leaders regard their closest neighbors with suspicion. Furthermore, because contiguity is often hostility in international politics, Kautilyan patterns, in which leaders look to the other side of their neighbors to find reliable allies, often result.[14] These tensions embedded within the regional structure often hamper efforts to use a regionalized sense of sovereignty to encourage greater accountability in internal matters.

Regions may be conflict systems or cooperation systems, depending on the nature of the component states and the manner in which security policies interact. The character, and even the definition, of a given region changes over time: Southern Africa, for example, has been transformed from a conflict system defined by the Front Line States' resistance to apartheid South Africa's hegemonic designs, to a regional economic and security community in which postapartheid South Africa plays a leading role.

THE HORN OF AFRICA. The Horn of Africa is defined by the security linkages between Ethiopia, the core state in the region, and its neighbors, Djibouti, Eritrea, Kenya, Somalia, and Sudan. As Ahmed Samatar explains, whether leaders like it or not, three broad factors tie the peoples of the region together: "spatial proximity, historical intimacy, and, most relevantly, common fate in the teeth of harrowing challenges."[15] No strong regional institution directs relations among the states in the Horn; rather, the regional system is characterized by a network of bilateral relations between Ethiopia and each of its neighbors.[16]

In part because of the nature of the region's structure, the Horn of Africa has been the site of serious inter- and intrastate conflict for decades. Ethiopia, a multinational state, and Somalia, a multistate nation, represent a contrast between two types of states that, according to I. M. Lewis, "inevitably creates a fundamental structural conflict of interests and aspirations which is more deeply grounded and refractory than the routine 'border problems' that plague interstate relations in Africa."[17] In the early 1960s the newly independent state of Somalia (formed by the unification of British Somaliland and Italian Somaliland) supported insurgencies among the ethnic Somalis in northern Kenya, French Somaliland (now Djibouti), and the Ogaden region of Ethiopia in an attempt to create a "Greater Somalia" that would encompass all ethnic Somalis.[18] This goal inherently created conflict between Somalia and each of its neighbors. In addition to these conflicts, Ethiopia and Sudan intervened by providing safe haven and logistical support to each other's insurgents. In the early 1990s, however, these interstate conflicts became eclipsed by state breakdown in Somalia and, to a lesser extent, Sudan, with serious spillover effects in Ethiopia, Eritrea, Djibouti, and Kenya.

The Horn of Africa has a regional organization, the Intergovernmental Authority on Drought and Development (IGADD), that has taken on the task of coordinating some regional resource issues.[19] More important for conflict management, its periodic summits have afforded heads of state the opportunity to meet and discuss political questions, including conflict issues. The 1986 IGADD summit, for example, served as the occasion for the leaders of Ethiopia and Somalia to begin talks that led to a detente and the demilitarization of their border. In the early 1990s the threat that conflicts in Somalia and Sudan might infect the transitions taking place elsewhere in the Horn compelled regional leaders to place security issues high on IGADD's agenda.[20]

In September 1993 IGADD took up the challenge of mediating an end to the brutal civil war in Sudan.[21] After a series of unsuccessful talks, some of Sudan's neighbors determined that the government in Khartoum was not interested in compromise and began to provide support for the insurgent Sudan People's Liberation Army (SPLA). Eritrea broke off relations with Khartoum and hosted a meeting of Sudanese opposition leaders, Ethiopia accused Khartoum of involvement in the assassination attempt against Egyptian president Hosni Mubarak in Addis Ababa, and Kampala charged that Sudan was supporting rebels in northern Uganda.[22] Eritrean president Isaias Afewerki was blunt: "The stability of the region depends on the regime's defeat. There is no more room for diplomacy, and no compromise."[23] Many observers believed that neighboring states were supplying arms to the SPLA.

The structure of the Horn of Africa system, therefore, characterized for the past thirty-five years by mutual intervention by proxy and bilateral conflictual relations between weak states, underwent a transformation as a number of states faced collapse in the early and mid-1990s. Ethiopia divided when the former Italian colony of Eritrea, that had been federated and then unified with Ethiopia, received its independence after a thirty-year civil war. The remainder of Ethiopia was experimenting with a new political system that invested significant political power in the ethnic or nationality group, raising the potential for the country either to become a loose federation of ethnic ministates or to splinter into numerous separate states. Somalia already had collapsed, the initial chaos followed by United Nations intervention and withdrawal in the south, and a new self-proclaimed but internationally unrecognized Republic of Somaliland in the north.[24] The unresolved civil war in Sudan led many southern Sudanese to advocate separation as a solution. Crossborder ethnic affiliation threatened to divide Djibouti, and rising tensions put the Kenyan state at risk as well.

EAST AFRICA. East Africa has had a long and often troubled history with regional cooperation. Kenya, Tanganyika (now Tanzania), and Uganda achieved independence with a common British colonial heritage and preexisting institutions of economic cooperation, including a customs union and jointly operated common services organization.[25] Disputes over the rules and institutions for regional economic cooperation dominated interstate relations in the 1960s and early 1970s. The three states signed the treaty that created the East African Community (EAC) in 1967 to institutionalize cooperation. The treaty characterized the community's goal as "accelerated, harmonious, and balanced development and sustained expansion of economic activities the benefits whereof shall be equitably shared."[26]

Each member state, however, had different views on what was balanced and equitable. The community quickly became mired in political differences between the member states and squabbling over the distribution of benefits, and as a result of these conflicts, eventually collapsed in acrimony in 1977. As Peter Anyang' Nyong'o has remarked, "Economically, the East African Community made a lot of sense; politically, it failed to survive because the claims of national sovereignty and the ideological divergence of the partners called for its collapse." John Ravenhill points out that the EAC was plagued by problems typical of cooperative ventures by developing countries, most notably, perceptions of unequal benefits and the inability to place regional cooperation above short-term national interests.[27]

More important than differences over the distribution of benefits, the EAC collapsed because it could not contain the tensions generated by the coup that brought Idi Amin to power in Uganda in 1971. "The Uganda problem" dominated East African regional politics and sparked both domestic and regional insecurity. Tanzanian leader Julius Nyerere refused to accept Amin's nominees to the EAC and supported the deposed Ugandan leader Milton Obote. Amin invaded northern

Tanzania in October 1978, and Nyerere responded by organizing Ugandan opposition forces and, ultimately, by sending his troops to depose Amin. The new Ugandan leaders, however, failed to create domestic security, and a new round of civil war broke out between the government in Kampala and the insurgent National Resistance Army (NRA). Kenyan leader Daniel arap Moi organized talks between Tito Okello's regime in Kampala and Yoweri Museveni's NRA in August 1985. The NRA, however, smelled victory and overran Kampala in January 1986, an action that Moi regarded as a personal affront. Moi and Museveni quarreled in the late 1980s with border skirmishes, charges of harboring and training each other's opponents, the expulsion of diplomats, and allegations that a Ugandan plane had bombed northwestern Kenya. In 1987 Kenya closed its border with Uganda, thereby depriving Uganda of access to the sea.[28]

Political power in East Africa has been highly personalistic, making long-term cooperation subject to competition for prestige among the individual leaders. Leaders have used bad relations with their neighbors as a rallying cry for national solidarity and as a tactic to paint domestic opponents as traitors working for outside interests. In November 1992, Kenyan president Daniel arap Moi, Tanzanian president Ali Hassan Mwinyi, and Ugandan president Museveni met in Arusha and decided to revive the East African Community. The three leaders discussed a joint military structure, in large part as a means of protecting their regimes against coup attempts, and perceived that there would be economic benefits from a regional organization, given the shift of investment from East Africa toward South Africa.[29]

Political developments and conflict in Rwanda and Burundi have often had consequences in East African states. Ethnic massacres in Rwanda in 1962 led thousands of Tutsis to flee into Uganda. Years later, some joined Ugandan insurgents in overthrowing the government in Kampala. Some of these same refugees, or their children, formed the Rwandese Patriotic Front (RPF), and in 1990 launched an invasion of northeastern Rwanda. In 1994 ethnic violence and political instability in Rwanda and Burundi led Tanzanian leader Ali Hassan Mwinyi to invite leaders from these two states (along with the leaders of Kenya, Uganda, Zaire, and Zambia, and OAU secretary general Salim Ahmed Salim) to discuss regional security. As a Tanzanian official explained, "without peace in Burundi and Rwanda, our countries will also not be secure."[30] Uganda and Kenya split over policies toward

Rwanda, with Kampala supporting the Rwandese Patriotic Front while Nairobi resisted international attempts to prosecute members of the old regime who were implicated in genocide.[31] The collapse of the state in Rwanda and the threat of collapse in Burundi led neighboring states to try to assume some of the responsibilities of sovereignty and fill the destabilizing vacuum of authority.

SOUTHERN AFRICA. The Southern African regional security system, defined here to include the members of South African Development Community (Angola, Namibia, South Africa, Botswana, Lesotho, Swaziland, Zimbabwe, Zambia, Malawi, Mozambique, and Tanzania), has been dominated by the southward drive of the forces of liberation from minority and colonial rule. As described by Thomas Ohlson and Stephen Stedman, the region has been an arena for three interlocked conflicts for thirty years: the struggles for independence in Zimbabwe, Mozambique, Angola, and Namibia; the attempt by South Africa to maintain white supremacy at home; and the related conflicts between South Africa and its neighbors as the apartheid government sought to prevent decolonization and thereby keep the forces of change at a distance.[32]

In contrast to most of the other regions, Southern Africa has significant intraregional economic links.[33] The transportation infrastructure, particularly the railroads, ties the states together, and there is a relatively regionalized labor market.[34] A fair amount of intraregional trade existed in the 1980s, despite sanctions against South Africa, and this undoubtedly will expand in the postapartheid 1990s. Sustainable regional development requires cooperation on resource issues, such as water projects like the Lesotho Highland Water Scheme.[35]

Patterns of relations in Southern Africa have been created by the contest between two competing visions of how the region should be structured: an apartheid South African concept of a constellation of states subservient to Pretoria, on the one hand, and a region unified by its opposition to racial privilege, on the other. South Africa's superior military power and its ability to both threaten and reward its neighbors compelled vulnerable regional leaders either to find some form of modus vivendi with Pretoria or to seek safety by joining other neighbors in a regional security coalition.

The South African Customs Union that tied Botswana, Namibia, Lesotho, and Swaziland to South Africa in a formal trade relationship, for example, represented an attempt to reach accommodation with Pretoria. On the other hand, South Africa's neighbors organized to pool their respective power and international voices in a common front against apartheid's threat. The regional states formed the Southern African Development Coordination Conference (now known as the Southern African Development Community), a functionalist organization that succeeded mostly in winning international assistance as a part of the antiapartheid struggle. Now that South Africa has joined the organization, a major transformation is required.[36] In August 1995 the first SADC meeting with South Africa in attendance produced agreement to share scarce water resources, but little progress toward the organization's goal of a common market.[37] As the Southern African regional system changes from a conflict to a cooperation system, the organization will need to develop new capacities as the facilitator of this regional cooperation.

Neighboring states have played critically important roles in peace settlements, indicating the regional nature of security in Southern Africa and the opportunities to strengthen responsible sovereign states through regional cooperation. Zambia and Mozambique pressured the Patriotic Front in Zimbabwe to accept the Lancaster House settlement and the Front Line States were instrumental in pressuring the South West African People's Organization (SWAPO) to accept agreements, and in bringing the conflicting sides in Mozambique together.[38] The threats made in 1994 by South Africa, Zimbabwe, and Botswana that reversed a coup in Lesotho, and the role that regional states played in pressuring RENAMO leader Alphonse Dhaklama to accept the results of the November 1994 election in Mozambique show that regionalized norms of behavior are developing, at least as regards governance. The antiapartheid Front Line States grouping was transformed into the Association of Southern African States (ASAS) with the admission of South Africa in 1994. The ASAS intends to act as a conflict management and peacekeeping instrument.[39]

WEST AFRICA. The West African regional system is characterized by Nigeria's predominance in terms of economics, military power, size, and population.[40] At the same time, Nigeria is often estranged from its smaller Francophone neighbors (often supported by Paris) who resist what they perceive as the imperious efforts of Lagos to organize the region without due regard to their interests. A conflict over status and leadership between Nigeria, on the one hand, and its Francophone neighbors, particularly Senegal and Côte d'Ivoire, on the other, has shaped, in part, the dynamics of conflict management efforts in West Africa.

The region is structured formally in the Economic Community of West African States, founded in May 1975, that now includes sixteen states from Mauritania to Nigeria.[41] ECOWAS has coordinated steps on such economic matters as telecommunications and the reduction of barriers to intraregional trade, while setting aside several more politically delicate issues, such as a subregional defense pact. Each of the member states continues to hold on to sovereignty, and when leaders perceive ECOWAS agreements as threatening regime stability, violations are not uncommon. For example, border closures have taken place despite ECOWAS's norms, including the Togo-Benin border in 1975–77, the Sierra Leone-Liberia border in 1983–85, and the Nigerian border in 1983.[42] In January 1983 and again in April 1985 Nigeria expelled millions of non-Nigerian workers, subverting the 1979 protocol on the free movement of persons, creating significant resentment among neighboring states, and destabilizing neighboring Benin in the process.[43] The organization has faced rivals, such as the West African Monetary Union (UMOA) and the Communauté Economique de l'Afrique de l'Ouest (CEAO), two organizations of Francophone states engaged in postcolonial cooperation and inspired, in part, by fear of Nigerian hegemony.[44] Yet despite these conflicts, ECOWAS has survived as a regional organization.[45]

Although the primary focus of ECOWAS is on regional economic questions, the Liberian crisis of 1989 forced West African leaders to recognize the need to intervene when political problems threaten the region. ECOWAS executive secretary Abass Bundu stated that "the Liberian crisis has demonstrated . . . that it is futile to talk about economic integration unless the environment in which you pursue such integration is peaceful and secure."[46] Benin's head of state, Nicephore Soglo, then acting president of the organization, articulated an obligation of neighboring states to intervene: "Each of our states in the sub-region constitutes a link in a chain of solidarity which can fail as soon as one of us is threatened with destabilization. No question linked to peace and security in our states can only be considered as one of national sovereignty."[47] The West African military intervention in Liberia (discussed in detail in chapter six below) revealed a number of characteristics of the regional security system. The role of Nigeria as the principal power in the region and the rivalry between Nigeria and the Francophone states were evident in the often controversial intervention.[48]

West Africa, therefore, is structured, in large part, by Nigeria's position in the region. Nigeria has been perceived by some of its neighbors as a threat, while simultaneously it has played the role of regional organizer. Political instability in Nigeria following the canceled elections of 1993 and the potential for serious internal conflict may lead to a change in the country's regional role. As has been the case in Central Africa and the Horn of Africa, a regional structure may fall into chaos if the core state itself is besieged with internal problems. This threat will remain for West Africa until the governance issue in Nigeria is settled.

CENTRAL AFRICA. Zaire is Africa's natural heartland, stretching from Sudan to Zambia, Congo to Tanzania. Like Ethiopia, Nigeria, and Algeria, Zaire is a potentially dominant power in its region. This potential compels its Central African neighbors to include Kinshasa in their security calculations. Zaire's weakness as a state, with poor communications, an incompetent military, an alienated population, and a political system based on institutionalized corruption, has prevented it from assuming this role. Until 1974 Zaire was on the front line of the anticolonial battle due to its border with Portuguese Africa, and its regional relations developed from this position. Thereafter it has had to develop a structure of relations with its neighbors, including several that were ideologically hostile.[49]

In the early 1960s Zaire (known as Congo until 1971) underwent a series of internal crises as precipitous decolonization threw the state into chaos. After a series of rebellions, mutinies, attempts at secession, short-lived regimes, external interventions, and a controversial and costly United Nations peacekeeping effort, Mobutu seized control in November 1965 and instituted a single party, authoritarian, corrupt, unitary political system.[50] By eliminating political freedom in Zaire, Mobutu forced opposition movements to organize in neighboring states. As a result, conflicts between Zaire and its neighbors flared up regularly in the 1970s and 1980s. In 1977 and 1978, for example, opposition groups operating out of northern Angola invaded Zaire's Shaba province. Zaire, in turn, supported opponents of the Popular Movement for the Liberation of Angola (MPLA) regime in Luanda.

The incoherence of Zaire, and the distraction of its conflict with forces in Angola, allowed the other potential members of a Central African regional system to pay less attention to Zaire. Leaders in Zambia sometimes shared Zaire's choices for political clients in places like Angola, but did not get involved in a similar conflict of mutual intervention by proxy. Zaire's neighbors to the east (Rwanda, Burundi, Tanzania, and Uganda) largely focused on East African issues. By 1994 reporters were describing Zaire as a completely collapsed state with much of its infrastructure reverting to the bush, government services completely absent, security forces on the rampage, and politics a stalemate between Mobutu and a divided, weak opposition.[51]

NORTH AFRICA. The states of North Africa clearly form another regional security system. The region shares a common culture and sense of identity, and the Arab Maghrib Union (UMA) has served as an organizational focus since 1989.[52] As a security system, the region is characterized by a structural rivalry between Morocco and Algeria. As in the conflict between Ethiopia and Somalia, Morocco and Algeria represent two competing organizing principles of the state: the historic Sharifian empire of Morocco versus the more recent concept of Algeria based on colonial boundaries and the politics of national liberation and self-determination. The two states fought a border war in 1963 and have used the decolonization of the Western Sahara as an arena in which to contest that rivalry.[53]

North African politics on occasion involves neighboring states to the south, for example, Libya's involvement in Chad and Sudan, and the Western Sahara conflict that drew in Mauritania and threatened to split the Organization of African Unity in the early 1980s. The internal political struggle for power that threatened to destroy the Algerian state in the 1990s, and similar threats to the other North African states, demonstrate that the region is not immune from the problems of instability that have troubled sub-Saharan Africa.

The major conflict that divides the region is the Western Sahara. On one side is Morocco, asserting historic claims over the sparsely populated region that predate the creation of the Spanish colony. On the other side, the Popular Front for the Liberation of Saguia el-Hamra and Rio de Oro (POLISARIO) struggles to assert the independence of the Saharan Arab Democratic Republic (SADR). Algeria provides critical support to Polisario, including refuge and arms, in a bid to limit Morocco's regional role. Mauritania at first supported Morocco's claims, but recognized the SADR in 1987. Libya, typically, has alternately supported and withdrawn its support at the whims of Muammar Qadhafi. Tunisia has attempted to remain neutral.[54]

The Western Sahara conflict is, in part, a proxy battlefield where Algeria and Morocco compete over being the primary power in the Maghreb. The issue provides Algeria leverage over Moroccan ambitions in the region.[55] For Morocco, it provides a useful issue on which to rally domestic political support. A United Nations mission to resolve the conflict by referendum bogged down in charges and counter-charges between Rabat and the POLISARIO over the determination of eligible voters and other aspects of implementing the agreement.[56] The Western Saharan conflict, therefore, was supported, in part, by the nature of the regional rivalry between its opponent and its patron.

In the early 1990s the Polisario's leadership underwent a reorganization as pressure from Morocco and defections took their toll. At the same time Algeria suffered from violent internal conflict as an Islamic movement known as the Front Islamique du Salut (FIS) fought for political power against a succession of weak military governments. On the other hand, Morocco managed to develop a relatively strong economy with a largely peaceful society. The resolution of the Western Sahara issue may require further internal developments in the parties. Their divergent political paths and varying degrees of stability likely will hamper North African cooperation in the coming years.[57]

Regionalization of Conflict

Most of the bloodiest conflicts in Africa have occurred within the borders of recognized states. As stated at the outset of this chapter, however, the regional context shapes the course of such conflicts, and internal conflicts have regional repercussions. Internal conflicts inherently draw in neighboring states in one manner or another.[58] This is particularly true in state systems such as Africa where sovereignty is weak, regime legitimacy is often under challenge, and borders are often porous. As Mohammed Ayoob puts it, "fragile polities, by definition, are easily permeable. Therefore, internal issues in Third World societies . . . get transformed into inter-state issues quite readily."[59] Weak African governments can rarely control their borders from smugglers and illegal population movements during times of peace. When the state is further strapped by conflict, people (refugees and insurgents) and contraband (weapons and the smuggled goods that sometimes finance insurgencies) cross with little restriction. Conflict in Africa, therefore, generally is rooted in local struggles but played out in regional arenas.

Governments and insurgents in Africa use the regional context to obtain the resources and support they need to pursue their military strategies. Neighbors can assist one or the other party by altering policies relating to safe haven, deliveries of military equipment, cross-border humanitarian relief operations, and a broad range of other activities that impinge on the course of the conflict. In the Horn of Africa, for example, insurgents and governments were able to sustain extremely high levels of fighting because they could extract resources in the form of military supplies, food aid, and remittances from the region and beyond.[60] Because the regional context shapes how parties to a conflict perceive their choices, changes at the regional level can help or hinder efforts to manage conflict.

Patterns of Regionalization

Regionalized conflicts may be analyzed along five overlapping but distinguishable dimensions: internal conflict regionalized as a result of spillover effects; internal conflict regionalized as a consequence of domestic politics pursued outside a state's borders; internal conflict regionalized by a neighbor's attempt to use it as an instrument to change a government's leadership or policies; interstate conflict over the sovereignty of borderlands and peoples; and regional conflict driven by status rivalries among states. Any specific conflict may play out on one or more of these facets, and many conflicts change over time and move into different dimensions. These five dimensions are arranged to suggest that the regional level of analysis includes issues of both domestic governance and international relations.

SPILLOVER EFFECTS. Internal conflicts in Africa often develop regional ramifications due to spillover effects as nearby states are threatened by the consequences of a neighbor's civil strife. Given weak sovereignty and permeable borders, instability from one internal conflict often is transmitted to neighboring states, particularly because the neighbor generally suffers from similar conditions. The connections between the violence in Rwanda and Burundi were tragically clear in 1993 and 1994. As Alex Shoumatoff characterizes it, the two states are "yoked by a common culture, language, and history. They are mirror images of a single nightmare, and they feed each other's violence; most people felt that it was only a matter of time—weeks, months, a year at most—before the aftershock of Rwanda would hit Burundi. (In fact, the killings in Rwanda were partly a reaction to an under-reported massacre last fall in Burundi, in which tens of thousands—perhaps even hundreds of thousands—were killed.)"[61] Whether in terms of refugees, arms flows, demonstration effects, or as the base from which opposition (including armed insurgency) is organized, neighbors are drawn into internal conflicts.

Evidence of spillover conflicts in Africa is abundant. Southern Africa faced regionwide instability as a result of the struggles against colonialism in Angola, Mozambique, Zimbabwe, and Namibia, and apartheid in South Africa. Conflict in Sierra Leone and the 1992 military coup were stimulated by the chaotic conditions brought about by the conflict in neighboring Liberia. In the early 1990s, the Somali conflict spilled into northern Kenya, the breakdown of security in northeastern Ethiopia following the overthrow of Mengistu in 1991 led some armed Afar militias to cross into Djibouti, where they joined with dissident forces, and Rwandan refugees in eastern Zaire created conflict when their presence disrupted local ethnic balances.[62]

The flight of refugees to neighboring countries is nearly always the direct and tragic consequence of internal conflict. Conflicts create refugees, and these refugees both stimulate additional conflict and hamper efforts to manage the conflict.[63] Africa has a ruinous number of refugees and internally displaced persons. Refugees pose a substantial economic and social burden on the host country, thereby further complicating domestic problem solving. Refugee camps also have traditionally served as important recruitment grounds for insurgencies and often have become pawns in interstate conflicts.

The permeability of borders in Africa applies to political ideas as well as insurgents, refugees, and arms. The literature on Africa has focused on the demonstration and diffusion effects of nationalism, coups d'état, and conflicts.[64] Political messages other than conflict, however, may also be transmitted across national borders. Julius Nyerere, for example, clearly anticipated in 1990 that Tanzania would soon face pressures to liberalize politics when he saw conditions changing in the region. Nyerere told local journalists that "when you see your neighbor being shaved, you should wet your beard. Otherwise you could get a rough shave."[65] The series of national conferences leading to political liberalization in Francophone Africa clearly were connected; activists in Cameroon, Congo, and elsewhere came to understand the potential of this form of activity from their neighbors in Benin.[66] Political change can "snowball" across a region as the message and momentum of reform in one state carry over into neighboring states.[67]

Gilbert Khadiagala has suggested that security may be conceived as a learning process as contagious as a coup or conflict. Multiparty elections in Namibia (November 1989) and Zambia (October 1991) greatly influenced both the regimes and opposition movements in Zimbabwe, Tanzania, and Malawi. Lesson-drawing by regional leaders takes place continuously, and policymakers can emulate successful neighbors or seek to avoid their mistakes. Officials trying to implement the 1992 peace agreement in Mozambique, for example, clearly drew lessons from the 1991 Angolan debacle. Which lessons are most appropriately drawn, however, is often a highly contested matter in conflict situations.[68] Political and military leaders in northern Somalia, the Oromo, Somali, and Afar regions of Ethiopia, and southern Sudan are all considering the precedent set by Eritrea's successful struggle for self-determination.

Unresolved refugee problems have provided the tinder for interstate conflict. Following ethnic massacres against the minority Tutsi group in 1962, thousands fled to neighboring countries. After lingering for decades, a group of Rwandans living in Uganda formed the Rwandese Patriotic Front and launched a major assault on government forces from their bases in Uganda in October 1990. Rwandese president Juvénal Habyarimana condemned the RPF as a foreign force, and many of the insurgents had served in Ugandan president Yoweri Museveni's National Resistance Army. Although the underlying source of the conflict was rooted in the struggle over political participation and power in Rwanda, the unresolved refugee issue provided the form in which the struggle was fought.[69]

In Mauritania internal ethnic, religious, and racial divisions stimulated a conflict with spillover effects in Senegal that generated a three-year border war. The deaths of two Senegalese in a 1989 grazing rights disagreement provoked riots against Mauritanians living in Senegal and the expulsion of Senegalese from Mauritania. The "Moorish" and pro-Arab Mauritanian government led by Colonel Maawiya Ould Sid'Ahmed Taya used the opportunity to deport large numbers of dark-skinned Mauritanians as well. Other "black" Mauritanians fled to Senegal as refugees. Interstate tensions increased, and Dakar accused Nouakchott of providing arms to rebels in the Senegalese Casamance region. Internal forces (radical Arabs in Mauritania, opposition groups in Senegal) seized on the issue and constrained the two governments from managing the conflict. Border skirmishes flared in 1990 and ineffective mediation efforts under OAU auspices failed. Diplomatic links between the two states were reestablished in April 1992 and the border reopened, but the issue of black Mauritanians and Senegal continued unresolved.[70]

One dimension of regional conflict, therefore, is derived from the porous nature of Africa's borders and the inevitable spillover and demonstration effects that are broadcast from one conflict to neighbors throughout a region. Completely preventing such ripple effects is not feasible, although more effective management of the movements of refugees and arms would help. Ultimately, better governance, more responsible sovereignty, and hence better management of internal conflicts will minimize the regional conflicts stimulated by spillover effects.

REGIONALIZED POLITICAL SPACE. Another aspect of a state's internal struggle for political power that has become regionalized relates to the pattern and consequences of opposition movements operating in exile. The single party and military governments that have ruled much of Africa since independence have prevented the organization of legitimate internal opposition, thereby dictating that alternative leaders and groups seeking to participate in government need to agitate and organize—often militarily—from outside the state. Politics in a given state, therefore, has often been pursued outside the state's borders, and tensions between neighbors have inevitably developed.[71] Although such conflict does not relate to border disputes or irredenta, the propensity of states to allow their territory to be used by their neighbors' political opponents has regionalized politics and conflict, adding an additional level of conflict to the domestic political competition. Because many African governments have prohibited domestic opposition, the "domestic realm" of a country's politics has often transcended the boundaries of the territorial state.[72]

The Shaba conflicts of the late 1970s illustrate the manner in which the disjunction between the political space of domestic politics and the legally sovereign territorial space of the state in question has created conflict. Conflict erupted between neighboring Angola and Zaire in 1977 and again in 1978 as a result of each state's harboring and supporting the other's opposition groups. Both states had experienced difficult and violent transitions to independence, and the losers in the struggle to control the new government sought, and readily received, refuge and support in the neighboring territory. Defeated military forces from the insurgency in the mineral-rich province of Katanga (later renamed Shaba) fled to Angola in the mid-1960s. These forces, organized as the Congolese National Liberation Front (FLNC) in 1968, acted as mercenaries for various parties during the Angolan civil war. Angolan nationalist groups similarly organized themselves in Zaire during the struggle against Portuguese colonialism. Zairian leader Mobutu Sese Seko's attempt to control the struggle failed when he backed the National Liberation Front of Angola (FLNA) against the victorious Popular Movement for the Liberation of Angola. Angolan dissidents, however, continued to use Zaire as a base of operations in their struggle against the MPLA government. Each state, then, harbored significant refugee and exile communities from its neighbor, as well as opposition movements that periodically crossed the border to raid and agitate among the disaffected. Neither party fully controlled the borderlands on which this activity was taking place, and each one blamed the other for any instability.[73]

In March 1977 a group of about 1,500 former Katanganese gendarmes and their followers invaded Zaire from their bases in Angola and advanced on the mining centers, meeting little resistance from the Zairian military. Moroccan troops flew to Mobutu's rescue and eventually repulsed the invasion. A second, more effective, invasion occurred in May 1978 and lasted until a force of French, Belgians, Moroccans, Senegalese, and other West Africans intervened.[74]

The Shaba invasions took place in an environment of multiple, interlinked conflicts: one among Angolan political movements; one among Zairian political movements; the interstate conflict between Angola and Zaire whereby each intervened in the other's affairs by proxy, through their respective support for each other's opposition; and the cold war conflict in which Zaire's patrons (principally the United States, France, and Belgium) competed with Angola's (most notably the Soviet Union and Cuba) for influence in the region. The regional dimension, whereby both the Angolan and the Zairian domestic political struggles took place partly outside their respective borders, made resolution of the internal conflicts more difficult.

Other examples of the domestic political realm incorporating space outside the borders of the state in question are numerous. Sudanese opposition groups organize politically in Cairo and run major food relief operations through nongovernment organizations in Kenya and Uganda. The African National Congress managed camps for political exiles and its military wing from Tanzania and elsewhere in southern Africa. The Zimbabwean opposition operated from Mozambique and Zambia until the Lancaster House agreements allowed them to organize at home, and the POLISARIO existed largely in Algeria, rather than the Western Sahara. If a regime liberalizes and permits legitimate opposition to operate at home, then the regional dimension resulting from exiled opponents will lose its relevance. States practicing more responsible policies at home will have little to fear from exile groups.

REGIONALIZED CONFLICTS TO CHANGE POLICIES. The first two dimensions—spillover effects and domestic politics pursued outside the target state—highlight the structure of regional relations in an African state system where sovereignty is weak, legitimacy is questioned, and borders are porous. A third dimension focuses on the regional implications of a policy decision by one government to support a neighboring insurgency in an attempt to change the neighbor's leadership or policies. Such regional aspects of a conflict reflect the conscious or instrumental decision of a neighbor, rather than a neighbor's involvement due to a common border or the inability to limit spillover effects.

As I. William Zartman points out, the attitude of a neighboring state to an internal conflict "may be either friendly or hostile, but scarcely indifferent."[75] A neighbor's interest in an internal conflict often leads to "conflict triangulation" among the insurgents, the home state, and the host state. For example, the Eritrean People's Liberation Front (EPLF) received safe haven and logistical support from neighboring Sudan in its struggle against Ethiopia. In response, the vulnerable Ethiopian regime provided sanctuary and sustenance to the insurgent Sudan People's Liberation Movement and Army (SPLM/A). Leaders in both Khartoum and Addis Ababa countered subversion from outside by reciprocating.[76] Zartman's findings suggest that triangulation of a bilateral conflict generally makes the chances for negotiation worse and makes conflicts more intractable.[77]

African states often use their relationship with a neighbor's insurgents to attempt to compel, coerce, or persuade that neighbor to change a policy or alter its leadership. The support for such insurgencies has been provided in a multitude of ways, including offering safe haven, providing access to radio facilities for propaganda purposes, serving as a conduit for arms or other supplies, training military forces, and diplomatic support. The weakness of most African states and their poor record on governance means that opposition groups are usually available if a neighbor is seeking to use this lever. Insurgents generally also seek the support of neighboring states; thus there is an offer of support and a willing recipient. As George Modelski has stated, "every internal war creates a demand for foreign intervention."[78]

In some cases vulnerable leaders will exaggerate an external threat in order to solidify their hold over their society and enable them to delegitimize internal opposition by characterizing it as the proxy of an external power. Ethiopia, particularly under Mengistu Haile Mariam, regularly labeled Eritrean insurgents as mere mercenaries of covetous Arab states. Idi Amin staged a border conflict and sent his army against Tanzania in 1978, in part to divert attention from his internal problems.[79]

In other cases the neighboring state has not merely offered support to an already existing insurgency movement, but has actively recruited and developed such a force explicitly to weaken, if not bring down, another regime. The Rhodesian Central Intelligence Organization, for example, initially created the Mozambique National Resistance (MNR) to weaken the Mozambican government. When Zimbabwe received independence in 1980, South Africa stepped in and used the MNR to devastate Mozambique and thereby limit Maputo's ability to contribute to the antiapartheid struggle.[80] Similarly, the Revolutionary United Front in Sierra Leone was created, in part, by Charles Taylor of the NPFL in order to hinder Sierra Leonean leader Valentine Strasser's ability to participate in the ECOMOG intervention against Taylor. Nigeria and Guinea sent troops to Sierra Leone to bolster Strasser, thereby replicating the conflict between ECOMOG and Taylor in a neighboring country.[81]

The internal upheaval in Uganda during Amin's brutal government had regional consequences as refugees fled to Tanzania and other neighboring countries, and Dar es Salaam allowed Ugandan opposition movements to organize on its territory. The regional context changed in late 1978, however, when Amin invaded Tanzania in an effort to control his splintering power base, punish opposition forces operating from exile in Tanzania, and divert attention from deteriorating internal conditions. Tanzanian leader Julius Nyerere struck back, sending his armed forces all the way to the Ugandan capital, Kampala, and deposing Amin. Tanzania sponsored a conference among the Ugandan opposition that created the Uganda National Liberation Front, led by Yusufu Lule, to take power in Uganda. Lule lasted only a few months, however. Tanzania's intervention succeeded in removing Amin, but could not rebuild the collapsed Ugandan state. Chaos and violence in Uganda continued to spill across its borders for years.[82]

Ethiopia and Sudan similarly used the presence of refugees and exiled opposition movements on their territory to attempt to influence each other's policies, and even bring down each other's regime. Leaders in Khartoum supported various Eritrean insurgent groups seeking independence, and the government in Addis Ababa, in turn, provided logistical support and safe haven for southern Sudanese insurgent groups. Both Khartoum and Addis Ababa had to govern incompletely integrated multiethnic populations in weak, poorly institutionalized states. Each was threatened by the other's policy of intervening by proxy in a mutually destructive game of tit-for-tat. Sudan and Ethiopia could counter subversion from the outside only by threatening to reciprocate. They, therefore, were reluctant to cut their ties to neighboring rebel groups. The ability to destabilize a neighbor, however, did not serve as a deterrent to conflict. Instead, a cycle of spiraling provocation disrupted the relationship: state weakness and vulnerability encouraged intervention by proxy. The resulting interstate conflict between Ethiopia and Sudan, therefore, seemed to result from their very similarities and common vulnerabilities.[83]

Finally, South Africa intervened in and destabilized its neighbors, in part, as a means to limit support for the African National Congress (ANC) and other antiapartheid groups. South African support for

RENAMO, for example, provided the leverage that forced Samora Machel to sign the Nkomati accords, ending Mozambique's support for the ANC. South Africa also used its support for the National Union for the Total Independence of Angola (UNITA) in Angola as a stick with which to pressure the Angolan government to limit its support for SWAPO in Namibia.[84]

In all of these cases the management of internal conflicts, whether between Ugandan political groups, Eritreans and Ethiopians, southern Sudanese and the government in Khartoum, MPLA and UNITA, or FRELIMO and RENAMO, was made more complicated by the involvement of a neighboring state. A neighboring government's motivation for supporting an insurgency is different than the motivation of the insurgency itself, thereby creating an additional layer of conflict to be managed. Although the fundamental basis of the conflict is internal political issues, interstate dynamics and forces from the regional level enter the equation for all parties, making conflict management more difficult.

REGIONALIZED CONFLICTS OVER SOVEREIGNTY AND PEOPLES OF THE BORDERLANDS. The next level of regionalization includes those aspects of conflict that relate to borders and questions of sovereignty. This dimension is more international, but is still linked to internal political issues because the attitude and sense of identity of the peoples who inhabit these borderlands, and often straddle the international frontier, is critical. In addition, the artificial nature of Africa's borders means that any state that is looking for a conflict with a neighbor can always find a border issue as the pretext.[85]

The conflict between Ethiopia and Somalia that twice broke into significant interstate warfare over the Ogaden region illustrates this dimension. Leaders in Ethiopia and Somalia have based their regimes on principles that have resulted in antithetical security goals. Ethiopia's security has been predicated on maintaining territorial integrity and building cohesion within its multinational population. These goals have required its regimes to insist on maintaining sovereignty and control over the Somalis who have inhabited the Ogaden. Somali leaders, in contrast, have aimed to create a "Greater Somalia" nation-state that would incorporate Somalis living not only in the Ogaden, but also in northern Kenya and parts of Djibouti. Actions by either Ethiopia or Somalia in pursuit of these conflicting conceptions of security increase the perceived insecurity of the other. The conflict, therefore, is structural, for the organizing principles of the two states contradict each other and implicate them so closely they can not simply ignore each other's existence.[86]

This tension between opposing principles of statehood and state identities has flared into periodic violence. At the 1963 OAU meeting, the Somali and Ethiopian representatives accused each other of seeking territorial aggrandizement across their common frontier.[87] In early 1964 the two states clashed along their border and engaged in a provocative propaganda campaign. The fighting escalated until Sudan, acting as a third party under the auspices of the OAU, mediated a cease-fire and established a demilitarized zone on both sides of the border. Tensions, however, remained high and each side accused the other of border violations.[88] Following the 1974 Ethiopian revolution, Somalia increased its support to the Western Somali Liberation Front insurgency in the Ogaden. In July 1977 Somalia directly invaded the Ogaden, hoping to exploit Ethiopia's postrevolution weakness to achieve its pan-Somali goal. Ethiopia successfully repulsed the Somali invaders with the help of massive Soviet and Cuban assistance. Kenya, which had its own reasons to fear an expansionist Somalia, vocally supported Ethiopia, but the regional security system did little to moderate the conflict.

Despite this enduring and seemingly zero-sum conflict over the Ogaden, there have been examples of accommodation and conflict management, if not resolution, between Ethiopia and Somalia. Somali prime minister Muhammad Haji Ibrahim Igal (1967-69) initiated a period of detente, in part because of the cost to both parties of the extended stalemate, the freedom of action which the new Igal government enjoyed in domestic politics, and Igal's ambition to join the East African Community.[89] In 1977 Moscow and Havana became more deeply engaged on the Ethiopian side of the conflict and tried to broker an agreement, but the gap between the two states remained too large to bridge.

By January 1986, both sides had concluded that the stalemate benefited neither party, and both wanted a settlement in order to concentrate their resources against internal threats. Mengistu and Siad met in Djibouti at the organizational meeting of the Intergovernmental Authority on Drought and Development. After a series of meetings and a military buildup on both sides of the border, the two agreed in

April 1988 to reestablish relations, withdraw troops from the border, exchange prisoners of war, and "refrain from the use or threat of force against the territorial integrity or political independence" of either state.[90] Both states had an urgent need to redeploy troops from the Ogaden in order to face internal challenges.

While the agreement left the major issue of sovereignty and border demarcation unsettled, it has held. The collapse of the regimes of Siad Barre and Mengistu Haile Mariam in 1991 led to tremendous internal turmoil in both states. The struggle for control of Mogadishu, the Somali National Movement's efforts to consolidate its authority in northern Somalia, and the multisided contest for control in Addis Ababa diverted attention from the Ogaden. The underlying conflict, however, remains unresolved and may flare up again once the internal transitions are complete. Furthermore, the explosion of conflict within Somalia following the detente with Ethiopia indicates that progress in reducing conflict at the interstate level may contribute to the release of pent up domestic conflict.

A second example of regional conflict over a contested border is that between Libya and Chad. Northern groups in Chad, reacting to the repression of a government run by southerners, formed the National Liberation Front of Chad (FroLiNaT) with Libyan support in 1965.[91] Libyan involvement on behalf of various northern factions escalated in the early 1970s, and from 1973 until 1987, Muammar Qadhafi's regime conducted a broad intervention. This ranged from political and diplomatic support for various armed factions within Chad to the large-scale involvement of Libyan armed forces. Tripoli claimed sovereignty over the Aouzou strip, an area with potentially rich mineral deposits, on the basis of an unratified treaty between Italy and France (the respective colonial powers of Libya and Chad). In addition, strong cultural links between the Toubou and Arabs on both sides of the border encouraged Qadhafi to see northern Chad as an appropriate sphere of influence. After an early tactical alliance, Chadian leader Hissene Habre broke with Qadhafi and won support from France and the United States in opposing Libya's designs on the Aouzou. Conflict between Habre (supported by France, the United States, Sudan, and Zaire) and Goukouni Oueddei's Transitional National Union Government (GUNT, supported by Libya) raged across the northern half of Chad in the early 1980s. Habre's forces decisively defeated Libya's clients in 1987, forcing Qadhafi to reconsider his Chadian adventure.[92]

In 1994 Libya accepted a decision handed down by the International Court of Justice in the Hague in favor of Chadian sovereignty over the Aouzou Strip.[93] Tripoli's acceptance of this adverse decision may have been influenced by the building pressure of international sanctions as a result of the Lockerbie bombing case. Regardless, if Libya withdraws its armed forces and administration from the Aouzou in accordance with the World Court decision, a long-festering interstate conflict over sovereignty may be resolved.[94]

A final contemporary example of contested sovereignty threatening to flare into regional war is provided by Cameroon and Nigeria. In 1994 the border between the two along the Bakassi peninsula flared up in a minor conflict. Both states claim the territory—the gateway to their oil fields—on the basis of a murky record of colonial boundaries and administrations. On December 31, 1993, Nigeria sent forces into the region to stop what it considered harassment of Nigerian citizens from Cameroonian gendarmes. The squabble seemed to be a test of strength and a means to shore up faltering domestic support, but tenuous internal political transitions created the worrisome possibility of miscalculation and blundering into a fight. Despite some threatening maneuvers and Cameroon's activation of its defense agreements with France, both states seemed committed to a negotiated settlement.[95]

STATUS RIVALRY. Interstate rivalries over rank and status make up the fifth dimension of regional conflict. Competition between states for leadership occurs in all state systems, unless a clearly recognized and accepted hierarchy is established. In Africa such jostling for position is ubiquitous because the state system is relatively new and power relations are only beginning to be worked out.[96]

Status rivalries form the backdrop to a number of the conflicts discussed above. The struggle to establish rank relations between Uganda, Tanzania, and Kenya contributed to the destruction of the East African Community in the 1970s. Rivalry for leadership in West Africa between Nigeria, on the one hand, and the Francophone states, on the other, adds an additional layer to the Liberian conflict, a dimension that has complicated ECOMOG's program of conflict management. Algeria's support for POLISARIO is, in part, motivated by Algiers' desire to prevent Morocco from consolidating its position as a rival power in the Maghreb.

In Southern Africa the transition toward nonracial democratic government in South Africa has transformed the structure of the region. Under apartheid, South Africa's lack of legitimacy in the region made its attempts to assert its status as the dominant power unacceptable. Since Nelson Mandela's inauguration as president in 1994, however, the new role that South Africa will play vis-à-vis its smaller neighbors is being determined. South Africa and Zimbabwe already are competing for leadership of the newly created Association of Southern African States.[97] Ohlson and Stedman speak of the "regional asymmetry in economic and military power" between South Africa and its neighbors as a latent source of regional insecurity. This asymmetry does not create conflict on its own, but it may indirectly encourage military solutions to political problems and the diversion of scarce resources into military spending.[98]

No conflict takes place exclusively in any one of these five dimensions. One indication of the complex dynamics that make conflict management such a difficult challenge is that rivals may compete and fight in a number of arenas, along a variety of dimensions. In the Horn of Africa, for example, a full understanding of the regional context and consequences of the Eritrean conflict would need to include the spillover effects of Eritrean refugees into Sudan, the manner in which Eritrean politics came to be organized from EPLF bases in Kassala and Khartoum, how Sudanese support for the EPLF and reciprocal Ethiopian support for insurgents in southern Sudan fed the conflict, and how the anarchic structure of the Horn of Africa encouraged interstate rivalry between Ethiopia and Sudan.[99] While the underlying source of conflict is generally internal and rooted in the struggle to make domestic sovereignty responsible and accountable, the regional dimensions influence the dynamics and the potential for conflict management.

Continental Norms and Conflict Management

One of the remarkable characteristics of conflict in Africa is that there have been relatively few examples of significant interstate war. In a newly independent state system with arbitrary borders and few accepted norms of international behavior, one might have expected frequent wars to establish regional dominance, and the development of hierarchies among the states as wars were fought to make abstract borders meaningful on the ground. The low level of military development at independence, the threat that redrawing boundaries posed for the majority of states, and the imperative to concentrate on state and nation building, however, limited international conflict.[100]

In addition, interstate conflicts in Africa have been managed, in part, by two norms established and defended by the Organization of African Unity. The OAU supports territorial integrity and the inviolability of the borders within which independence was attained, and noninterference in the internal affairs of other African states. On the question of borders, African leaders and analysts have argued that altering any borders would open Pandora's box and bring all state boundaries into question.[101] As Jeffrey Herbst points out, "the stability of African borders is remarkable, given the consensus that these borders are arbitrary, that most countries have only a limited ability to defend their boundaries, and that there seem to be many groups that would welcome wholesale changes of African frontiers."[102] The strong consensus on territorial inviolability, based in the norm of *uti possidetis*, has served to organize how the African state system responds to attempts by dissident groups to change boundaries, with few defections since the creation of the OAU in 1963. Most African boundary disputes have been resolved without resort to force. This is a significant, even remarkable, accomplishment, and it has contributed to the reduction of conflict on the continent.[103]

Respect for the noninterference norm, enshrined in article III of the OAU charter, developed in a political environment where few states had the interest, means, or opportunity to pursue territorial aggrandizement.[104] Despite early predictions that Africa would suffer a multitude of conflicts over its colonial borders, the failure of early challenges reinforced the norm of inviolability.[105] Boundaries may generate conflict when they create a disjunction between the interactions of a sociocultural or economic system, on the one hand, and a political system, on the other. In most of Africa, however, political boundaries have rarely been seen on the ground, and social interactions have continued without regard to the juridical distinctions.

The OAU's norm of territorial integrity has shaped, in part, the dynamic of certain conflicts. The position made Somalia's actions to change the borders in the Horn to coincide with ethnic realities illegitimate in the African state system. This illegitimacy reduced Somalia's ability to win international support, and strengthened the positions of Ethiopia and Kenya. The norm of noninterference reduced (but did not completely eliminate) African support for the Biafran side of the Nigerian civil war, and limited support for such unilateral actions as Libya's involvement in Chad and Tanzania's in Uganda.

In the 1990s the OAU's commitment to the status quo of borders was challenged by Eritrea and Somaliland. For twenty-eight years the norm of the inviolability of recognized borders weakened the Eritrean struggle for independence. Once the Eritrean People's Liberation Front gained control over the territory and presented the organization with a fait accompli, the OAU accepted its independence. The OAU took extraordinary measures to make Eritrea a narrow exception and held on tightly to the general rule. At the same time, the OAU vigorously opposed the Republic of Somaliland's declaration of independence and passed a resolution at its June 1991 meeting that reaffirmed the indivisibility and territorial integrity of the Somali Republic.[106] The resentment of the leaders of the Republic of Somaliland to this decision made it extremely difficult for the OAU to play an effective role in responding to the Somali conflict. The OAU's strong reaction probably influenced other international actors to keep Somaliland at a distance, thereby hindering the efforts of other external institutions to engage in conflict management.

The OAU's norm against external interference in the internal affairs of an African state was designed to protect vulnerable states from neo-imperial meddling, but has had the effect of protecting authoritarian regimes. This is illustrated by the OAU's reaction against Tanzania's intervention to remove Idi Amin from Uganda. Most African leaders were privately pleased to be rid of Amin, who had become an international embarrassment and shame on the continent. Few, however, publicly applauded the Tanzanians because most feared that the precedent of intervention threatened their own regimes. Nyerere received public criticism at the OAU summit in July 1979 from Sudan's president Jaafar Nimeiri and Nigeria's Olesegun Obasanjo. The Nigerian leader condemned the invasion as "a dangerous precedent of unimaginable consequences."[107] African leaders, however, have reconsidered this norm in the 1990s, as evidence of the destabilizing consequences of internal conflicts has mounted.

Regional Security Organizations

The creation and strengthening of regional organizations may promote more regularized interaction among African states, and thereby encourage conflict management and more responsible sovereignty. An examination of the role that regional security organizations have played suggests, however, that they are most successful when they are motivated by a common threatening neighbor, and when regimes perceive the organizations as a tool to preserve the survival of their rule, not more responsible sovereignty. Regional organizations will be limited in their ability to promote responsible sovereignty, governance, development, and justice, and thereby address the root causes of conflicts, to the extent that they are composed of member states under the control of authoritarian regimes who use their sovereignty irresponsibly.

A number of regional organizations were created to counter external threats and seem to act primarily to protect regime survival. In Asia, the Association of Southeast Asian Nations (ASEAN) was organized to oppose the threat posed by Vietnam, and the members of the Gulf Cooperation Council (GCC) organized to counter the threat from revolutionary Iran.[108] Leaders in Southern Africa explicitly organized their regional security through the Front Line States and the Southern Africa Development Coordinating Committee in opposition to the hegemonic designs of South Africa.[109] Regional organizations, therefore, may polarize rather than unify regions.

Furthermore, regional organizations may inhibit, rather than encourage, action to address some of the fundamental challenges facing Africa. Amitav Acharya has argued that regional organizations are often supported by vulnerable leaders who see them as useful for resisting domestic challenges.[110] This suggests that regional organizations made up of authoritarian states will impede the building of a new, more just, and democratic order based on responsible sovereignty. During the 1993 summit of the Intergovernmental Authority on Drought and Development Sudanese leader Bashir urged the organization to work for a solution to the conflict in Sudan. He hoped, however, that a regional effort would prevent "interference in the internal affairs in African countries," suggesting that he perceived IGADD involvement as a means to forestall the intervention of other powers with greater leverage.[111] Rather than increasing pressure to use sovereignty more responsibly, the regional organization was perceived as shielding against such pressure. Once Ethiopia, Eritrea, and Uganda grew sufficiently concerned to use IGADD to pressure Bashir, however, the Sudanese leader denounced the organization and declared, "We shall resolve the war in Southern Sudan through the barrel of a gun."[112]

The Economic Community of West Africa Monitoring Group in Liberia demonstrates that regional organizations have the capacity to act in an effective manner when leading regional powers feel threatened by a conflict. As detailed below (see chapter six), internal conflict and state collapse in Liberia in 1990 led to the creation of a West African military intervention force. As Nigerian president Ibrahim Babangida put it, the West African leaders recognized that if they allowed the security situation to degenerate, "it would affect the entire West African sub-region."[113]

The ECOMOG intervention suggested that regional organizations can transform some conflicts, but that such intervention inevitably generates a new series of disputes. Whether the new conflicts will be less destructive and more susceptible to management depends on the dynamics of a given context. ECOMOG was able to operate, in large part, due to Nigeria's ability and willingness to provide leadership and military resources. A number of West Africans perceived Nigeria's intervention as motivated by a hidden agenda to dominate the region.[114] ECOMOG was able to deny Taylor victory, but had greater difficulty in imposing a long-term political solution. In the end, the United Nations and the Organization of African Unity became more involved, and with this additional leverage a cease-fire was proclaimed in August 1993.[115]

Because regional organizations favor certain actors (most often states) more than others (such as insurgents or civil society), they seldom provide the best context for addressing the underlying sources of conflict. In fact, the asymmetrical nature of internal conflicts that hinders management is precisely a result of an insurgent party's seeking recognition as the equal of the state, while the state resists accepting the insurgents as its equal.[116] Regional organizations provide a useful forum for discussions and can facilitate conflict management when all parties are genuinely seeking to reduce conflict and increase responsible sovereignty. The structure of such organizations and the nature of the states that are their component parts prevent them from playing a larger role.

Regional organizations in Africa also contribute to conflict management by establishing norms and rules that supplement, and sometimes expand upon, the OAU norms. In 1978 ECOWAS member states, for example, signed a protocol on nonaggression avowing that "Member States declare and accept that any armed threat or aggression directed against any Member State shall constitute a threat or aggression against the entire community." This provision allowed ECOWAS to respond to the internal conflict in Liberia that had generated regionally destabilizing implications, and some have suggested that this model could be adopted by other regional organizations, such as SADC.[117] Moreover, regional organizations increasingly cite democracy as a fundamental norm against which state behavior will be measured. For example, ECOWAS, at the Abuja summit of 1991, adopted a declaration of political principles that committed member states to the observance of democratic ideals and respect for human rights.[118]

Ultimately, though, regional organizations often cannot distance themselves enough to serve as an effective forum for managing conflicts within their midst. Since member states often also face threats from insurgents, they are unlikely to pressure a government to accede to insurgents' demands. The historical evidence in the Horn, for example, indicates that parties to conflict have looked outside the region, most notably to the United States, to guarantee agreements and mediate settlements.[119]

In Southern and West Africa, tentative regional cooperation has developed out of functional cooperation. As communications and interactions increased, and institutions dedicated to multilateral coordination grew in competence, state leaders came to recognize the benefits that could be derived from greater regional cooperation. In Southern Africa common perceptions of a regional threat from apartheid South Africa greatly stimulated coordination. In West Africa, Nigeria's ability to pay the leadership costs of cooperation, and the benefits of the larger markets resulting from the cooperation of the smaller states in the region, provided an initial basis from which to build.

In the Horn of Africa, in contrast, fundamental conflicts among the governments hindered even the most basic functional cooperation for many years. Only in the early 1980s and with the prodding of the United Nations Environment Program did leaders in the Horn establish the Intergovernmental Authority on Drought and Development. IGADD initially focused on resource questions as an initial issue area that then could be used to produce momentum for more wide-ranging cooperation.[120]

IGADD played a positive role in reducing regional tensions in the late 1980s, when Ethiopia and Somalia used the 1986 summit to begin exploring ways to reduce their conflict. IGADD did not play a mediating role as an organization, but it provided a "nonpolitical" occasion that allowed the two countries to begin their talks. In the early 1990s IGADD became the focus of regional efforts to manage the conflict in southern Sudan. The organization charged four member states (Kenya, Uganda, Ethiopia, and Eritrea) led by Moi to broker talks among the regime in Khartoum and two factions of the SPLM/A. Talks took place in Nairobi in January, March, and July 1994. The neighboring states, particularly Ethiopia and Eritrea, fearing that the Sudanese government was promoting Islamic fundamentalist opponents to their rule, had a particular interest in moderating Khartoum's behavior. In addition, each of the four states charged with the talks suffered from spillover effects as brutal offenses and the denial of food to southern Sudan created huge flows of refugees across their borders.[121]

Functionalist and neofunctionalist arguments suggest that regional organizations can help to manage conflicts by "tying up states in a tight web of functional relationships."[122] Regional organizations that are created to manage questions of economic and technical cooperation, the functionalists argue, may provide the basis for more political forms of interaction, resulting in spillover effects that can address conflict.[123] In addition, they suggest that regional identities will develop as authority is increasingly shifted to regional organizations. As the lessons of the East African Community demonstrate, however, economic integration need not encourage political cooperation, but may reinforce political differences. Joseph S. Nye, Jr. has argued that regional integration schemes in the developing world often produce overpoliticization of issues, rather than permitting technocratic solutions as in the industrial world.[124] Yet despite these flaws, minimalist organizations have demonstrated a great capacity to survive.[125]

Finally, the relationship between geographically focused organizations, such as ECOWAS, SADC, and IGADD, and more inclusive, continental institutions, such as the OAU or the innovative Conference on Security, Stability, Development, and Cooperation in Africa, remains vague and open to question. Coordination among such organizations so that each one does what it can do best will only develop with discussion and experience over time. In the end, however, the impact of regional and continental organizations is limited by the nature of their membership. Organizations composed of states will only be as representative and responsive as their components. Responsible sovereignty at a regional level is best able to increase accountability and manage conflict when the region consists of states that have the willingness and capacity to govern with accountability and use their sovereignty responsibly.

Conclusions—Future Roles for Regional Organizations

The regional context of a specific conflict shapes the dynamics of the struggle and offers opportunities for management. The regional level of analysis, therefore, is critical to a full understanding of any specific conflict. Conflicts arise at multiple levels simultaneously, and the regional dimension generally is not the most important. For successful conflict management, therefore, initiatives at each level should do what they can do best and attempt to reinforce and complement the others. In Southern Africa, for example, the agreements to limit external support for insurgents, the regional settlements that led to the disengagement of South Africa from Namibia, and the internal transitions in Namibia, Angola, Mozambique, and South Africa all interacted with each other, and the outcome of any settlement was shaped, in part, by the success or failure of the others. In the Horn of Africa, success in managing the interstate conflict between Ethiopia and Somalia in 1988 resulted in additional conflict within Somalia and Ethiopia, rather than reinforcing efforts to improve governance and manage the internal conflicts. Similarly, the resolution of the conflict between Ethiopia and Sudan following the downfall of Mengistu Haile Mariam in 1991 led the government in Khartoum to escalate its war in southern Sudan.

For African regional security systems to produce a less violent, more cooperative climate that helps to manage conflict, agreement must be reached on the definition and identity of the constituent actors or states. In the Horn of Africa, for example, John Harbeson has argued that "the international politics . . . has largely been a struggle of competing actors to establish just such settled identities."[126] The legitimacy of actors and the definition of borders must be established. Such agreements will require the development of solutions to internal political conflicts and the institutionalization of systems of governance that encourage participation and inclusion, rather than resistance and alienation. More responsible sovereign states will encourage regional organizations that can reinforce—but not by themselves create—accountability. Regimes and states that are recognized as legitimate by both their own people and neighboring states will reduce each state's vulnerability and provide each with a cushion of security to encourage it to run the risks implicit in cooperating in regions where distrust has been enduring and intense.[127] Internally stable states are needed to serve as the "fulcrum" of regional security.[128] Peter Anyang' Nyong'o has noted that regional cooperation requires domestic processes and social forces that create an "enabling environment."[129]

Along with the resolution of internal political struggles and the creation of more stable, legitimate states, Africa needs regional structures that include shared rules, norms, expectations, and, eventually, strong institutions. If rules could be agreed upon that set limits to acceptable regional behavior, as have been developed in the ASEAN region in Asia and are being drawn up in West and Southern Africa, then insecurity from next door would be substantially reduced.

For Africa to develop into a less violent continent, improved governance will be required. In the future, governance will need to take place on multiple levels, with different structures, rules, and actors playing greater or lesser roles depending on the issue area.[130] New regional organizations, norms, and patterns of behavior constitute only one level at which new forms of nonviolent interaction are needed. Perhaps the most important will be the state level, where democratic and accountable governments and healthy civil societies must be established. As argued above, regional organizations built on functionalism cannot, by themselves, act to reduce internal conflicts.

In the past centralized, irresponsible, authoritarian bureaucracies seized control of decisionmaking to the disadvantage of both regional or international cooperation, and local autonomy. The breakdown of such regimes, most notably in Somalia, Ethiopia, Sudan, Liberia, Angola, Rwanda, and Zaire, suggests that the old focus on the state as the most appropriate context for the regulation of social and economic activity must be reevaluated.

While some legitimate authority and responsibility will continue to reside at the level of the state, new structures or "regimes" need to be created at the local, regional, and global levels. Increased capacity to govern and coordinate at the local and regional levels will both provide a check on authoritarian state power and avoid overburdening the state, thereby discouraging the state from becoming oppressive and preventing it from collapsing. One issue area may require more management from the local level, while another may demand more regional coordination; nearly all issues, however, have implications and consequences for each of the multiple sites of decisionmaking. Key questions in the coming years, therefore, will be how these different levels interrelate and cooperate, who will participate and in what manner, and how each level will be accountable to the people who are subject to its decisions.

6

International Actors

*D*URING the cold war confrontations of the 1970s and 1980s, the United States and the Soviet Union were critical actors on the African scene, intervening directly or indirectly in many of Africa's conflicts. At times, as in Angola, these interventions exacerbated the struggle on the ground between the army and insurgent forces. However, with the waning of adversarial relations between the great powers and their adoption of more pragmatic perceptions of each other's intentions in the late 1980s, the situation changed dramatically. At that point, the great powers, with enormous political and economic resources at their disposal, were in an advantageous position to cooperate in settling regional conflicts. But in the next phase of the evolution of world politics, that cooperation too has waned, as Russia sees less reason for interaction with Africa, and with that the United States has lost some of its interest as well.

It is important to explore the implications of this shift in great power roles for the management of conflict in Africa. In the changing world context of the 1990s, Africa has little choice but to confront a wide variety of clashes on the continent and to do so increasingly on its own. In Francis Deng's words, the "aggravating external factor" had been removed, but so had "the moderating role of the superpowers, both as third parties and as mutually neutralizing allies."[1] Given Africa's resource constraints, who can assume the mantle of peacemaker when state actors fail to govern responsibly? There are certainly many skillful African diplomats and intermediaries ready to take on a variety of management activities. However, mediatory skill is not likely in itself to prove sufficient to bring about a return to routinized politics. Skill must be complemented with leverage in order to overcome the stalemates that plague many conflict situations and to push the process of peacemaking through to a constructive conclusion (that is, where norms ensure regular relations and human dignity).[2] The leverage required in each encounter is a function of the difficulty of the problem to be dealt with. In the current context, there may be sufficient third-party actors on hand to deal with disputes of moderate intensity, but when it comes to conflicts over the legitimacy of the basic rules themselves, there would appear to be a dearth of mediators "with muscle" who are prepared to intervene actively in bitter intrastate or interstate encounters.

Where the issues at stake lead potentially to high levels of conflict, as in South Africa, Sudan, and the countries of the Horn of Africa, then the objective conditions for peacemaking would not seem encouraging.[3] Unlike the relatively successful regimes discussed in the West African volume, the capacity of state authorities in high conflict situations to govern responsibly and effectively is stretched to the limit.[4] What causes certain of these conflicts to become intense? In many countries economic performance is weak and indecisive, the political rules have yet to gain full legitimacy, and religious, ethnic, and regional identity groups sometimes disagree among themselves about the application of the rules of the game, with highly destructive consequences in terms of their commitment to the state and its purposes. As a result of the colonial experience, political memories on the ground complicate the process of constructing overarching rules acceptable to the various African leaders and their constituents and lead to a distancing of African societies from potential nonregional, third-party actors. The result at times is institutional fragility in the face of sharp economic and social disjunction; where grievances are not dealt with effectively, grave individual and group insecurity accrues and results in intense conflict between state and societal interests.

Who, then, are likely to emerge as the institutional agents of conflict management in Africa? And what are the anticipated results of their efforts in terms of reconciling sovereignty and responsibility? In probing these interrelated issues, it will be necessary to start first by analyzing the extent to which a mediator's status and power contributed to a successful peacemaking outcome. Certainly the data on mediatory initiatives point to the advisability of being cautious about the capacity of third-party interveners to resolve conflicts between and within states. With such general difficulties in mind, how critical is the role of the major powers and other external agents in the settlement of

Africa's various confrontations, and what accounts for their ability to advance the negotiating process? Second, why, after a laborious and seemingly successful effort, have some of these agreements collapsed during the implementation or postagreement, peace-building stage? Third, having fallen apart, what possibilities exist for creative diplomacy to renew a commitment to the peace accords? In the conclusion, the issue of the quality of the agreements themselves will be examined. Do the adversaries accept the preexisting or newly worked out rules of the game? Put another way, does peace "signify normalization, or is it merely a glorified nonbelligerency?"[5] Peace agreements are a beginning, hopefully leading to a process of ongoing negotiations. Hence, conflict management is viewed as an iterative process that may be able to create unanticipated opportunities for "fairness" and empathy as the parties learn through interaction with one another over time.

The Limits of Mediation

Before looking at the response agents, it is important to provide a cautionary note about what can be expected realistically from peacemaking (particularly mediatory) efforts. International negotiation and mediation may be necessary to bring about peaceful relations, but they are by no means likely to prove sufficient in all instances. One option open to state elites, as in Nigeria during the Biafran confrontation, is the attempt to eliminate the opposition by means of force and the securing of capitulation. According to Stephen Stedman, forty-one out of sixty-eight civil wars in the twentieth century (including Uganda [1966, 1987], Burundi [1972], and Nigeria [1970] among the African states) were terminated in this manner. The other option for securing peace—that is, mediation—was effective in only a minority of instances, with some twenty cases in the Stedman sample (including Sudan [1972], Angola [1975], Zimbabwe [1980], and Namibia [1989]) being ended in this manner.[6] In the abstract, negotiation may hold out the possibility of mutual gains solutions and a shrinking of the distance between adversaries, but it is often extremely difficult to put into effect.

Another data set, collected by Daniel Frei, points up a related finding: interstate conflicts tend to be more amenable to mediation than state-insurgent struggles. Clearly, where grievances involving ethnic, nationality, or religious identity groups are at issue, it is particularly difficult, although not impossible, to find overarching compromise formulas that satisfy both state elites and insurgent groups.[7] In the Sudan, a northern-led state and southern-based insurgent leaders did successfully reach a settlement of their differences in 1972, only to see the fragile accord break down by 1983 and with it the renewal of heavy fighting. The difficulty of mediating disputes with a communal dimension stems in part from the high level of insecurity and emotion surrounding such encounters and the evident reluctance that state elites exhibit for negotiating with—and thereby giving a measure of legality and international respectability to—these movements. Hence Daniel Frei and others contend that interstate conflicts, where the legitimacy of the state is not in question (such as in the Algerian-Moroccan negotiations of the 1980s), are more open to facilitation by external actors than civil wars.[8]

Agencies of Intervention

In undertaking mediatory initiatives in African interstate and sub-state conflicts, what are the key variables that seem likely to contribute to successful outcomes? In attempting to come to grips with this question, it will be useful to disaggregate the mediatory process by concentrating first on the prenegotiation and negotiation stages and looking later at the implementation stage. This section will therefore examine the pressures that third parties bring to bear on adversaries to negotiate their differences, mediatory action under the auspices of other institutional agents, direct mediation, and military intervention followed by mediatory activity. Importantly, however, the various stages of the mediatory process are intertwined, with the negotiation of agreements linked to implementation processes. Thus warring state and ethnic elites are not likely to commit themselves to an agreement, with all its potential insecurities regarding inclusion in the political, bureaucratic, and military institutions of the new regime, unless a third-party mediator can be anticipated who will be able to enforce the terms of the settlement.

Pressure on Adversaries to Negotiate

In the 1990s, the notion of diplomatic or military intervention by one state in the affairs of another to restore order and pursue humanitarian objectives has become more and more accepted practice.[9] As Organization of African Unity (OAU) Secretary General Salim Ahmed Salim observes, interventions can be preemptive or can come after conflict has occurred:

> The basis for 'intervention' may be clearer when there is a total breakdown of law and order, as in the case of Liberia, and where, with the attendant human suffering, a spill-over effect is experienced within the neighbouring countries. . . . However, preemptive involvement should also be permitted even in situations where tensions evolve to such a pitch that it becomes apparent that a conflict is in the making.[10]

The purpose of the intervention is a key to its possible acceptance by the international community. Propaganda attacks, the training of insurgents against neighboring countries (Ghana's Kwame Nkrumah), the provision of military supplies (Ethiopian support to the southern Sudanese insurgents in various periods), and military incursions (South Africa's extended forays into Angola, Rhodesia's attacks on guerrilla forces in Mozambique, Libya's intervention in Chad, and Somalia's dispatch of forces to Ethiopia) have all raised considerable misgivings among African governments and citizens. However, a number of constructive interventions are also worth noting. These include appeals for humanitarian action, sanctions against inequitable treatment and violations of civil liberties (among these, South Africa, Rhodesia, Uganda), and peacemaking initiatives (for example, Daniel arap Moi's efforts to mediate the conflict in Uganda [1985–86], Emperor Haile Selassie's arbitration during the Sudanese negotiations of 1972, or the initiative taken by an OAU peacekeeping force, working alongside a Tanzanian diplomatic team, to facilitate talks between the Rwanda government and the rebel Rwandese Patriotic Front), some of which have been widely applauded. If a number of these efforts have played a significant role in shifting the preferences and perceptions of the actors about the need for compromise (notably the roles played by Haile Selassie in the Sudanese negotiations or U.S. Assistant Secretary of State for African Affairs Chester A. Crocker in the Angolan settlement of 1988), others (such as Zaire's President Mobutu Sese Seko's initiative to make peace between the Angolan government and the National Union for the Total Independence of Angola [UNITA], or the attempts made by Moi, President Robert Mugabe, and President Hastings Banda to intercede in the ongoing civil war in Mozambique) produced little change.[11]

Pressures of a nonmilitary type seek to raise the costs on governments that persist in pursuing policies viewed by the international community as grievously harmful to the well-being of other states or to a significant section of the target state's own citizenry. Such pressures take various forms: exhortations, denunciations, the closure of embassies, freezing of assets, trade embargoes, the termination of assistance programs, and so forth. They may also involve programs with a military dimension, such as limitations placed on the use of military assistance (U.S. aid to Somalia and the Sudan) and a ban on the export of military equipment (UN resolutions on Rhodesia and South Africa). During Idi Amin's regime, the U.S. Congress sought to protest the "savage abuses of the Uganda people" by placing an embargo on coffee imports in 1978. Angry protests against apartheid practices in South Africa came from the OAU, the United Nations, and a variety of countries, and, in 1993, intense public pressures were directed by UN, nongovernmental organizations and Western and Arab governments against Sudanese human rights violations (including charges of "ethnic cleansing" against the Nuba people in Kordofan Province).[12]

Although the South African and Sudanese governments have responded substantively or possibly only symbolically to such pressures, moving by stages toward peace talks with their adversaries (Convention for a Democratic South Africa [CODESA], Abuja),[13] such diplomatic exhortations and protests were hardly decisive in changing the preferences of state decision elites. Sanctions can cramp and isolate a regime, and World Bank and International Monetary Fund pressures may be able to dramatize and protest the failure of effective governance on some occasions (as shown in chapter 4), but in the end the political actors themselves must change their preferences and perceptions and develop new norms and routines of encounter—or be compelled to do so by overwhelming force from some internal or external actor. In the case of Uganda, for example, external military intervention proved to be the determining factor, for Idi Amin's regime fell before a combined invasion of Tanzanian forces and returning Ugandan troops.

Because the legitimacy of great power military actions can be expected to remain in doubt as well as their preparedness to accept the human and financial costs of interventions in the years ahead, the United Nations or African regional organizations such as the Economic Community of West African States (ECOWAS) can be expected to play a leading role in interceding in Africa's disputes. In light of such trends, the American-led humanitarian intervention in Somalia in 1992–94 will probably come to be regarded as something of an exception. But in the complex post–cold war environment of the present, the initiative in peacemaking has clearly been assumed by Africa's leaders. And not only are they working through such traditional institutions as the United Nations and regional organizations to achieve this goal, but they are launching new initiatives, such as the Intergovernmental Authority on Drought and Development (IGADD) and the Africa Leadership Forum's proposal for a Conference on Security, Stability, Development, and Cooperation in Africa (CSSDCA). As chapter 5 shows, IGADD had provided a forum for talks on reducing tensions between Ethiopia and Somalia in the 1980s and for a series of efforts to mediate between the Sudanese government and the two Sudan People's Liberation Army (SPLA) factions in the 1990s.[14] With respect to CSSDCA, General Olusegun Obasanjo and his colleagues hope that through this medium Africans will be able to provide a comprehensive framework for helping troubled governments cope in a responsible manner with problems of security, stability, economic integration, and socioeconomic transformation. "There is, indeed, the urgent requirement to prevent conflicts and disputes from escalating into armed hostilities," declared the 1991 Kampala Forum. "This calls," it stated, "for the strengthening of conflict resolution mechanisms for negotiation, mediation, conciliation and arbitration at the governmental, political and diplomatic levels, within the framework of intervention."[15]

At Cairo in June 1993, the OAU heads of state and government, seeking to ensure that their organization would play "a central role in bringing about peace and stability in the Continent," established a mechanism for conflict prevention, management, and resolution.[16] In doing this, the African leaders at the OAU summit gave the organization's secretary general greater authority to become involved in internal conflicts on the continent while they were still at an early stage. Throwing off the lethargy that had marked the last two decades, African leaders were seizing the initiative—and just at the juncture that Westerners were displaying an evident fatigue at being drawn into Africa's internal conflicts. Yet in the years ahead, it will be necessary to invest heavily in making the OAU secretariat a more effective organization, creating an early warning credibility, training and equipping a standby military unit, and promoting improved links between the OAU and both the United Nations and subregional organizations. The enforcement of peace agreements is necessarily an expensive proposition but well worth the investment.

Mediation under the Auspices of Other Institutional Agents

Indirect mediatory activity, the backing by a state or states of a mediatory effort mounted under the auspices of another actor, can take various forms, including the encouragement of international observer missions, support for private, unofficial conciliators or mediators, or formal third-party mediatory efforts led by other states or regional or international organizations. To be sure, the line between indirect mediatory activity and direct mediation is sometimes fuzzy. However, it can provide important insights into the dynamics of the peacemaking process, for behind-the-scenes actors may prove critical to successful outcomes (such as the significant agenda-setting role played by Russian and American observers in the Portuguese-led mediation effort at Bicesse in 1990–91).

NONOFFICIAL MEDIATORS. In several instances, governments have also worked alongside or supported the efforts of private mediators as peacemakers in African conflicts (for example, the World Council of Churches [WCC]/All Africa Conference of Churches [AACC] in the Sudanese negotiations of 1971–72, and the Roman Catholic lay organization Sant Egidio and the Roman Catholic archbishop of Beira in the Mozambican negotiations in 1989). Unofficial mediators can at times contribute importantly to the negotiation process, communicating between the rival parties, clarifying misperceptions and misinformation, identifying points of contention, influencing preferences, recommending compromises, and even helping to set agendas. Unburdened by the particular interests of states, unofficial mediators, acting privately and without extensive media attention, can sometimes play a useful role in bringing the disputants to the negotiating table and helping them to understand their opponent's position on the issues in contention. The nonofficial mediator's independence from any government is the source of that person's or organization's strength.

Not being a state, such a mediator can deal with rebel and government alike and can be used or dismissed without loss of face or major diplomatic incident.

However, the room for maneuver gained by such actors comes at a distinct cost in terms of promoting agreements through the effective use of pressures and incentives. Occasionally the private mediator has attempted to act as a catalyst in the mediatory process. For example, the Liberian Council of Churches, in an effort to encourage negotiations between the government of President Samuel K. Doe and the National Patriotic Front of Liberia (NPFL) insurgents over the council's proposed three-stage peace plan, helped organize demonstrations in Monrovia in 1990 to pressure the Doe administration to manage its conflict in a more conciliatory manner.[17] The WCC/AACC team in the Sudan was obviously reticent about attempting to influence the outcomes of negotiations, but at the final meetings at Addis Ababa in 1971–72 it became more active, offering formulas for the two sides to discuss, slowing the pace of negotiations when it appeared necessary, and building a consensus for the agreement.[18]

Although the contribution of unofficial mediators is potentially significant, it is important not to expect too much from these agents in resolving Africa's conflicts. Acting alone, they are clearly limited in what they can achieve. The backing of state actors therefore becomes critically important. Such support takes two main forms: state encouragement to undertake peacemaking initiatives and a parallel or collaborative relationship during the negotiating process. Jimmy Carter's initiative in promoting a dialogue between the Ethiopian government and the Eritrean Peoples' Liberation Front (EPLF) illustrates the links between private mediators and their state backers as well as the kinds of achievements an unofficial actor can be expected to produce. As a past president of the United States, Carter obviously had exceptional stature and access to people in high places, something he used effectively to bring the main protagonists together at Atlanta. Importantly, his initiative took place with the tacit approval of the Bush administration and against the backdrop of increasing superpower cooperation on ending regional conflicts.[19]

The Atlanta talks illustrate both the opportunities and limitations following from nonofficial efforts to help others manage conflict in a responsible way. Although the Ethiopian government and the EPLF had fundamentally different conceptions of what the negotiating process entailed, they nonetheless came prepared to talk about the issues that divided them. Under Carter's aegis, agreement was reached on ten of the thirteen procedural points discussed at the meetings, including the nature of the delegations, possible sites for further meetings, the agenda, relations with the media, public discussions of the issues, and the official language to be used. A number of points tied to substantive issues (including the role of the chair, the nature of the mediation process, the staff at the disposal of the mediator, and the number and composition of the observers) were left for later deliberations. At the follow-up session at Nairobi, however, the process reached a dead end, largely because of Ethiopian fears that UN attendance as an observer would internationalize the Eritrean cause.[20] The unofficial mediator had succeeded in initiating a dialogue but lacked the political capabilities to overcome the stalemate.

The second type of state backing for unofficial mediation takes the form of a parallel or collaborative relationship between them on peacemaking initiatives. The relationship may well be an asymmetrical one, with the powerful state actor playing the more decisive role at critical junctures, but the joint nature of the enterprise is evident throughout. An example of such asymmetry emerges from the Sudanese negotiations of 1971–72. Although the WCC/AACC was effective in enhancing communication between the Sudan government and the Southern Sudan Liberation Movement at Addis Ababa, it was limited in its abilities to overcome a deadlock and to guarantee that the parties would abide by the terms of an agreement. At the point that a deadlock arose over the critical issue of the future composition of the army, it was necessary to turn to a state leader, Emperor Haile Selassie, to intercede in the crisis. The emperor agreed, somewhat reluctantly, to use his good offices to attempt to settle the question. Acting more as an arbitrator than a mediator, the emperor, taking advantage of the aura of respect he was accorded, proposed to split the difference between the contending parties. He recommended that half of the armed forces in the south consist of southern troops and half of northern troops. Concessions were made accordingly by each of the bargaining parties, leading to an agreement along the lines the emperor proposed.[21] Why had the emperor succeeded in moving the negotiations out of deadlock? Backed by a state prominent and highly active in regional affairs, he was in a very strong position to influence the two parties to reassess their preferences. On the one hand, the emperor could alarm the

Nimeiri government with renewed Ethiopian assistance to the SSLM; on the other hand, full implementation of the agreement he signed with Sudanese President Jaafar Nimeiri would result in diminished military supplies to the SSLM, thereby pressing the southerners to adopt a conciliatory stance regarding the peace accord. In this case, therefore, the state and unofficial mediators cooperated in an effective manner to yield an impressive result in reconciling sovereignty with responsibility.

Somewhat less asymmetrical was the collaborative relationship of the public and private mediators in the Mozambican negotiations. In the 1980s, several states, distressed over the destructiveness of the war between the Mozambican government and the Mozambique National Resistance (RENAMO) and concerned over its effects on relations throughout the southern African region, took a series of initiatives aimed at easing the conflict. In seeking national reconciliation between the warring Mozambican parties, U.S. diplomats also worked with the leaders of other states in the region to promote a settlement of the civil war. An effort in August 1989 by Kenya's President Daniel arap Moi and Zimbabwe's President Robert Mugabe to mediate the conflict held out some promise, for these important regional actors had considerable influence with the RENAMO and Mozambican government authorities respectively. However, the Moi-Mugabe attempt to manage the conflict soon lost its impetus. Whereas RENAMO insisted upon its recognition as a condition for negotiations, the Mozambique Liberation Front (FRE-LIMO) government demanded that it be recognized as the valid ruling authority in the country.[22] With the gap between the adversaries remaining wide, the two African mediators, allied as they were with one of the local rivals, soon lost the confidence of the opposing party.

In these circumstances, new intermediaries acceptable to both sides became essential, and the rival parties agreed, in the summer of 1990, to begin direct talks in Rome under the joint mediation of two private, third-party actors, the Sant Egidio community, a Roman Catholic lay organization, and Archbishop Goncalves of Beira, as well as a state actor—the Italian government. Archbishop Jaime Goncalves had maintained close contacts with RENAMO leaders for some time, while the Italian government had friendly ties with the Mozambican government. The private-public mediating team, backed by an active U.S. observer group, proved effective in the many rounds of negotiations that followed.[23] They worked out the complicated arrangements on a cease-fire, the withdrawal of Zimbabwean and Malawian troops from the country, the confining of RENAMO and government troops to predetermined assembly points, the integration of the armies, the demobilization of the remaining forces, multiparty elections to take place by the end of 1993, and United Nations and international verification and supervision of the General Peace Agreement. The timetables for demobilization, disarmament, and the unification of armies seemed too compressed, the 7,000-troop peacekeeping force was too immobile and lacking in aircraft capacity, and the transition process was highly dependent on generous external funding (estimated at $503 million) for the United Nations' Operation in Mozambique (UNOMOZ) and for the elections.[24] Even so, the October 1992 peace agreement followed up by the October 1994 national elections represented an important beginning in the attempt to return to normal relations. Certainly, the unofficial mediators deserve much credit for taking the initial steps to communicate between the rival parties, offering to host the talks in Rome and clearing up misperceptions that the parties held about one another. However, as U.S. diplomat Jeffrey Davidow stressed regarding their role in the Rome talks, a nongovernmental group "can only go so far."[25] At a certain point, outside governments and international organizations necessarily became involved, bringing their political pressures and economic resources to bear in overcoming the reluctance of the parties to commit themselves to a peace accord and in enforcing the final contract. The strengths of the private and public mediators proved coextensive in this case, with constructive results in terms of a final agreement and a commitment to implement it.

OBSERVER AND MONITORING MISSIONS. In principle, observer and monitoring missions are neutral agents engaged in verifying referendums and elections, capacity building, the development of democratic institutions, and monitoring political violence. All of these functions are included in the dynamic of peacemaking. For fair and legitimate elections, effective party systems and active and responsible civil societies are part of the ongoing process of regularizing intergroup relations and encouraging state responsiveness. External states have made use of a variety of private and public monitoring institutions, often funding and encouraging such diverse institutions as the Commonwealth Observer Group, the Carter Center, OAU monitoring teams, the African-American Institute, the International Republican Institute, and the National Democratic Institute. The UN Observer Mission to South Africa (UNOMSA), which was on the scene monitoring evidence of political violence before the April 1994 elections in South Africa, was active in helping to manage the conflict. Not only did UN observers make recommendations to local officials on the handling of security matters immediately after the murder of Chris Hani, but they urged the militant Pan-Africanist Congress to participate in the meetings of the national peace commission.[26] Election monitoring teams have validated elections and promoted democratic organizations and practices; at times, moreover, they have gone beyond this role to mediate between rival interests. Thus Carter Center officials held discussions with representatives of the opposing parties following the disputed 1992 elections in Ghana where proposals were put forward to both sides encouraging them to create informal political structures to facilitate participation by the opposition, to use the current constitution as a basis to judge the conduct of the government in power, to deal with the problems that arose during the elections (such as the electoral register and the voter identification system), and to promote an enhanced capacity for democratic participation and administration.

THE ENCOURAGEMENT OF ANOTHER STATE OR INTERNATIONAL ORGANIZATION. Besides supporting observer and monitoring missions and working in collaboration with nonofficial mediators, indirect mediatory activity can also involve a state's encouragement of a peacemaking effort led by another state or international organization. With the end of the cold war, this approach is likely to prove more and more the norm. In the United States—the world's sole remaining military superpower—a "declinist" view is increasingly in fashion, leading some public officials to pull back from peacekeeping commitments and to speak openly of the limits of American power and resources.[27] The reluctance of the Clinton administration to be drawn into Bosnia and its withdrawal of American troops from Somalia stand as warnings that American policymakers are likely to be very cautious about major new initiatives in Africa.

To gain an insight into the cooperative relations that take place between the formal mediator and major supporting actors, indirect mediatory activities at the state, regional, and global levels must be examined. In focusing on indirect U.S. backing for Britain's efforts to mediate in Rhodesia (Zimbabwe), Russian and U.S. support for Zairian and Portuguese mediation in Angola, the OAU in Rwanda, and the United Nations in the Western Sahara and South Africa, one must analyze the dynamics of the relationship between mediatory actors. In all these situations, it is apparent that the lead state or multistate mediator plays a critical role in initiating the deliberations, guiding the process to an agreement, and helping to enforce the postaccord, peacebuilding process. In part, this ability to assume the role of manager is based upon the actor's favored historical or geopolitical position as a former colonial power, a middle-sized (and hence nonthreatening) country, or an international organization. Such circumstances strengthen the formal mediator's claim to legitimate intervention. However, because such countries or international bodies lack the resources to orchestrate the peacemaking process on their own, they often rely for success upon the economic support of a powerful state actor or actors. A complicated mediatory relationship results, which may nevertheless prove very effective in advancing joint purposes.

The Rhodesian independence negotiations of 1979, which followed a long process of British and American efforts to negotiate an end to the destructive internal war between several African nationalist movements and Ian Smith's breakaway regime, concluded as very much a British-orchestrated show. With the world community refusing to accept Smith's unilateral declaration of independence, Britain continued to be regarded as the colonial power. This status contributed in no small way to the extensive "leverage" that the third-party mediator wielded in its dealings with the parties during the critical Lancaster House peace negotiations.[28] The Lancaster House conference was organized and guided by Britain's Foreign Secretary, Lord Carrington, and his team, who used their positions to control the conference agenda, set deadlines, deal with issues on a step-by-step basis, and submit drafts that served as the cornerstone for further deliberation.[29] The British promise of fair elections was regarded as a credible one by the Mozambican leadership (especially President Samora Machel), who did not see any reason to allow the Patriotic Front forces to continue using its territory as a safe sanctuary in light of it. This change of perceptions led the Mozambicans to be able to pressure Patriotic Front leader Robert Mugabe to trust the British-orchestrated peace process.

During the Lancaster House negotiations, not everything proceeded

as Carrington planned. At one critical juncture, when future constitutional arrangements were under discussion, it became necessary for
the British to try to overcome an impasse by offering to grant financial
assistance for land resettlement and redistribution to an independent
Zimbabwe—provided the Patriotic Front leadership agreed to the proposed arrangements. At this time U.S. diplomats, who had been observing the proceedings at close hand, came to the support of the
British mediators. They offered financial grants to an independent
Zimbabwe for such broad purposes as agriculture and education. This
offer proved very timely, for it helped to keep the conference from
breaking down over the land issue. The American initiative was not,
as described in the press, specifically intended for a buyout of white
farmers, although everyone knew that money was fungible and could
in fact be used for such purposes. By enabling the Patriotic Front
negotiators to save face on this sensitive issue, the American offer of
side-payments made an important contribution to keeping the British-
led peacemaking effort on track (although, largely in response to Zimbabwean criticisms of American foreign policy, the United States reduced and then, in 1986, cut off aid to Zimbabwe for two years).[30]

State support for mediatory action by another state was also evident
in Angola following the successful conclusion of the international negotiations between the Angolan government, Cuba, and South Africa
in 1988. The 1988 agreement left several issues unresolved, particularly
a settlement of the ongoing civil war between the Angolan government
and UNITA. In keeping with the provisions of the Angola/Namibia
Accords, Cuban and South African troops did withdraw from these
countries on schedule, leaving the two Angolan adversaries increasingly to their own devices. With neither of the rival parties having
much of a chance of winning a decisive military victory at that time,
a political solution appeared to be the only way out of a mutually
hurting stalemate.

The first venture at peacemaking between the two adversaries was
taken on by Zaire's President Mobutu Sese Seko, with the quiet backing of the Soviet Union and the United States. With encouragement
from several governments in the region, Mobutu organized an African
summit initiative at Gbadolite in June 1989 aimed at bringing the Angolan civil war to an end. Throughout the seven-hour, closed-door
meeting, Mobutu met separately with the two main leaders, UNITA's
Jonas Savimbi and Angola's President José Eduardo dos Santos, to gain

their consent to a very general summit declaration providing in principle for a cease-fire and national reconciliation.[31] Given the hasty way
in which the agreement was hammered out and the vagueness of the
resulting principles, it was not surprising that the accord proved extremely difficult to implement. The antagonists held contrasting views
of Savimbi's alleged consent to go into exile and to the integration of
UNITA's civilian and military personnel into the MPLA-state and
party organizations. Although a series of minisummits were held in
an attempt to thrash out the discrepancies in viewpoint, it did not take
long before the stalemate gave way to new military engagements in
the Mavinga area.

With the failure of the follow-up summits, it became apparent to
dos Santos that the Gbadolite process had stalled. He therefore called
for the acceptance of a new third-party intermediary. Portugal, the
former colonial power, stepped into the situation, and from mid-1990
onward chaired a series of talks between representatives of the Angolan government and UNITA. This time the two great powers took a
very active stance in support of the Portuguese-led mediation effort.
U.S. Assistant Secretary of State for African Affairs Herman Cohen,
with Soviet approval, gave quiet, behind-the-scenes assistance to Portuguese Deputy Foreign Minister Durao Barroso's efforts to generate
a set of basic principles acceptable to both sides. Then, in a concerted
effort to buttress the Portuguese mediation effort, Soviet Foreign Minister Eduard Shevardnadze conferred with Savimbi while U.S. Secretary of State James A. Baker met in public with the Angolan Foreign
Minister. Following this open, conciliatory display, the two great powers sponsored a meeting in Washington, D.C. In the end, this meeting
produced the so-called Washington Concepts Paper—a conceptual
framework for the Portuguese-mediated talks. The Washington agreement on basic negotiating principles gave a new impetus to the flagging
deliberations taking place at Bicesse. With U.S. and Soviet observers
in attendance at subsequent rounds of deliberations at Bicesse, the
negotiators came to an agreement on such knotty issues as the formation of a national army, the setting of dates for the cease-fire, the
timing of multiparty elections, and the international monitoring process. Not only did the great powers play an important role in pushing
the parties to sign the interim cease-fire accord, but they also took part
in the Joint Political-Military Commission that oversaw the (ultimately
ill-fated) transition process. Working under the auspices of the Portu-

guese mediator, then, the great powers were in a strong position to influence the Angolan government and the insurgents to deal with a number of the incompatibilities between them on the means of structuring party competition. The outside powers had intervened to help manage the conflict. However, their ineffectiveness in implementing the agreement combined with Savimbi's irresponsible actions in reigniting the war led to another round of internal destruction, followed by a UN-led initiative at Lusaka to hammer out the details for what will, it is hoped, prove a more enduring peace.

Meanwhile, at the subregional and regional levels, various African interstate institutions have played important roles in reducing conflict. Based largely on consensus, these organizations provide "an institutionalized forum that facilitates the mutual adjustment of member states' policies and actions within an evolving framework of general norms and operating practices."[32] With their legitimacy well grounded—as African actors seeking to encourage stable relations on the continent—these bodies are likely to prove indispensable as agents of peacekeeping, peacemaking, and peace-building in the years ahead. Among the many examples of such African-based initiatives in recent years were those orchestrated by the OAU in Rwanda. In October 1990, the Rwandese Patriotic Front (RPF), a largely Tutsi force, crossed from Uganda and began a major assault upon government positions in the country. The predominantly Hutu government resisted the attack, with sharp encounters resulting in the north around the district capital of Ruhengeri. Meanwhile, government forces retaliated against Tutsi in other parts of the country, detaining many civilians and assaulting and killing others.[33] As the war ground on inconclusively, Rwandese President Juvénal Habyarimana came to accept the international character of the conflict. Following a meeting in Dar es Salaam with the leaders of Tanzania, Burundi, Uganda, and Zaire, he agreed to let Mobutu make a start at drawing up the terms of a peace accord.[34] In time, this initiative was followed by the OAU's decision at its 1992 meeting to dispatch a monitoring force to the area.

What followed was an informal OAU/U.S. collaborative effort at peacekeeping and peacemaking. The OAU provided a fifty-five-person military observer group composed of Senegalese, Nigerian, Malian, and Zimbabwean troops to monitor the cease-fire and patrol the no-man's-land between the contending forces. Meanwhile, the Bush administration, recognizing the OAU's difficult financial situation, provided $500,000 to help fund the OAU peacekeeping operation.[35] The Tanzanians were also the main facilitators in the various rounds of negotiations held at Arusha in the 1992–93 period. By early 1993, the main terms of a peace accord had been negotiated, including a cease-fire, a partial demobilization of some 30,000 government and RPF troops, the integration of the remaining RPF and government forces into a new, unified army, and constitutional provisions on a mutual veto and power sharing in future cabinets and the National Assembly.[36]

Despite these apparently constructive efforts by the international community to help Rwanda exercise sovereignty in a responsible way, the informal OAU-U.S. collaborative effort (supplemented by a June 1993 Security Council decision to deploy UN peacekeepers along the five main crossing points at the Uganda border to search for lethal weapons) found itself overtaken by events in 1994.[37] When President Juvénal Habyarimana was killed in an airplane crash, it triggered an attack by hardline Hutu elements in the military upon Tutsi civilians and other perceived opponents of the regime, resulting in the massacre of some 500,000 to 1 million people.[38] The peace agreement negotiated between the Hutu-led Habyarimana government and the predominantly Tutsi RPF played a role in the planned violence that followed. Extremist Hutu elements in the military, particularly the Interahamwé, strongly resented the agreement's compromises providing for an extraproportional inclusion of the Tutsis in the government. With relations poisoned for the time being between the main political-ethnic interests and the Hutu leaders and army encamped in Zaire as refugees, it would appear that a negotiated peace between the main rivals will be difficult to recreate in the period ahead.

Direct Mediation

As already noted, it has been prudent for powerful state actors to intervene in African conflict situations under the auspices of various unofficial, medium-power state, or international organization actors. This hesitancy by the major powers to take the lead in peacemaking activities reflects both their awareness of African sensitivities in the postcolonial period and their reluctance to take on new and possibly far-reaching assignments. Such mediators must be prepared for a heavy and prolonged commitment of energy and resources if they are to shift the mind-sets and strategies that accompany adversarial encounters.[39] At times, however, these powerful global actors have concluded that direct third-party intervention was in line with their national interests. Thus, even though American policymakers show an increasing preference for behind-the-scenes supportive action, they have nonetheless been prepared to assume the lead in mediating conflicts in Ethiopia (1990–91), Zaire (1992), Sudan (1989–90), and Angola/Namibia (1976–88). The United Nations, perceived by many as a more disinterested agent, has also become increasingly visible during the post–cold war period as a direct third-party intervener, interceding prominently in the long-simmering disputes in South Africa, Western Sahara, Angola (1993–94), and Mozambique. Although severely constrained economically, this international body seems destined to play a more active mediatory role in the years ahead.

GREAT POWER INITIATIVES: THE UNITED STATES AS MEDIATOR. Unlike the United Nations, U.S. policymakers can command enormous resources to promote a responsible management of sovereignty. Nevertheless, not all U.S. mediatory initiatives have produced conclusive results. With Mobutu's hold on power in doubt and the possibility of Zairian instability becoming a matter of alarm, U.S. Assistant Secretary Herman Cohen mediated an agreement between Mobutu, Prime Minister Etienne Tshisekedi wa Mulumba, and Archbishop Laurent Monsengwo (the president of the High Council of the Republic) on a power-sharing arrangement during the 1992–94 transition period. The agreement, never signed, gave Mobutu extensive authority over the appointment of the ministers of defense and foreign affairs, while assigning the handling of day-to-day affairs to the prime minister. The Cohen initiative represented a kind of high-risk, preventive diplomacy, inevitably fragile where the parties to the accord disagreed over whether each had the right to be consulted regarding appointments and where they refused to act in a conciliatory manner toward one another. In fact, after accepting the compromise on power sharing, Mobutu refused to abide by its terms, leading to the breakdown of the agreement and a continuance of social disorder.

Another inconclusive U.S. mediatory effort took place in the Sudan, where American mediators intervened at various times to protect the distribution of relief supplies and to facilitate the peace process. Upon taking office in 1989, the Bush administration announced a concerted effort to settle the long-running Sudanese civil war.[40] In February 1989,

Secretary of State James A. Baker publicly urged the Sudanese government and the Sudan People's Liberation Movement (SPLM) to put peace first and agree to an early cease-fire.[41] Prime Minister Sadiq el Mahdi resisted proposals for international mediation, although in time he did come to support an internal agreement to freeze Sharia, the Islamic laws, which had been the main stumbling block.[42] This is widely recognized as a pivotal factor behind the military coup staged by factions of the army under the leadership of General Omar al-Bashir in alliance with the National Islamic Front on June 30, 1989.

In the months that followed, Francis Deng, who had undertaken previous peace initiatives in association with General Olusegun Obasanjo, visited Khartoum for talks with the leaders of the revolution. Taking advantage of a request from Khartoum to meet with Deng about the possibility of reactivating the Obasanjo/Deng peace initiative, U.S. Assistant Secretary of State Herman Cohen invited Deng to meet with him. At the meeting Cohen suggested that Deng (and, it was hoped, Obasanjo) proceed to the Sudan and that they propose the idea of a withdrawal of Khartoum's troops from the south and the establishment of a civilian administration there, with the SPLA confined to agreed positions. Obasanjo did in fact join Deng on this mission, where they met separately with government and insurgent leaders and presented the idea of "disengagement."

In light of their talks in the Sudan, Deng and Obasanjo formulated a comprehensive proposal based on disengagement and federalism and then, having reported to Cohen, suggested that the next move was for the U.S. assistant secretary to meet with the parties and convey his ideas directly to them. Accordingly, Cohen went to the region in March 1990 and met al-Bashir and John Garang, the chairman of SPLA/SPLM, where he proposed a cease-fire and disengagement of forces, the establishment of a monitoring group, and the convening of a national constitutional conference. There was much ambiguity about what "disengagement" entailed.[43] Cohen wrote that he "suggested that the government withdraw a large number—perhaps half—of its troops in the south. At the same time the SPLA would pull back to a set distance from all government-held areas in the South."[44]

In its new form, the proposals did not appeal to either side. Although they did not openly reject Cohen's ideas, the parties made counterproposals that reasserted their optimal positions. Southerners, in particular, were disappointed that the new proposals required only a partial pullback of government units, with the SPLA troops withdrawing a specified distance from the government-held areas. Cohen subsequently put forward new variants of the original disengagement scheme, including the demilitarization of Juba, federalism, a military pullback, and multiparty democracy, but to no avail.[45] Achieving little in the way of results from these direct mediatory efforts, U.S. officials appeared to resign themselves to quiet, behind-the-scenes support of Nigerian leader General Ibrahim Babangida's abortive attempts to mediate the civil war with meetings at Abuja in 1992–93.

If peace initiatives the United States made in Zaire and the Sudan were inconclusive, its role in facilitating regime transition in Ethiopia was more in line with what one expects of a great power's intervention. With the failure of the Carter Center's efforts to promote a dialogue between the Ethiopian government and the EPLF at meetings in Atlanta and Nairobi, the U.S. government became more directly involved in mediating the conflict. In October 1990 and February 1991, Assistant Secretary Cohen held talks in Washington with the Ethiopian government and EPLF delegations but again proved unable to narrow the differences. Then, as the government contingents were routed in the field and the insurgent forces of the Ethiopian People's Revolutionary Democratic Front (EPRDF) approached the perimeters of Addis Ababa, Mengistu Haile Mariam fled the country. Thereupon Cohen, at the request of the caretaker government and the opposition movements (the EPRDF, EPLF, and the Oromo Liberation Front), convened a meeting of these various organizations in London on May 27, 1991, to work out a cease-fire and transition to a new regime.

The situation on the ground was now deteriorating rapidly. EPRDF troops remained on the outskirts of Addis Ababa, honoring a pledge to Cohen not to enter the city before the commencement of negotiations. Upon learning that the interim government was losing control over its troops and anxious to spare the city the destruction that accompanies house-to-house combat (as in Mogadishu), Cohen seized the initiative and publicly recommended that the EPRDF be allowed to move into the capital "in order to reduce uncertainties and eliminate tensions."[46] The interim government, unable to prevent the occupation of the city, watched helplessly as EPRDF units took charge on the night of May 27–28.[47] Clearly, the EPRDF would have succeeded in crushing resistance by government troops with or without the American intervention. What the U.S. third-party effort did accomplish under these turbulent conditions, however, was not a mediation of differences between the parties but the facilitation of a relatively smooth regime transition—no small achievement in terms of advancing a future responsible sovereignty in that country.

No doubt the most successful direct mediatory initiative U.S. mediators undertook in Africa was the facilitation of international negotiations in Angola and Namibia. These mediatory efforts can be deemed successful in promoting sovereignty, for foreign troops were withdrawn and Namibia gained its independence. Nevertheless, the Angola-Namibia accords of 1988 may have been viewed as something of a unique event. They followed a critically important shift in the balance of forces on the ground in Angola and offered the various international actors an opportunity to use their leverage to extricate themselves from a costly regional conflict on honorable (or at least face-saving) terms.[48] This is not likely to be repeated in post–cold war times. With the great powers reducing their involvement in Africa, further U.S. peacemaking initiatives will most likely emphasize the leading role of local actors and take an indirect form.

The critical negotiations to end the deadlock and bring about an international settlement gained momentum in late 1988, when the Angolan government accepted the idea of linking a phased withdrawal of Cuban forces from Angola with Namibia's independence.[49] The Angolans and South Africans remained far apart in their thinking on the timetable for Cuban redeployment and withdrawal, aid for the UNITA insurgents, and the terms for South Africa's disengagement from Namibia, but U.S. Assistant Secretary of State for African Affairs Chester Crocker nonetheless concluded that a ripe moment had arrived for a major third-party peace initiative.[50] What followed was an eight-month effort to overcome the regional deadlock through peaceful means. With Crocker in the chair, the representatives of Angola, Cuba, and South Africa met in London in May 1988 to explore the Angolan proposal for a four-year withdrawal of Cuban forces. This was followed by sessions in Brazzaville, Cairo, and New York, where persistent behind-the-scenes Soviet and American communications between these adversaries, and even some pressures on their allies, resulted in the acceptance of general principles on Namibia's independence, a phased Cuban withdrawal, verification, and formal recognition of the U.S. mediatory role.

At the Geneva talks that came after, the conferees issued a joint statement announcing a de facto cessation of hostilities and a series of steps, including proposed dates for Namibia's independence and for the exit of Cuban and South African troops from Angola. Then, at successive meetings in the fall, the parties narrowed the gaps between them on the issue of Cuban troop withdrawal, agreeing that the pull-out would take place over a twenty-seven-month period and that two-thirds of these soldiers would leave during the first year, with the remainder being redeployed by stages to the north. With this thorny question behind them, the negotiating parties tackled the remaining points of contention still outstanding—the verification procedures and the language of the protocol.

The possibilities of a settlement were advanced by several factors coming together at the same juncture: a change in the balance of military power on the ground, a sense of war weariness on the part of those directly involved in the fighting, and a shift of great power perceptions of the costs and benefits of regional conflicts in the third world. If these preconditions helped encourage the parties to move to an international peace accord, they did not carry over to the related task of reconciling the Angolan government and the UNITA guerrilla forces. Direct mediation by a great power had its limits at this point, with the Soviets and Americans displaying a lower sense of urgency about using their resources to bring about a return to responsible governance between the internal antagonists. Only as the great powers ranked the matter somewhat higher on their order of priorities did they come to exert significant influence on their respective allies to sign the Bicesse Accords—and even then they chose to act indirectly, under the auspices of a Portuguese mediator.

THE UNITED NATIONS AS MEDIATOR. As an organization of "sovereign" states, the United Nations is dependent upon its membership for approval of its actions as well as for financial and military backing. When the membership is divided about the purposes of a particular intervention, or when UN peacekeepers lack sufficient force to maintain order or to implement their policies, the organization may suffer a serious loss of credibility. Not surprisingly, therefore, the killing of twenty-three Pakistani soldiers and the wounding of fifty-seven others (including three Americans) in Somalia in an ambush by General Mohamed Farah Aidid's faction in June 1993 put the credibility of UN peace enforcement on the line and was followed by a series of U.S.-

led retaliatory measures. Unlike an American mediatory initiative, then, a UN undertaking gains strength largely from its moral standing in the eyes of the world community and its ability to make "symbolic payoffs"; however, as a resource-strapped organization, it may lack equivalent material resources to facilitate agreements between the adversaries or to offer the kind of security guarantees needed to implement the agreement.[51]

The difficulties encountered by the United Nations in facilitating a smooth transition of regimes is exemplified by its efforts to oversee a referendum in the Western Sahara. With the emergence of a military stalemate between Moroccan and Popular Front for the Liberation of Saguia el-Hamra and Rio de Oro (POLISARIO) forces in 1983, both the United Nations and the OAU launched a series of new initiatives to find a solution to one of Africa's most intractable conflicts.[52] Their efforts were given a boost in 1988 as Saudi Arabia used its good offices to promote talks between the adversaries and as the two regional giants, Algeria and Morocco, reestablished diplomatic relations. With the conflict seemingly closer than before to resolution, the UN Secretary General, Javier Perez de Cuellar, put forward, and the parties agreed to, a plan that included a cease-fire and referendum on self-determination.[53] However, with Morocco able to sustain the war for the foreseeable future, the peace plan did not provide a framework for terminating the hostilities and setting up a credible referendum.

With no apparent end to the war in sight, the UN Security Council adopted a series of resolutions to bring the dispute to a halt. In resolution 658 of 1990, the council set up a UN Mission for the Referendum in Western Sahara (MINURSO), charged with supervising a cease-fire and supporting the administration of a referendum.[54] MINURSO's composition and procedures were outlined in detail in UN Security Council Resolution 690 of 1991, and a Special Representative on Western Sahara, Johannes Manz, was appointed to oversee the monitoring of the cease-fire and referendum processes.[55] By mid-September, UN observers arrived in the Western Sahara and were dispersed around the ten observation posts. However, the date for the formal cease-fire, September 6, came and went. In December, Secretary General de Cuellar reported that substantial differences existed between Morocco and POLISARIO, particularly over the identification process to be used during the referendum. Further delays and new fighting occurred, leading to Manz's resignation and a loss of confidence in the UN-led peace process. An essential precondition for MINURSO's successful achievement of its task—the full cooperation of the two main parties to the dispute—was lacking. Both sides seek acceptance of procedures that would improve their position before a referendum, with the result that an internationally certifiable process continues to be difficult to implement.

A more encouraging example of effective UN facilitation of a change to responsible governance occurred during the South African run-up to the 1994 elections. By June 1992, the Convention for a Democratic South Africa (CODESA) II negotiations were brought to a halt as South Africa faced escalating violence, particularly a massacre at Boipatong township south of Johannesburg, where Inkatha Freedom Party supporters, armed with spears, knives, and guns, randomly murdered forty-two of the predominantly ANC residents.[56] Observing that there were 373 deaths and 395 injuries during that month alone, Mandela told the UN Security Council that the violence amounted to "a cold-blooded strategy of state terrorism," and the ANC withdrew from the second plenary session of CODESA II.[57]

As the storm clouds gathered and the effort to resolve political differences by peaceful means faltered, the international community moved cautiously to restore confidence in the peace process. Previously, South African church and business leaders had played an important mediatory role as violence threatened the constitutional talks between the government and the ANC in April 1991. Moreover, the National Peace Accord of September 1991, which provided for the Regional Dispute Resolution Committee and the Local Peace Committees to settle disputes by negotiating with the parties concerned, attempted to promote an easing of tensions at the grass-roots level.[58] As important as these internal mediation efforts were, the international community decided it was necessary to intervene formally in South Africa's peace process to deal with the violence of June 1992 and the evidence of a breakdown in the negotiations.

Even though it was not the only international actor to take a hand, the United Nations certainly played the most important role. Declaring itself concerned over the rising violence and its consequences for peaceful negotiations, the UN Security Council unanimously adopted a resolution in July inviting the secretary general to appoint a special representative to recommend "measures which would assist in bringing an effective end to the violence and in creating conditions for negotiations leading towards a peaceful transition to a democratic, non-racial and united South Africa."[59] In accordance with this authorization, the secretary general appointed Cyrus R. Vance, the former U.S. secretary of state, as his special representative. After arriving in South Africa, Vance met with de Klerk and members of his cabinet and then with leaders of the major political parties, the homelands, and civil society.

Upon Vance's advice, the secretary general wrote to de Klerk, Mandela, and the Inkatha Freedom Party leader, Chief Mangosuthu Buthelezi, expressing his concern that the mass demonstrations planned for August 3 could take a violent turn. Mandela assured the secretary general that the ANC would do all it could to avoid violence. Mandela also requested that the United Nations consider sending some ten observers to witness the demonstrations. State President de Klerk and his cabinet colleagues declared that they had no objection to this proposal, and de Klerk went on to suggest that the UN observers should act in coordination with the National Peace Secretariat.[60] In light of this agreement, Secretary General Boutros-Ghali did dispatch international monitors to South Africa to observe mass action throughout the country. In addition, concluding that the National Peace Accord of September 1991 needed to be strengthened, Boutros-Ghali recommended that the United Nations make available some thirty observers to serve in close association with the National Peace Secretariat to further the purposes of the accord. The Security Council welcomed this initiative and authorized the dispatching of a fifty-member (increased to one hundred in September) UN Observer Mission in South Africa (UNOMSA) team.[61]

On arrival in South Africa, the UNOMSA team attended political rallies, observed meetings of the peace committee, and remained in close contract with the National Peace Secretariat staff. It also made recommendations to local officials on the handling of security matters following the murder of African nationalist leader Chris Hani and urged active participation by the Pan-Africanist Congress and others in the nationwide peace commission.[62] These efforts were supplemented by other outside observer groups on the scene—most prominently, the European Community, the Commonwealth, and the OAU. The United Nations and other observers were important to the peace process as they provided a stabilizing influence and gave useful guidance to the local parties. By working closely with Peace Accord Committee officials, the UN monitors strengthened the legitimacy of these officials and their activities.

Nevertheless, as important as this observation and advisory role was in promoting responsible sovereignty in South Africa, there were strict limits to its reach. The UN observers were circumscribed by their mandate, for they could not exert pressure officially. As impartial observers, moreover, they could provide information, but they were not permitted to judge this information or intervene formally in the conflict.[63] In fact, the approach of the April 27, 1994, elections revealed all the strengths and weaknesses of international monitoring. The UN team strove as effectively as it could to monitor political marches and rallies and in some cases to mediate between contending parties, but in the end, as political violence surged before the elections in the former homelands and Natal province, it became necessary for President F. W. de Klerk to declare a state of emergency in the KwaZulu homeland and the surrounding Natal province. In that event, the brunt of ensuring that campaigning and voting proceeded peacefully fell on the shoulders of the national police and army, and the election monitors were described as "increasingly powerless to defuse local conflicts."[64] The upshot is to raise questions about the credibility of UN and other international monitors in future high-conflict situations.

Military-Diplomatic Intervention

In the post–cold war period, peacekeepers may feel themselves obliged to act in a forceful manner to restore sovereignty and responsibility. In doing so they frequently become peace enforcers, occupying a "failed state" to ensure that relief supplies can be delivered to the populace at large (Somalia) or to maintain order and reestablish regular relations between state and society (Somalia, Liberia).[65] When undertaking these initiatives, the line between food delivery and political order becomes hazy. Regularized state-society relations are required if humanitarian relief is to be delivered to its intended recipients over an extended period. Hence peace enforcement requires joint military-diplomatic action to restore the state's capacity for effective leadership and to bring about a return to responsible sovereignty.

Certainly, peace enforcement in collapsed state situations involved unique choices. In both Somalia and Liberia, the interveners brought considerable military force to bear on the militias in the target territory. If U.S. and UN involvement in Somalia differed from the Economic

Community of West African States Monitoring Group's (ECOMOG's) intervention in Liberia in terms of the relatively greater financial resources available to the U.S.-backed global organization in Somalia, they were similar in the reluctance of the interveners to take casualties. Overwhelming force without a willingness to risk substantial troop losses meant a general inability to win a decisive victory. Hence the peace enforcement efforts in Somalia and Liberia dragged on for lengthy periods, raising questions about the credibility of the United Nations and regional organizations to cope with situations where sovereignty itself is at risk.

In the future, the Somali humanitarian intervention may come to be seen as something of an exception in terms of the extent of U.S. unilateral action under the auspices of the United Nations. Earlier opportunities for preventive diplomacy by the international community had been missed—for example, 144 moderate political leaders called for a national reconciliation conference in May 1990 to bring an end to the atrocities and to establish a multiparty system.[66] With hostilities continuing and the food delivery system becoming increasingly problematic by January 1991, the Security Council requested that a special coordinator be appointed to supervise the relief effort and encourage the warring parties to agree to a cease-fire. In March, UN mediators succeeded in gaining the concurrence of the two main contending leaders, General Aidid and Ali Mahdi, to a cease-fire and UN monitoring of the accord.[67] The provision on UN monitors was not put into effect until June, when fifty international observers were deployed in the Mogadishu area to watch over the cease-fire.[68] Under pressure from Ambassador Mohamed Sahnoun, the UN special representative, the warring factional leaders agreed to the stationing of an additional 500-person UN security force, subsequently airlifted to Somalia on U.S. aircraft. This security force proved woefully insufficient in its ability to protect the relief shipments throughout the country, and the Security Council passed a resolution authorizing a further deployment of 3,500 personnel of the UN Operation in Somalia (UNOSOM) in December 1992.[69] Sahnoun began negotiating with the militia leaders over this increase in UNOSOM number.[70] When the militia leaders responded rather diffidently to these appeals, the special representative decided to terminate his assignment and force the issue of an increased UN role in peacekeeping and national reconciliation.

It was the inability of the United Nations to cope with the factional skirmishes that led the United States to decide on intervening directly in the Somali crisis. Ambassador Robert Oakley remarks on the Bush decisions as follows:

> The U.S. would have made it a UN peacekeeping operation, but at that point neither the UN Secretary General nor the UNSC was willing to see the UN accept the sort of muscular mandate, rules of engagement and command and control arrangements upon which we rightly insisted. Thus it became a UN-endorsed but U.S.-led consortium operating on its own.[71]

Seeing little alternative to an American-led military intervention, the Bush administration dispatched a 25,000-person U.S. contingent to the country in December 1992 (with the first phase of the intervention ending in May 1993). Bush outlined limited objectives for the force: to ensure a safe environment for the delivery of relief supplies and, by implication, to begin the process of national reconciliation.[72] Although this action in Somalia sets something of a precedent in Africa for employing military contingents to ensure food deliveries to the starving, questions abounded over the operation's ability to deal with such problems as disarmament and national integration. Because of this book's attention to international mediation and conflict resolution, it will be appropriate to focus on the longer-term objectives of national reconciliation and peacemaking. In essence, the problems in Somalia, with its clan-based rivalries over access to scarce resources and positions of influence in state institutions as well as ethnoregional antagonisms (for example, the Isaak rebellion against the Barre regime), are essentially political in nature.[73] If U.S. and UN peace enforcement units could promote the conditions for positive change, they could not be expected to create political legitimacy through the use of military force alone.

In part, the fragility of the peace process reflected the strategy of peacemaking employed by the international community. From the outset, UN and U.S. diplomats faced a difficult choice between basic alternatives: to foster negotiations among the powerful militia leaders on the scene, or to reach out and encourage the development of civil society—that is, those organizations standing between state and society, which are distinct from but which relate to both.[74] In the Somali context, this includes such groups as clan elders, religious leaders, professionals, women's organizations, intellectuals, and others. Inevitably the first route was attractive to American authorities because it was quicker and easier to implement. On the downside, however, it meant dealing with the very people who had been the source of the breakdown and ending with some kind of pacted elite arrangement that was far less democratic than the more inclusive civil society route.[75]

The diplomatic process that followed the U.S.-led military intervention represented a cautious effort to contain the most destructive elements of the conflict—in particular, seizing some of the weapons controlled by the militia leaders and thereby forcing them into the political arena. Although the American team did mediate some of the local conflicts on its own, such as that between Ali Mahdi and Aidid, the main task of negotiating a nationwide peace accord fell to the United Nations, and especially to Ethiopian leader Meles Zenawi, with the Americans playing a supporting role. In March 1993, the fifteen main factional leaders assembled in Addis Ababa under UN sponsorship to try to work out a comprehensive settlement. They agreed to set up a Transitional National Council that would include the various clan leaders plus three elected representatives (one of whom has to be a woman) from the country's eighteen regions. The council would serve as a legislative body; it was authorized, however, to establish an independent judiciary as well as to create elected local and regional councils.[76]

The fragility of the elite pact soon became evident as the main part of the American forces left Somalia and were replaced by units from other countries. General Aidid, recognizing the increasing vulnerability of the UN force, appears to have sanctioned the ambush of the Pakistani troops on June 5, raising questions about the credibility of the UN operation and causing the United States to respond with heavy air and ground assaults on Aidid's military positions in Mogadishu. A ferocious street battle took place on October 3, leaving eighteen U.S. soldiers dead and seventy-eight wounded and an estimated five hundred to one thousand Somali casualties. Fatigued with its peacekeeping and peace enforcement roles in Somalia, the United States declared the mission a success and withdrew in phases from the scene, to be followed shortly after by a winding down of the UN presence. Peace enforcement in this case clearly relied on overwhelming force and the willingness to use it. However, as the intermediary with muscle disengaged, the gains in national reconciliation were undercut.

Thus the external force sent to help the Somalis exercise their sovereignty in a responsible manner had failed on both accounts.

The existence of overwhelming force and the will to use it was also in question in the case of the ECOWAS intervention in Liberia. In this instance, the 1980 military coup led by Master Sergeant Samuel K. Doe quickly gave way to a regime of terror and repression, not only against the formerly dominant Americo-Liberian community but also against the Gio and Mano peoples in Nimba county. Terrible atrocities committed by government (largely Krahn) soldiers led to the emergence in 1989 of a guerrilla force commanded by Charles Taylor—and a further cycle of atrocities against Doe's Krahn and Mandingo supporters. When Taylor's National Patriotic Front of Liberia (NPFL) launched an assault upon Doe's Armed Forces of Liberia (AFL) in Nimba county in late 1989, a war broke out, escalating shortly afterward into a merciless struggle between adversaries. With the United States refusing to be drawn into the civil war, ECOWAS decided in the summer of 1990 that it was necessary to intervene to halt the worsening crisis in and around the capital city. "We knew," declared President Babangida, "that if we allowed the situation to degenerate . . . it would affect the entire West African sub-region."[77]

A five-nation peace enforcement group from Nigeria, Ghana, Guinea, Gambia, and Sierra Leone was dispatched to Liberia in August. Later, a Senegalese contingent joined this core group (only to depart in January 1993 to help ensure order during the Senegalese elections). ECOMOG created what amounted to a "safe sanctuary" in parts of the Monrovia area—separating the beleaguered government forces (Doe having been captured and killed) from both the NPFL insurgents and a breakaway insurgent force, the Independent National Patriotic Front of Liberia led by Prince Yeduo Johnson.

Although better equipped and militarily superior to the NPFL forces, the ECOMOG contingents did not find it easy to establish their superiority. Until February 1993, concludes a correspondent for *Africa Confidential*,

ECOMOG's military performance against the NPFL had been lacklustre, reflecting the calibre of commanding officers, the training of the soldiers and the initially poor logistics. While the Senegalese . . . and Ghanaian troops were regarded as the most effective, the Nigerian troops had been criticised as 'unmotivated' and 'poorly-led' by Western diplomats. Under the more aggressive leadership of ECOMOG Field Commander Adetunji Olurin, the Nigerians' performance appears to have improved considerably.[78]

In the months after landing, ECOMOG units consolidated their position in Monrovia and extended their hold over the area just beyond the city limits. For the next two years, an uneasy cease-fire was maintained between ECOMOG and Taylor's insurgents, with the former dug in around the capital city and the latter controlling the rural hinterland and its natural resources. Taylor strongly questioned the neutrality of ECOMOG, contending that it countervened its mandate by siding with elements from Doe's former army—the United Liberation Movement of Liberia (ULIMO).[79] By October, with the war along the Sierra Leone border against ULIMO going poorly, Taylor broke the cease-fire agreement and launched an attack on the ECOMOG units in Monrovia. This attack was condemned by the UN Security Council.[80]

ECOMOG reacted strongly to the NPFL attack, moving from a peacekeeping to a peace enforcement mode. Now viewed as a victim rather than an initiator of violence,[81] it went on the offensive—and with significant results. In conjunction with a naval blockade and air attacks on Taylor's positions, the revivified ECOMOG force captured the international airport at Robertsfield, the Firestone plantation, and, in April 1993, the flourishing port city of Buchanan. The capture of Buchanan was especially important as it enabled ECOMOG to tighten the blockade on NPFL imports and exports. Yet these successes did not amount to anything like a knockout blow, for the NPFL continued to control more than 50 percent of the country. NPFL could still engage in trade relations across its borders, and it retained some capacity to mount assaults upon ECOMOG positions.[82] Moreover, the intensity of the ECOMOG attack was criticized in the international press.[83]

So long as ECOMOG adopted only a defensive stance, protecting the city of Monrovia and its environs from NPFL probes, it was difficult to extract a conclusive agreement from Taylor and make him abide by its terms. On paper, Côte d'Ivoire's President Felix Houphouët-Boigny appeared to move ahead in his efforts to broker a peace accord between the NPFL and Amos Sawyer's internationally recognized interim government.[84] After several failed efforts to secure Taylor's acceptance of a cease-fire, agreement on a government of national unity, and the holding of general and presidential elections, progress was achieved at Yamoussoukro, Côte d'Ivoire, in September 1991 in bridging the wide gulf between Taylor and Sawyer.[85] With Houphouët-Boigny acting as mediator, the two sides agreed that an expanded ECOMOG force would be permitted to supervise the assembling and disarming of local military units, with an eye to facilitating national elections. The agreement was ambiguous about who would actually conduct the disarming exercise—the militias themselves or ECOMOG—and what would happen to the arms;[86] even so, the September meeting represented a first serious effort to negotiate the rules for a return to responsible sovereignty. At subsequent meetings at Yamoussoukro, attempts were made to enlarge on the specifics of ECOMOG's role in monitoring the disarmament of the military forces and organizing the elections throughout the country. Although Taylor agreed to the Yamoussoukro accords, he nonetheless resisted the application of all its terms, including plans to set up a buffer area along the border with Sierra Leone, the reopening of the roads, and the disarming of his troops.[87]

Frustrated over Taylor's continuing obstruction and determined to force compliance with the accords, ECOMOG decided to take more forceful action. With resistance from some of the French-speaking African countries, the ECOWAS heads of state and government endorsed a proposal at its July 1992 meeting in Dakar to impose comprehensive sanctions against the Taylor-held areas of Liberia. In November 1992, the Security Council gave its blessing to the ECOWAS efforts to bring about a settlement. It reaffirmed its belief that the Yamoussoukro IV Accord of October 30, 1991, offered "the best possible framework for a peaceful resolution of the Liberian conflict." The Security Council, though failing to support comprehensive sanctions, called for an embargo on deliveries of military equipment to all military forces in Liberia—except to the ECOWAS peacekeeping contingents. This resolution also brought the United Nations more directly into the conflict resolution process, for the Security Council requested that the secretary general dispatch a special representative to Liberia to evaluate the situation and to report back to it with recommendations.[88] The weight of the United Nations had now come down firmly on the side of ECOWAS and its peace plan.

This support for ECOMOG did not stop Taylor from launching a new assault on the peacekeepers. The greatly strengthened regional organization responded in a forceful manner, however, and significantly expanded its perimeters. In March 1993, the Security Council again reaffirmed its backing for the Yamoussoukro process and went on to declare "its readiness to consider appropriate measures in support of ECOWAS if any party is unwilling to cooperate in implementation of the provisions of the Yamoussoukro Accords, in particular the encampment and disarmament provisions."[89] Clearly the coalition of mediators (ECOWAS, the OAU, and the United Nations) was now in a stronger position to gain assent for the Yamoussoukro agreements. In response to this changed situation on the ground, Taylor appeared to shift his position once again, accepting the July 25, 1993, Cotonou agreement provisions on a cease-fire and the disarming and demobilization of all combatants. The implementation of the Cotonou conference provisions on disarmament and the installation of an all-party Liberian National Transitional Government (LNTG) proved slow and difficult, particularly as the animosities between the rivals remained strong. However, as the mediators, supported by the United States, pressured the various parties to agree to the so-called Triple 7 Agreement signed in Monrovia on February 5, 1994, the path toward a fragile settlement was set in place. The NPFL secured assent to its demand that the LNTG be installed before the beginning of disarmament, and the expanded ECOMOG forces (now broadened to include troops from Uganda and Tanzania) committed themselves to deploying their forces throughout the country. The threat of a pullout of forces was sufficient to extract the Monrovia agreement from the warring factions (now increased to seven), but not to break the impasse over demilitarization and representation in the LNTG.

Seeing no end to the conflict and increasingly fatigued with the heavy financial costs of peacekeeping, a disheartened Jerry Rawling, president of Ghana and ECOWAS chairman, warned the Liberian representatives at talks in Accra that the international community might pull their troops out if they failed to seize this opportunity to move toward peace.[90] Spurred on by warnings from Ghana, the United States and the United Nations, and pressured by marchers in Monrovia demanding that the factional leaders return home with a peace agreement, the NPFL, United Liberation Movement for Democracy in Liberia (ULIMO-K), and AFL chiefs, with other factional strongmen looking on, signed the Agreement on the Clarification of the Akosombo Agreement. The main parties (with some dissent) agreed to a five-member Council of State that included representatives from NPFL, ULIMO, AFL, the Liberian National Conference (LNC), and a traditional chief elected by the NPFL and ULIMO. They also reaffirmed the Cotonou and Akosombo agreements as frameworks for peace and agreed to work with ECOMOG and the UN Observer Mission in Liberia (UNOMIL) to create safe havens and buffer zones throughout the country. Although a cease-fire did go into effect on December 28, 1994, violations were reported shortly afterward. The Akosombo agreement had failed to address the issue of disarmament and to end the dispute over the composition and chairmanship of the collective Council of State.

With the peace process deadlocked over the exercise of executive power, a determined Rawlings, with support from the United Nations and other West African states, used heavy pressure from a coalition of mediators to push the warring parties to sign a compromise agreement at Abuja, Nigeria, in August 1995.[91] With the UN and ECOWAS states threatening to withdraw their observers in September if no progress toward peace had been achieved, the majority of Liberian leaders at Abuja agreed to a mandatory cease-fire and a six-person Council of State for a one-year transitional period consisting of an independent chairperson and five vicechairpersons with equal status. Howeover, Abuja II is inevitably a shaky basis for peace. With Bonecuelt Johnson, a general and leader of a ULIMO breakaway faction refusing to sign the agreement because the mediators failed to name his protégé chief of staff, this agreement, like its ten predecessors, appeared to suffer from the problem of credible commitment. As OAU representative Canaan Banana commented on the problem of implementation: "Agreements in Liberia are not in short supply, what is in short supply is the determination and commitment to implement them."[92]

In brief, then, a mediator's status and power and preparedness to use that power do make a difference in third-party efforts to advance the negotiation process. It was the mediator with strength—Haile Selassie in the Sudanese negotiations of 1972, Britain in the Zimbabwe independence negotiations, the United States in the Angolan international negotiations of 1988, the coalition of mediators under UN leadership in the Liberian negotiations of August 1995—who controlled agendas or influenced the adversaries, causing them to reexamine their preferences. In the cases of the United Nations in Somalia and

South Africa, the OAU in Rwanda, the Portuguese in Angola (at Bicesse), and the Italians in Mozambique, the legitimacy of the international organization, small state, or private mediator became linked directly or indirectly to powerful state actors supportive of a peaceful change. In the post–cold war era Angola-type lead roles by powerful states may not be appropriate in attempting to deal with Africa's internal disputes, but in this event a successful intervention may require that the leading part be played by an international or regional organization actor, with the powerful external actor in a supportive position.

The Problems of Postagreement Peace Building

Compromises struck during negotiations inevitably structure the course that elite interactions will take in the ensuing period. At times, such compromises reduce outward expressions of conflict without coming to grips with the factors giving rise to the conflict in the first place. If competition and conflict are to be bounded and channeled along manageable lines, the rules of the game must be known and accepted by the major political actors. To fail to understand that the negotiation of a settlement is closely joined to the administrative effort to put the agreement into operation is to take some risks with incoherence during the transitional stage.

Not only is the structuring process critical but the implementation of agreements is also central to outcomes. Africa's record in this regard is decidedly mixed. If agreements were successfully consolidated in Namibia and Zimbabwe, where multiparty elections legitimated the negotiations and provided some slack for the transition process,[93] some of the peace agreements laboriously hammered out by various international interveners have weakened or dissolved during the implementation stage. The breakdown of the 1972 Sudanese Agreement, the 1975 Alvor Agreement, the 1985 Nairobi accord on Uganda, the Bicesse Accords, the Zairian political compromise, the 1993 Rwanda accords, and ten Liberian agreements are all examples of such lost opportunities in the African context. Clearly, implementation is part of the larger peacemaking process, not a separate and distinct phase. To fail to develop a realizable plan for demobilization, disarmament, and the reintegration of militias in Somalia was to risk placing the fragile, elite power-sharing pact worked out under UN auspices in March 1993 in serious jeopardy. The two processes of careful peacemaking and effective implementation are intertwined. Successful conflict resolution requires simultaneous attention to both if it is to achieve settlements that are sustainable.

In several instances, the United Nations, the United States, and others concentrate more on facilitating peace accords than implementing them. A number of possible explanations for this come to mind, including the faith than many Western analysts have in the sanctity of agreements, intolerance of alternative strategies for dealing with conflict, absorption in the drama of negotiations, impatience with extended implementation processes, inability to gain a commitment from both sides to the agreement, involvement in internal bureaucratic politics, and concern over the human and financial costs associated with long-term peace enforcement activities.[94] Among the most dramatic illustrations of this gap between negotiating and administrative skills in recent times was the orchestration of the Angolan (Bicesse) settlement and its tragic aftermath.

In the Bicesse negotiations in 1991, the Angolan government sought to lengthen the period before national elections, but agreed, at UNITA's insistence, on a Portuguese-recommended compromise of approximately eighteen months after the signing of the cease-fire.[95] Both sides continued to hold grim perceptions of each other's intentions, but each went ahead with the elections—assuming that it would be victorious. With dos Santos receiving 49.57 percent of the presidential vote (and Savimbi 40.6 percent), Savimbi charged election fraud and, recognizing the likelihood of a defeat in a second round, refused to proceed with the run-off election. Heavy fighting resumed, with UNITA quickly gaining the initiative and seizing extensive territories.

The UN-administered transition in Angola proved flawed. With the United Nations trying to resolve conflict on the cheap, it provided too thin a presence on the ground to dissuade Savimbi from defecting. In all, there were only 400 UN cease-fire monitors in Angola, a woefully insufficient number to ensure the disarming of the combatants and to verify that the troops had actually gathered at the prescribed assembly points. The Bicesse Accords, which provided for the unification of the government and UNITA armies following the cease-fire, declared that,

By the time the elections are held, only the Angolan Armed Forces shall exist; there may be no other troops whatsoever. All members of the present armed forces of each party who do not become members of the Angolan Armed Forces shall be demobilized prior to the holding of elections.[96]

In fact, the two military forces were only partially integrated before the elections; moreover, it remained unclear whether the armies would have continued to be loyal to the new command structure in the event that the civil war flared up again. Finally, it is important to note that there was no means of breaking a deadlock at the meetings of various observer organizations set up to oversee the elections.[97]

This lamentable experience contrasts markedly with that in Namibia in 1989 where the United Nations Transition Assistance Group (UNTAG) effectively performed the role of third-party enforcer, controlling the movement to independence, monitoring the South African-appointed administrator-general government at the central and regional levels, and attempting to ensure that the elections were conducted in a free and fair manner.[98] In seeking to build public confidence in the transition process, UNTAG dispatched a relatively large force of 4,650 troops to oversee the elections in a country of some 1.4 million people. The secretary general projected a budgeted cost of $416 million, although actual requirements only came to $367 million; by comparison, in Angola, with an estimated population of 9.4 million, UN expenses came to a mere $132 million.[99] Moreover, in Namibia the contending parties adopted essentially pragmatic perceptions of one another. Indications of such pragmatism include the following: national elections came after agreement on a constitution, the elections for a constituent assembly protected minority interests through a party list system of proportional representation, and the constitution dispersed power among the rival parties.[100]

It seems apparent that the United Nations and other international observers were fully alert to the shortcomings of the implementation process following the Bicesse Accords in Angola, and they have attempted to build preventive measures into the follow-up Lusaka Protocol of 1994 to guard against a similar failure. The UN secretary general remarked in his report of May 1993 that if the Angolan adversaries agreed to end their hostilities, "It would be necessary not only to redeploy observers expeditiously to all parts of the country, but also *to expand their number very rapidly,* as the present strength would clearly be inadequate to the task."[101] In essence, the Lusaka Protocol represents a continuation of the Bicesse process, providing for a cease-fire, the deployment of monitors, the withdrawal of South African mercenaries, the formation of an integrated national army, national reconciliation, and the consolidation of democracy.[102] The negotiators at Lusaka made several adjustments to promote both sovereignty and responsibility. Not only did they plan to put 7,000 observers and peacekeepers at the major flashpoints, but they provided in detail for power sharing at all levels of government. New elections would be held when the UN representative on the scene decided that the time was appropriate. It was the best that could be achieved under difficult political circumstances. With both sides continuing to show considerable mistrust of each other's intentions, the strong third-party enforcer is necessary to build confidence on both sides by making certain that they live up to the terms of the contract. Yet, even with a respected third-party mediator on the scene, suspicion and hostility between the adversaries remains evident. Not surprisingly, therefore, the 1994 peace agreement remains a fragile one.

In practical terms, the Angolan precedent (with the breakdown of the Bicesse Accords) was highly instructive for those engaged in implementing agreements elsewhere.[103] In Mozambique, where the UN Operation in Mozambique (UNOMOZ) presided over another transition process following a peace accord, a highly effective UN Secretary General's Special Representative, Aldo Ajello, chaired the various peace process oversight commissions and actively mediated between the rival parties on the issues of elections, demobilization, the police and military forces, and humanitarian relief. What was true regarding the long negotiations over a peace agreement applied to the postagreement peace-building process as well: the third-party intervener maintained sufficient leverage to guide the process to a safe landing.[104] To push the peace process along, Ajello extended financial assistance to the weaker party, Resistência Nacional Moçambicana (RENAMO), seeking to bring it to a position of equivalence with the government of the Frente de Libertação de Moçambique (FRELIMO) in order to build its confidence and encourage it to make concessions at the bargaining table. At times, moreover, when the parties appeared, for tactical purposes, to stonewall the implementation negotiations, Ajello did bring some pressure to bear to overcome the impasse.[105]

To cope with its complex assignment, the United Nations budgeted $330 million for the UNOMOZ operation. It planned on sending some 7,500 police and military peacekeepers to enforce the demobilization and disarmament of the combatants and the creation of a unified army before the holding of elections. However, because of financial constraints, the number of military peacekeepers was scaled back in February 1994.[106] In most respects, the Mozambican transition went smoothly. The General Assembly voted an advance on the budget of $140 million, and a sizable number of the UN peacekeepers did arrive in Mozambique in the spring of 1993. However, the continuing suspicions that the two parties had about one another and the unwillingness of RENAMO's officials to attend the meetings of the various commissions set up to supervise the implementation of the Rome accords led to long delays in the demobilization of forces and the creation of a unified army. Moreover, the overly optimistic date set for the elections had to be put off until October 1994, over a year after originally scheduled. In the end, however, the cease-fire held up, the elections took place, and the losing party (RENAMO) abided by the results.[107] After sixteen years of debilitating civil war, UNOMOZ had succeeded in connecting sovereignty with responsibility.

Conclusion

Where the sovereign state fails to manage conflict effectively and governance breaks down, the responsibility for dealing with disputes may fall for a limited time on external agents. In that event, they seek to help the rival parties return to regularized rules of relationship, the essence of successful governance. The South African negotiations are something of an exception to this generalization as both the government and ANC rejected an externally mediated all-party conference of the type that took place at Lancaster House in 1979; yet even here, one sees UN observers, church groups, and business interests playing an important facilitating role at key junctures. The question therefore is, what agent of international intervention is likely to be appropriate in the varied circumstances of contemporary Africa? Clearly, the setting differs widely from one context to another. Some private, small state, or international organization mediators possess considerable legitimacy as interveners. In addition, they often show great skill in communicating with and negotiating between adversaries. However, their lack of political and economic resources means they tend to be limited in the pressures and incentives they can bring to bear and are therefore unable to push the deliberations through to a successful conclusion. In other cases, such as the international negotiations in Angola, skill is combined with leverage, enabling the great powers to cooperate in negotiating an end to a divisive regional dispute. Nevertheless, because the latter situations are special in their links to the cold war, they are likely to be less and less relevant to the changing circumstances of the twenty-first century.

What becomes apparent, then, is the need for a new combination of actors for the years ahead, one that unites the skills and legitimacy of such organizations as the United Nations and OAU or well-placed unofficial or small-power mediators, with the leverage of a great power. Such a joint mediatory effort may be difficult to create and may prove limited in its capacity to deal with recalcitrant leaders, such as Charles Taylor in Liberia or Jonas Savimbi in Angola, but it nonetheless represents the most effective leadership available in an increasingly disunited and anarchic African continental order. Certainly, some logical candidates for such a role may hesitate to take on the responsibilities involved. The United States, for example, is currently feeling overwhelmed by its domestic and international responsibilities and is not eager to accept demanding new assignments as global policeman or peacemaker. Other potential actors also seem reluctant to assume lead roles as peacekeepers or mediators, regarding such commitments as costly and possibly illegitimate interventions in the affairs of other countries or regions.

Despite the difficulties in creating a coalition of mediators including an international organization or small state on the one hand and a great power on the other, there may be few effective alternatives in the post–cold war era for dealing with African conflicts. Driven by an overriding desire to promote global stability, the powerful actors in today's world appear likely to place restraints on their desire for business as usual and to engage in peacemaking initiatives aimed at preventing the spread of local conflicts to the region. As already noted, these efforts may prove insufficient in many instances, as warring parties carry on the fight to eliminate their adversaries or to force their capitulation. In a limited number of cases, however, further successes in OAU or UN-led peacemaking initiatives can be envisaged.

The problem here is that even where the leverage that such coalitions can bring to bear is sufficient to facilitate a practical, mutual-gains formula to end the fighting, it may not be adequate to ensure justice. The problem of conflict resolution and justice was examined in chapter 1, but it is important to note the dilemmas of peacemaking under conditions of weak governance and limited economic resources. In contemporary South Africa, negotiations led to power sharing and limitations on central government action, as the African majority agreed on a diffusion of power to reassure minority interests, stabilize the economy, and hasten the transition to majority rule. If curbs on majority action prove too effective, however, it may weaken the majority's respect for the agreement as the African masses come to feel that a political settlement cheated them of effective redistribution—and economic justice.

Hence, the quality of agreements becomes critical. These settlements cannot be viewed as static in nature, restraining movement toward more just distributional patterns. In addition, they cannot cope with the challenge of national reconciliation if they keep the contending rivals in separate containers. Agreements become possible when the contending interests, assisted by third-party facilitators, recognize that the existing forms of conflict are mutually destructive and show sensitivity toward each other's basic fears and wishes. The realism necessary to hammer out a responsible settlement is most likely to gain assent when it avoids pushing either adversary to make major concessions. In avoiding such concessions, however, the accord often places a higher priority on the accommodation of different interests than on justice as such. The result is likely to be a very unstable process of transition. Yet as Giuseppe Di Palma comments regarding regimes that are only minimally democratic, "An anemic democracy may still be capable of producing its own new blood."[108] Put in terms of conflict management procedures, the new peace accord may be quite imperfect, but it can make a contribution to good governance if it is followed by ongoing negotiations and renegotiations over time.

In the end, such an iterative process must transform the original pact and develop new rules of encounter perceived as just by the majority. If that does not happen, the founding pact is likely to be prone to disruption. Pragmatism, conceived as adjusting to the demands of powerful group interests, is not likely to prove a sufficient basis for responsible sovereignty in and of itself. Rather, bargaining encounters can at best help to create a stable environment in which an iterative bargaining process can take place, leading over the years to more constructive and, it is hoped, more just rules of relationship. Otherwise the social contract is likely to remain elusive, and with dire consequences in terms of predictable interactions among groups and between these groups and the state.

7

Conclusion

SOVEREIGNTY AS responsibility means that national governments are duty bound to ensure minimum standards of
security and social welfare for their citizens and be accountable both
to the national body politic and the international community. Seen
from this perspective, developments in Africa reflect a wide range in
the performance of governments. On the positive side, recent events
in South Africa signify a remarkable accomplishment in the creation
of conditions conducive to the exercise of responsible sovereignty in
the context of a multiracial society. South Africa is now a promising
nonracial, democratic model, not only for Africa, but indeed for the
world. At the opposite end of the spectrum are countries like Liberia,
Rwanda, Somalia, Sierra Leone, and Sudan, characterized by acute
ethnic violence or civil wars and a general disintegration of governance, public order, and personal and national security. In many parts
of the continent, hundreds of thousands, indeed millions of people,
are being lost in internecine warfare. Starvation, often the result of
man-made causes, abounds. Economic conditions have degenerated,
and states have collapsed or are becoming dysfunctional. In some
countries, only foreign humanitarian assistance is sustaining life at a
basic level. In between the models of South Africa and the failed or
failing states are states with a broad range of successes and failures in
discharging the responsibilities of sovereignty. But hardly any African
country can claim total success.

Relating the theme of sovereignty as responsibility to the challenges
of conflict resolution presupposes that managing conflicts is central to
nation building and development. Although economic and social development are among the major challenges facing Africa, a process of
self-sustaining growth and development is not possible without the

211

enabling environment of peace, security, democracy, stability, and respect for fundamental human rights. Conflict management clearly, therefore, is fundamental.

While these challenges fall within the domestic jurisdiction and therefore national sovereignty, neighboring states, and indeed the international community, cannot be indifferent to conditions in a given country, especially when the consequences of state performance affect their own situations and interests. States are therefore accountable not only to their own national constituencies, but also to the regional and international communities from which they are inseparable.

The urgency of seeing sovereignty as responsibility in relation to the challenges of preventing, managing, or resolving conflicts is underscored by the fact that most contemporary conflicts in the world are predominantly internal and Africa is the region most affected. Internal conflicts in Africa, as elsewhere in the world, often involve racial, ethnic, cultural, or religious cleavages that reflect severe, sometimes zero-sum, crises of national identity, usually manifested in a wide discrepancy between group identities and the official identity structures or frameworks of the state. As a result, the bases for participation in the political, economic, social, and cultural life of the country become factionalized and exclusive rather than inclusive to all groups. Those who fall outside the official identity framework fail the test of citizenship and become marginalized. These groups are likely to be seen as part of the opposition and therefore as the enemy.

The cases of Rwanda, Burundi, and Sudan demonstrate the brutal consequences of entire groups' being identified as "the enemy." Those who suffer the humanitarian consequences of conflict fall into a vacuum of the moral responsibility that is normally associated with the state. International humanitarian agencies are often called on to provide the necessary protection and assistance to fill this vacuum. Under those conditions, national sovereignty itself becomes violently contested.

Responsible sovereignty must first and foremost ensure for citizens peace, security, and stability through a system of law and order that enjoys broad-based support and therefore legitimacy. This, in turn, requires postulating guiding principles subsumed in the concept of human dignity conceived of not as a utopian vision, but as a political demand for which people are often prepared to risk their lives. An element of people's outrage at the indignities of the political, economic, or social situation and the defense of the status quo by those responsible for the indignities is nearly always behind internal conflicts. The quest for human dignity usually translates into a struggle for recognition, respect, and equitable participation in the political, economic, social, and cultural life of the country.

Within the framework of universal values, a major objective of responsible sovereignty should be the establishment of a system of just and fair distribution of power, wealth, and other moral and symbolic values. Conflicts that degenerate into widespread violence essentially reflect a breakdown of public order and the legal system designed to protect it. A normative approach to this crisis must address the concept of law as an instrument of control and the degree to which it lives up to the overriding goals of human dignity, at least to the pragmatic extent of ensuring functional legitimacy, all of which ultimately depend on a system of international accountability.

Although the institutional expression of the principles of human dignity varies according to the context and the prevailing culture, the fundamental values involved are universal and are now enshrined in the Universal Declaration of Human Rights and in the International Covenant on Civil and Political Rights and the International Covenant on Economic, Social, and Cultural Rights, as well as in other human rights instruments, both international and regional. For the most part, they have also been incorporated in national constitutions and legal norms. The essence of human rights law is the recognition of the inherent dignity and equality of all human beings and the setting of common standards for the articulation and protection of their rights without regard to race, ethnicity, religion, culture, or gender. This is particularly important to conflict management since internal conflicts often pit racial, ethnic, cultural, and religious groups against one another in a manner that is inherently discriminatory. Management of identities under those circumstances becomes a major component of the challenges confronting governance. It must be stressed that it is not the mere fact of the differences that generates conflicts, but the inequities or injustices of value production and distribution based on those differences. This often results in people's identifying themselves more with their exclusive groups than with the nation as a whole. Indeed, it has been argued that while Africans easily uphold their tribal identities and their continental identity as Africans, identification with the nation remains problematic for the overwhelming majority of Africans.[1]

In Africa's conflicts the issue of identity lies in several factors: the diversities of the racial, ethnic, religious, and cultural groups incorporated into the nation-state; the gap between the symbolic and substantive definition of the national framework and the way groups define themselves or are defined by others; the disparities, inequalities, and gross injustices implied in this gap; and the reaction of those marginalized or disadvantaged by the identity configuration and stratification.

The remedies required emanate from these factors and should include: defining national identity to be equitably accommodating to all the contending groups; developing principles of constitutionalism or constitutive management of power that creatively and flexibly balance the dynamics of diversity in unity to promote national consensus and collective purpose; designing a system of distribution or allocation of economic opportunities and resources that is particularly sensitive to the needs of minorities and disadvantaged groups and induces them to see unity as a source of security and enrichment and not of subjugation and deprivation; and through all these measures, to challenge every group to recognize that it has a distinctive contribution to make to the process of nation building by using its own cultural values, institutional structures, and a self-propelling sense of purpose within the framework of the nation. This is only possible in a context of equitable unity or just pluralism.

Where ethnic, cultural, and religious identities correlate with geographical boundaries, a large measure of autonomy, federal or confederal devolution of power, combined with power-sharing arrangements may be the appropriate solution to the identity problem. In the contemporary age, however, urbanization, migrant labor flows, intermarriage, and displacement due to conflict often intermesh identity and territorial boundaries. What is needed is not so much a constitutional label as a specific distribution of powers and allocation of responsibilities. If the parties cannot agree on principles to preserve even a framework of loose unity, then, in the interest of peace and security, alternatives to the unity of the nation-state as defined by the colonial powers should be revisited. And just as the international community was a factor in drawing the colonial borders, it should be involved in reconsidering those borders, with higher objectives in mind than were behind the colonial demarcation of African state borders. The decision to recognize Eritrea's independence while refusing Somaliland's claim represents an ad hoc adjustment to political and military facts on the ground rather than new international norms regarding borders.

The fact that the collectivity of the international community through the United Nations is involved in the process should remove or at least minimize the colonial connotation. The need for the involvement of the international community is heightened by the fact that in most destructive internal conflicts, the state is itself a party and not an impartial manager of conflicts. Conflict management is a function of regulating and mediating the demands individuals and groups make not only on each other but also on the government, which then both governs and negotiates its own relations with civil society and various identity groups. In cases of state collapse the need for a conflict manager is also great.

Stipulating substantive and procedural norms for the regulation and negotiation of demands provides the road map and the signposts for reconciling, harmonizing, or otherwise managing potentially conflicting relations and resolving conflicts. Setting standards to guide political and economic interaction among the participants and the regulatory function of governance is only a first step; institutional arrangements and enforcement mechanisms are crucial to the realization of the postulated objectives. The crisis of conflict emanates from the failure of sovereignty to discharge its management responsibilities. Building the institutional capacity for civil society (including its various identity groups) to negotiate and mediate differences and potential incompatibilities within itself and also with the government is the sine qua non of a successful system of governance with its political, economic, and social processes.

The rationale for sharing the responsibilities of sovereignty does not rest merely on altruistic motives, but also on mutual interests grounded in the fact that both the causes and consequences of conflict nearly always affect others, particularly at the regional level. Indeed, conflicts in Africa transpire on multiple levels, from local and state to regional and global. As a result, opportunities for improving conflict management also are found on multiple layers and may involve a variety of actors and agencies. Efforts at all levels need to be coordinated in order for each to reinforce and complement the others. This type of "layered response" has the advantage of allowing each participant to use its comparative advantage and permits one agency to pick up a problem when another becomes bogged down.[2] Conflict management, like security, needs to be analyzed holistically, with special attention to the linkages among the different levels of analysis and the relationships among agents of management at different tiers.[3]

The most fundamental arenas of struggle in which conflict management capacity urgently needs improvement are at the state and local (provincial, city, village) levels. The regional and international levels, as currently constituted, are dependent on states for their fundamental structure. Stable states, based on effective regimes regarded as legitimate and just by their populations, are therefore the fulcrum of more effective regional and international conflict management systems. Collective regional action is more likely to be effective when based on domestic stability, similarity of goals, and a consequent collective sense of purpose. Good governance—and hence well-developed conflict management capabilities—at the state and local levels is a necessary though not sufficient prerequisite to well-managed regional relations. Regional and international efforts at conflict management and resolution can supplement but not supplant national initiatives because questions of nation building, development, and democracy are primarily fashioned and resolved within the arena of nation-states.[4]

The regional and international levels, however, can reinforce and strengthen state and local conflict management systems. This has not been the general pattern historically. In the past, states more often exploited neighboring insurgencies to weaken the regime next door, and cold war–driven arms flows interfered with the ability of African states to manage their own affairs without recourse to warfare. In the contemporary international climate, however, these dynamics seem to be changing. External powers such as the United States no longer fund client states or insurgencies to serve as proxy forces in a global competition for influence. The West seems more interested in limiting its involvement than seeking out new clients. Within Africa, heightened concern about spillover effects and the high costs of internal conflicts has led to efforts to use regional organizations to encourage conflict management rather than accentuate the struggles. Regional initiatives in several conflict situations are examples of recent attempts by Africans to bring order to their regions: by the Economic Community of West African States (ECOWAS) through the Economic Community of

West Africa Monitoring Group (ECOMOG) to help manage or at least contain the Liberian civil war; by the Southern Africa Development Community (SADC) in Lesotho and Mozambique; and by the Intergovernmental Authority on Drought and Development (IGADD) to mediate in Sudan. As states have come under increased pressures and demands, leading some to collapse, external actors are seeking ways to support or reinforce conflict management at the state level.

One way to improve the capacity for conflict management in Africa is through the development of norms and rules of behavior. The African state system has demonstrated the usefulness of norms to manage international conflict. The strong consensus on territorial inviolability, based in the norm of *uti possidetis*, shaped Africans' view of and response to attempts by dissident groups to change boundaries. There have been few defections from this doctrine since it was explicitly adopted by the OAU by the Assembly of Heads of State and Government in Cairo in 1964.[5] This standard succeeded in discouraging some forms of conflict, but it must be noted that the norm made others— such as the Ethiopian-Eritrean conflict and the chronic civil war in Sudan—less manageable.[6] Norms and rules, of course, are means to achieve an end. The effectiveness and desirability of any rule must be judged against the normative goals of justice and dignity, not stability or management for its own sake.

While the institutionally supported continental norms of territorial integrity and noninterference played an important part in managing a limited set of problems amenable to collective diplomacy and self-restraint on the part of sovereign states, these norms proved inadequate as instruments for containing and preventing internal conflicts and their regional spillover effects. In the 1990s, therefore, political leaders and scholars engaged in policy discussions in Africa and beyond are struggling to develop new norms that will assist in the management of violent internal conflicts. The decision by the OAU at the 1994 Cairo Summit to set up a "mechanism for preventing, managing, and resolving conflicts in Africa" suggests that the organization may be preparing itself to move more creatively and effectively into issues previously out of bounds as internal affairs of member states.

Conflict management and stability in Africa will benefit in the long run from clearly articulated norms and guidelines supporting improved governance, democratization, and respect for the rights of minorities.[7] Norms at the regional and continental level with regard to the responsibilities of sovereignty involving such issues as democracy (respect for election results, tolerance for opposition, independence of the judiciary, freedom of the press and association, and respect for minorities) will help managers of Africa's internal conflicts in the same way that support for territorial integrity helped managers of Africa's interstate conflicts in the 1960s and 1970s. By providing markers and yardsticks that help establish acceptable behavior, the rules of the game are made clearer and violators more effectively identified, penalized, and isolated. Prior stipulation of the norms could indeed be an inducement for good governance and therefore prevention of conflicts.

The proposed Conference on Security, Stability, Development and Cooperation in Africa (CSSDCA), promoted by former Nigerian head of state General Olusegun Obasanjo, suggests a laudable series of norms to advance security and development and calls for greater participation by nongovernment groups. The plan in its general principles also recognized sovereignty and "the rights inherent in the territorial integrity and political independence of all other African states."[8] The fundamental conflict between narrow traditional notions of sovereignty and new regional norms therefore remains unresolved.

In addition, the relationship between geographically focused organizations such as ECOWAS, IGADD, and SADC and more inclusive, continental institutions such as the OAU and the proposed CSSDCA remains vague and open to question. Coordination among such organizations so that each one does what it can do best will only develop with discussion and experience over time. In the end, however, regional and continental organizations are limited in their effect by the nature of their membership. Organizations composed of states will be only as representative and responsive as their components. Hence the importance of the supplementary role of the international community. Indeed, the international community has recognized that increasing the operational capacity of regional organizations to manage conflict is a critical policy objective. The United States, for example, has provided funding for the OAU's conflict resolution efforts and encouraged other regional organizations, such as ECOWAS in Liberia and IGADD in Sudan, to develop additional capacities. The Western Friends of IGADD, which include Canada, Italy, the Netherlands, Norway, the United Kingdom, and the United States have also supported the regional peace initiative in Sudan.

In addition to providing the context and rules of the game that may promote conflict management, regional and international agencies can provide critically important mediators that may permit conflicting parties to find a way out of their conflicts. Mediatory skill, however, must be complemented with leverage to overcome the mutually damaging stalemates that plague many African conflict situations. It was mediators with strength—such as Haile Selassie in the Sudanese negotiations of 1972, Britain in the Zimbabwe independence negotiations, the United States in the 1988 Angolan talks—who were able to exert pressure on one or another of the parties to alter their preferences and accept an agreement. Skill alone is not likely to prevail in situations where high levels of conflict are present unless buttressed by the active support of strong third-party participants as mediators with muscle.

In the post–cold war world it may not be appropriate for powerful extra-continental participants to assume the lead in dealing with Africa's internal disputes. Outside powers such as the United States or European states may have the leverage but often lack the political will, interest, and commitment to play the mediating role effectively. In addition, they lack the legitimacy for such a role. As a consequence, they seem likely to channel their efforts to achieve a more stable and humane world under the auspices of the United Nations and such African regional bodies as ECOWAS, IGADD, SADC, and OAU. Such linking of great power and multilateral organization leadership seems efficacious, for it combines the moral legitimacy of the international organization with the fiscal and military capabilities of the strong states.

In some cases unofficial mediators may play important roles. Among their functions is facilitating negotiations, communicating between the rival parties, clarifying misperceptions and misinformation, identifying points of contention, influencing preferences, recommending compromises, and sometimes setting agendas. The room to maneuver that these unofficial mediators bring comes at the cost of lacking the economic and military resources of the great powers. Unofficial mediators normally are not in an effective position to influence the perceptions and preferences of the antagonists—hence the need for collaboration between them and forms of mediation with leverage.

One of the most important factors for policymakers to consider is the need to give much greater attention to the process of implementing agreements. In recent years, some of the peace agreements laboriously hammered out by various international interveners have weakened or dissolved during the implementation stage. It is clear that implementation is part of the larger peacemaking process, not a separate and distinct phase. Successful conflict management requires attention to all phases of the mediation process—prenegotiation, negotiation, and implementation—to show lasting results.

Where postagreement peace building fails, as in Angola, where renewed civil war broke out following the September 1992 elections, the options open to the United Nations, or its backers, are extremely narrow. Yet even someone as recalcitrant as UNITA leader Jonas Savimbi cannot insulate himself entirely from international pressures. Clearly, if exhortation, conciliation, or the desire to be included in the ruling coalition do not prove sufficient to bring Savimbi to compromise, then some form of coercive pressure may be imperative.

The international intervention in Somalia (1992–94) provides ample and tragic evidence of how difficult it is to use external force to assist political reconciliation and the rehabilitation of political institutions. The United States and United Nations tried two political strategies in Somalia. On the one hand, they sponsored meetings and negotiated agreements among the principal warring factions, the so-called warlords. On the other hand, they encouraged alternative voices from the ranks of traditional elders, women, local NGOs, professionals, and intellectuals to assume leadership roles. These two tracks, however, undercut one another, resulting in militia leaders' using force to prevent alternative leaders from emerging. When the international community was unwilling to use its force to protect the alternative leadership, the process of political reconciliation collapsed again into armed struggle.[9]

Pragmatism, conceived as adjusting to the demands of powerful interest groups, is not likely to prove a sufficient basis for peace in and of itself. Rather, bargaining can at best help create a stable environment in which an iterative negotiating process can occur, leading over time to rules and relationships that are more just. Such just rules of encounter are most likely to emerge where norms on some form of democracy, development, and equitable distribution emerge. Sustained systems and methods of conflict management require coordinated action on all of these levels and themes.

Although the issues of sovereignty and the root causes of conflict must be addressed as a critical prerequisite to intervention, formulation of credible operational principles is also essential. These principles relate to institutional mechanisms and strategies for action, both preventive and corrective. Appeal to external sources of protection and assistance, however, is inimical to the exercise of national sovereignty, especially by vulnerable governments. The more deficient the performance of a government, the more vulnerable to external scrutiny, and the more likely it is to plead sovereignty as a barricade. The outcome of the tug of war between conventional notions of sovereignty and the concerns and involvement of the international community, especially in situations of grave humanitarian consequences, explains the ambivalence now confronting the international community on the limits of national sovereignty. But the war is certainly not being won by those governments that are attempting to barricade themselves against warranted international scrutiny. Governments are increasingly called on to demonstrate responsibility or risk forfeiting their sovereignty.

The most critical question posed with respect to the masses of people who fall victim to humanitarian tragedies and gross violations of human rights as a result of internal conflicts is where to place responsibility for meeting their pressing and most compelling needs for protection, assistance, and transition into sustainable development. While the fundamental assumption is that the national government has the primary responsibility for taking care of its citizens, in internal conflicts the country is severely divided and the government itself is likely to be a party to the conflict. In other cases, the state has collapsed and there is no government to assume the necessary responsibilities of sovereignty. The affected population nearly always is forced to identify with one or the other. Often it is not even a matter of choice, but of belonging to either of the parties on the basis of race, ethnicity, religion, culture, or political ideology. Since the victims of internal conflicts are often members of the groups challenging the status quo and therefore the government, there is an inherent tension between the responsibility of the government toward its citizens and the tendency to identify groups with the adversary and therefore deny them the protection and assistance they expect from their government. As a result, the affected population falls into a void of responsibility usually associated with sovereignty, which in itself is often the focus of the contest. Whom can they count on to provide them with their fundamental needs for protection, assistance, reconstruction, and development?

Any attempt to answer the above question in the context of both the assumed national sovereignty and international concern must build on a number of basic assumptions. The first assumption is that although the state is under pressure from above and below, it will continue to be a central factor in national and international affairs. The framework of the state is part of global interdependence that has both international and national dimensions. The global dimension embraces subregional, regional, and international contexts, while the national envisages internal structures—central, provincial, district, and local. Humanitarian and human rights problems emanating from internal conflicts need to be analyzed and responded to at those multiple levels—the global, regional/continental, sub-regional, state, and local levels.

The second assumption is that the national framework is dominated by the laws, policies, and actions of the central government, which, while pertinent to the maintenance of law and order, favor the status quo. Citizens are therefore forced to choose between conformity and various forms and degrees of opposition, sometimes culminating in armed rebellion. Civilians who sympathize or are otherwise identified with such opposition become perceived as adversaries rather than as citizens to be protected. For those falling into the cracks of the national identity crisis or orphaned by state collapse, the only alternative source of protection, relief assistance, and rehabilitation toward a self-reliant development has to be the international community, both intergovernmental and nongovernmental.

The third assumption is that the existing legal and institutional frameworks for making available these alternative sources are fundamentally constrained by the state orientation of the international system and its commitment to national sovereignty. This presents something of a dilemma. On the one hand, the cooperation of the states is needed to move the international system to respond to the call of the needy within the framework of national sovereignty. On the other hand, the mere fact that the international community is needed implies the failure of national sovereignty and the exclusive dependency on the state for the welfare of its citizens.

The fourth assumption flows logically from the third: As long as the international system remains state oriented, any policies and strategies to help a population within the framework of national sovereignty must first aim at winning the cooperation of the government.

Where a government refuses to cooperate, thereby exposing large numbers of citizens to suffering and maybe death, the international community and intergovernmental or nongovernmental participants must make it clear that such a state of affairs ultimately threatens global order and will not be tolerated. The challenge thus is seeking policies, norms, and strategies that strike the delicate balance between what is expected of the state in exercising the responsibilities associated with sovereignty and international measures aimed at complementing national efforts or remodeling the features of governments to live up to their responsibilities.

The international community will therefore have to articulate specific legal standards that all governments are expected to adhere to and that have sufficiently broad legitimacy to motivate enforcement activities. These legal principles could be supplemented with guidelines or a code that would be more accessible to policymakers and other participants and would have sufficient political and moral authority to guide their performance.

The basic guiding principle for reconciling these positions is to assume that governments, under normal circumstances, strive to ensure for their people an effective governance that guarantees a just system of law and order, democratic freedoms, respect for fundamental rights, and general welfare. If they are unable to provide adequate protection and assistance for their people, they will invite or welcome foreign assistance and international cooperation to supplement their own efforts. The controversy arises in the exceptional cases when the state has collapsed or the government is unwilling to invite or permit international involvement, while the level of human suffering dictates otherwise. This is often the case in civil conflicts characterized by racial, ethnic, or religious crises of national identity in which the conflicting parties perceive the affected population to be part of the enemy. International concern and involvement become moral imperatives essentially to fill the vacuum of moral responsibility created by such cleavages.

Notes

Preface

1. John H. Herz, *The Nation-State and the Crisis of World Politics: Essays on International Politics in the Twentieth Century* (David McKay, 1976).

2. Boutros Boutros-Ghali, *An Agenda for Peace: Preventive Diplomacy, Peacemaking and Peace-keeping* (New York: United Nations, 1992), p. 7.

3. Organization of African Unity (OAU), *Resolving Conflicts in Africa: Proposals for Action* (Addis Ababa: OAU Press and Information Series 1, 1992), p. 3.

4. For a treatment of the treaty of Westphalia, see Gene M. Lyons and Michael Mastanduno, "Beyond Westphalia? International Intervention, State Sovereignty, and the Future of International Society," summary of a conference at Dartmouth College, 1992.

5. "The Endless Wait for Justice," *World Press Review*, March 1995, p. 12. In this article, Shahryar Khan, the UN secretary general's special representative in Kigali, is reported as saying, "The world has spent $700 million on emergency aid to Rwanda—'milk, power, and jerrycans.' By contrast, the Justice Ministry has received two payments—$27,000 from the Germans and $1 million from the Belgians—and two typewriters."

6. Jeffrey Z. Rubin, Dean G. Pruitt, and Sung Hee Kim, *Social Conflict: Escalation, Stalemate, and Settlement*, 2d ed. (McGraw-Hill, 1994), p. 4; Thomas C. Schelling, *The Strategy of Conflict* (Harvard University Press, 1960), p. 15; Jessie Bernard, "The Sociological Study of Conflict," in the International Sociological Association in collaboration with Jessie Bernard and others, *The Nature of Conflict: Studies on the Sociological Aspects of International Tensions* (Paris: UNESCO, 1957), p. 38; Raymond Aron, "Conflict and War from the Viewpoint of Historical Sociology," p. 179; John Powelson, *Institution of Economic Growth: A Theory of Conflict Management in Developing Countries* (Princeton University Press, 1972), p. 34; and Lewis A. Coser, *The Functions of Social Conflict* (Free Press, 1956), p. 8.

7. Richard Sandbrook, *The Politics of Africa's Economic Stagnation* (Cambridge University Press, 1985), p. 33.

Chapter One

1. See Hurst Hannum, *Autonomy, Sovereignty, and Self-Determination: The Accommodation of Conflicting Rights* (University of Pennsylvania Press, 1990), pp. 14–19; Gene M. Lyons and Michael Mastanduno, "Beyond Westphalia? International Intervention, State Sovereignty, and the Future of International Society," summary of a conference at Dartmouth College, 1992, p. 6; and Jarat Chopra and Thomas G. Weiss, "Sovereignty Is No Longer Sacrosanct: Codifying Humanitarian Intervention," *Ethics and International Affairs*, vol. 6 (1992), p. 95.

2. John Austin, *Lectures on Jurisprudence*, cited in Dennis Lloyd, *Introduction to Jurisprudence* (London: Stevens and Sons Limited, 1959), pp. 134–37; and W. Michael Reisman and Aaron M. Schreiber, *Jurisprudence: Understanding and Shaping Law* (New Haven Press, 1987), pp. 270–80. See also W. Friedmann, *Legal Theory*, 4th ed. (London: Stevens and Sons Limited, 1960), pp. 211–13.

3. Friedmann, *Legal Theory*, p. 211.

4. Lon L. Fuller, "Positivism and Fidelity to Law—A Reply to Professor Hart," *Harvard Law Review*, vol. 71 (February 1958), p. 634; see also H. L. A. Hart, "Positivism and the Separation of Law and Morals," *Harvard Law Review*, vol. 71 (February 1958), pp. 593–629.

5. F. H. Hinsley cited in Chopra and Weiss, "Sovereignty Is No Longer Sacrosanct," p. 103.

6. Fuller, "Positivism and Fidelity to Law," p. 646.

7. Ibid., p. 660.

8. General Assembly, "Universal Declaration of Human Rights," A/810 (United Nations, December 10, 1948), "International Covenant on Economic, Social and Cultural Rights," A/6316 (United Nations, December 16, 1966), and "International Covenant on Civil and Political Rights," A/6316 (United Nations, December 16, 1966). See Frank Newman and David Weissbrodt, *Selected International Human Rights Instruments* (Cincinnati: Anderson Publishing Co., 1990) pp. 11–15, 16–24, 25–41.

9. W. Michael Reisman, "Through or Despite Governments: Differentiated Responsibilities in Human Rights Programs," *Iowa Law Review*, vol. 72 (January 1987), p. 391.

10. Richard B. Lillich, "Sovereignty and Humanity: Can They Converge?" cited in Louis Henkin and others, *International Law: Cases and Materials*, 3d ed. (West Publishing Co., 1993), p. 19.

11. Friedrich Kratochwil cited in Lyons and Mastaduno, "Beyond Westphalia," p. 6.

12. W. Michael Reisman, "Humanitarian Intervention and Fledgling Democracies," *Fordham International Law Journal*, vol. 18 (March 1995), p. 795. See also W. Michael Reisman, "Coercion and Self-Determination: Construing Charter Article 2(4)," *American Journal of International Law*, vol. 78 (July 1984), pp. 642–45, and "Sovereignty and Human Rights in Contemporary International Law," *American Journal of International Law*, vol. 84 (October 1990), pp. 866–76.

13. Hart, "Separation of Law and Morals," pp. 603–04.

14. Nicholas Onuf cited in Lyons and Mastaduno, "Beyond Westphalia," p. 10. As one major power put it, concern about the externality of humanitarian intervention can be addressed by reformulating the issue cooperatively as "humanitarian solidarity."

15. See Roberta Cohen, "Comments on Jack Donnelly's Paper, 'National Sovereignty and International Intervention: The Case of Human Rights,' at Dartmouth College-United Nations Conference on National Sovereignty and Collective Intervention, 1992. See also Roberta Cohen, "Remarks to the Collapsed States Workshop," Johns Hopkins University, School of Advanced International Studies, 1996.

16. Alice Henkin, ed., *Human Dignity: The Internationalization of Human Rights* (New York: Aspen Institute for Humanistic Studies, 1979), p. v. See also Francis M. Deng, *Protecting the Dispossessed: A Challenge for the International Community* (Brookings, 1993), p. 1.

17. See Deng, *Protecting the Dispossessed*, pp. 1–20.

18. David J. Scheffer, "Toward a Modern Doctrine of Humanitarian Intervention," *University of Toledo Law Review*, vol. 23 (Winter 1992), p. 259.

19. Refugee Policy Group, *Human Rights Protection for Internally Displaced Persons: An International Conference* (Washington, June 1991), p. 7.

20. Ibid., p. 7.

21. Louis Henkin, "International Law: Politics, Values and Functions," 216. Rec. Des Cours 24–28 (1989-IV), cited in Henkin and others, *International Law*, p. 16.

22. Louis Henkin, "The Mythology of Sovereignty," cited in Henkin and others, *International Law*, p. 19.

23. W. Michael Reisman, "Haiti and the Validity of International Action," *American Journal of International Law*, vol. 89 (January 1995), p. 83.

24. For further information see Francis M. Deng and Larry Minear, *The Challenges of Famine Relief: Emergency Operations in the Sudan* (Brookings, 1992).

25. Economic and Social Council, UN Commission on Human Rights, *Responses of Governments and Agencies to the Report of the UN Special Representative for Internally Displaced Persons*, E/CN.4/1993/SR.40 (United Nations, 1993). Although the statement did not refer to the study on internally displaced persons or the specific issue of a mechanism for their protection and assistance, China supported the appointment of a special representative on internally displaced persons.

26. E/CN.4/1993/SR.40.

27. Economic and Social Council, UN Commission on Human Rights, *Responses of Governments and Agencies to the Report of the UN Special Representative for Internally Displaced Persons*. E/CN.4/1993/SR.41 (United Nations, 1993), pp. 4–6.

28. Economic and Social Council, UN Commission on Human Rights, *Situation of Human Rights in the Sudan: Report of the Special Rapporteur, Mr. Gaspar Biro, Submitted in Accordance with Commission on Human Rights Resolution 1993/60*, E/CN.4/1994/48 (United Nations, 1994), p. 15.

29. *Response of the Government of Sudan to the Interim Report Prepared by Mr. Gaspar Biro*, A/C.39/22.

30. Biro, *Situation of Human Rights in the Sudan*, p. 15.

31. *Response of the Government of Sudan to the Interim Report Prepared by Mr. Gaspar Biro*, A/C.39/22.

32. Kimberly Stanton, "Pitfalls of Intervention: Sovereignty as a Foundation for Human Rights," *Harvard International Review*, vol. 16 (Fall 1993), p. 16.

33. UN press release SG/SM/4560, April 24, 1991, cited in Lyons and Mastanduno, "Beyond Westphalia," p. 2. Portions of the statement are also cited in Scheffer, "Toward a Modern Doctrine of Humanitarian Intervention," p. 262.

34. Javier Perez de Cuellar, *Report of the Secretary-General on the Work of the Organization* (New York: United Nations, 1991), p. 12.

35. de Cuellar, *Report of the Secretary-General*, p. 13.

36. Boutros Boutros-Ghali, *An Agenda for Peace: Preventive Diplomacy, Peacemaking, and Peacekeeping, Report of the Secretary-General Pursuant to the Statement Adopted by the Summit Meeting of the Security Council on 31 January 1992* (New York: United Nations, 1992), p. 9.

37. Boutros Boutros-Ghali, "Empowering the United Nations," *Foreign Affairs*, vol. 71 (Winter 1992/93), p. 99.

38. Scheffer, "Toward a Modern Doctrine of Humanitarian Intervention," pp. 262–63.

39. Council of Ministers, *Report of the Secretary-General on Conflicts in Africa: Proposals for an OAU Mechanism for Conflict Prevention and Resolution*, CM/1710 (L.VI) (Addis Ababa: Organization of African Unity, 1992), pp. 12–13.

40. Ibid., pp. 12–13.

41. Ibid., p. 12.

42. Ibid., p. 12.

43. Note by the President of the Security Council, S/25344 (United Nations, February 26, 1993), p. 2.

44. Ibid.

45. Lyons and Mastanduno, "Beyond Westphalia," p. 31.

46. General Assembly, World Conference on Human Rights, *Vienna Declaration and Programme of Action*, A/Conf. 157/23 (United Nations, 1993), p. 5.

47. Ibid., p. 4.

48. Stephen John Stedman, "Conflict and Conflict Resolution in Africa: A Conceptual Framework," in Francis M. Deng and I. William Zartman, eds., *Conflict Resolution in Africa* (Brookings, 1991), pp. 367–68.

49. William Graham Summer, *Folkways*, 3d ed. (Ginn and Company, 1940), pp. 27–28.

50. Donald Rothchild, "Regime Management of Conflict in West Africa," in I. William Zartman, ed., *Governance as Conflict Management: Politics and Violence in West Africa* (Brookings, forthcoming).

51. Preliminary report of the Arusha Consultation, cited in Francis M. Deng, "Reconciling Sovereignty with Responsibility: A Basis for International

Humanitarian Action," in John W. Harbeson and Donald Rothchild, *Africa in World Politics: Post–Cold War Challenges*, 2d ed. (Westview, 1995), p. 303.

52. Ibid.

53. Boutros-Ghali, *An Agenda for Peace*, p. 9.

54. Ibid., pp. 9–10.

55. Deng, "Reconciling Sovereignty with Responsibility," p. 304.

56. Boutros-Ghali, "Empowering the U.N.," p. 99.

57. One source supports that rather than a conflict with sovereignty, humanitarian intervention should be viewed cooperatively as "humanitarian solidarity." Chopra and Weiss, "Sovereignty Is No Longer Sacrosanct," p. 108.

58. See Cohen, "Human Rights Protection for Internally Displaced Persons," pp. 16–18.

59. Note by the President of the Security Council, S/25344.

60. The International Committee of the Red Cross (ICRC) generally maintains that the issue is one of implementation and not of gaps in the existing law. See Michel Veuthey, "Assessing Humanitarian Law," in Thomas G. Weiss and Larry Minear, eds., *Humanitarianism across Borders: Sustaining Civilians in Times of War* (Lynne Rienner, 1993), pp. 125–49.

61. For a discussion of this issue with regard to internally displaced persons, see Economic and Social Council, Commission on Human Rights, *Internally Displaced Persons: Report of the Representative of the Secretary-General, Mr. Francis M. Deng*, E/CN.4/1995/50 (United Nations, 1995), p. 37.

62. See Richard B. Lillich, "Forcible Self-Help by States to Protect Human Rights," *Iowa Law Review*, vol. 53 (October 1967), pp. 347–51; John Norton Moore, "The Control of Foreign Intervention in Internal Conflict," *Virginia Journal of International Law*, vol. 9 (May 1969), pp. 261–64; and Steven E. Goldman, "A Right of Intervention Based upon Impaired Sovereignty," *World Affairs*, vol. 156 (Winter 1994), pp. 124–29. See also Theodor Meron and Allan Rosas, "A Declaration of Minimum Humanitarian Standards," *American Journal of International Law*, vol. 85 (April 1991), pp. 375–81, for a threshold below which humanitarian intervention might be triggered; and Scheffer, "Toward a Modern Doctrine of Humanitarian Intervention," p. 265.

63. See John Steinbruner, "Civil Violence as an International Security Problem," in Francis M. Deng, *Protecting the Dispossessed: A Challenge for the International Community* (Brookings, 1993), pp. 154–59.

64. Ibid.

65. Ibid.

66. Ibid.

67. See Larry Minear, "A Strengthened Humanitarian System for the Post–Cold War Era," Hearings before the House Select Committee on Hunger, cited in Larry Minear, Thomas G. Weiss, and Kurt M. Campbell, *Humanitarianism and War: Learning the Lessons from Recent Armed Conflicts*, Occasional Paper 8 (Providence, R.I.: Thomas J. Watson Jr. Institute for International Studies, 1991), pp. 32–49.

68. Boutros-Ghali, *An Agenda for Peace*, pp. 7–8.

69. For a more elaborate discussion of these phases as applied to the crisis of the internally displaced, see Economic and Social Council, Commission on Human Rights, *Alternative Approaches and Ways and Means within the United Nations System for Improving the Effective Enjoyment of Human Rights and Fundamental Freedoms, Note by the Secretary General*, E/CN.4/1993/35 (United Nations, 1993), and the revised version of that study in Deng, *Protecting the Dispossessed*. The study was considered by the Commission on Human Rights at its forty-ninth session, its findings and recommendations endorsed, and the mandate of the special representative of the secretary general extended for two years to continue to work on the various aspects of the problem as presented in the study.

Chapter Two

1. John P. Powelson, *Institutions of Economic Growth: A Theory of Conflict Management in Developing Countries* (Princeton University Press, 1972), p. 13.

2. I am grateful to Karim Mezran for these comparisons.

3. World Bank, *Sub-Saharan Africa: From Crisis to Sustainable Growth* (Washington, IBRD, 1989), p. 60. The World Bank definition uses "nation," a technical term of a different meaning. Note that there is no confusion between governance, thus defined, and good governance. The definition is properly neutral although Bank usage has slipped into an unhelpful elision since its original discussions. See also Deborah Brautigam, *Governance: A Review* (Washington: World Bank Policy and Review Department, 1991); and World Bank, *Managing Development: The Governance Dimension* (Washington: World Bank, 1991). Goren Hyden's oft-cited definition is more uncertain and ambiguous, in Hyden and Michael Bratton, eds., *Governance and Politics in Africa* (Westview, 1992), p. 7.

4. See I. William Zartman, ed., *Collapsed States: The Disintegration and Restoration of Legitimate Authority* (Lynne Rienner, 1995); Francis M. Deng and I. William Zartman, eds., *Conflict Resolution in Africa* (Brookings, 1991).

5. Ernest Barker, ed., *Social Contract: Essays by Locke, Hume, and Rousseau* (Oxford University Press, 1962); and Maurice Cranston and Richard Peters, eds., *Hobbes and Rousseau: A Collection of Critical Essays* (Anchor Books, 1972).

6. Jeanne Toungara, "Generational Tensions in the Parti Démocratique de Côte d'Ivoire," *African Studies Review*, vol. 38 (September 1995), pp. 11–39, and "Inventing the African Family: Gender and Family Law Reform in Côte d'Ivoire," *Journal of Social History*, vol. 28 (Fall 1994), pp. 37–61.

7. See H. Peyton Young, *Equity in Theory and Practice* (Princeton University Press, 1994); and I. William Zartman and others, "Negotiation as a Search for Justice," *International Negotiation*, vol. 1 (March 1996), pp. 1–20.

8. See Myron Weiner, *The Politics of Scarcity, Public Pressure and Political Response in India* (University of Chicago Press, 1962).

9. Meaningless violence is indeed an aspect of current African conflict, just

as it is of modern Western urban alienation; see Howard W. French, "Africa's New Guerillas: Pillage, No Politics," *International Herald Tribune*, February 20, 1995, p. 8.

10. All three country studies in the West Africa volume in this series affirm that the demands and conflicts two generations later are essentially the same as in the immediate independence period; in I. William Zartman, ed., *Governance as Conflict Management: Politics and Violence in West Africa* (Brookings, forthcoming). On issue realignment, see V. O. Key, Jr., "A Theory of Critical Elections," *Journal of Politics*, vol. 17 (February 1955), pp. 3–18; and Peter F. Nardulli, "The Concept of Critical Realignment, Electoral Behavior, and Political Change," *American Political Science Review*, vol. 89 (March 1995), pp. 10–22.

11. On the land deal and the courts, see Timothy D. Sisk, *Democratization in South Africa* (Princeton University Press, 1995).

12. On the importance of political parties and their limitations in Southern Africa, see Thomas Ohlson and Stephen John Stedman with Robert Davies, *The New Is Not Yet Born* (Brookings, 1994), chap. 7.

13. On union government and reactions, see Naomi Chazan, *An Anatomy of Ghanaian Politics: Managing Political Recession, 1969–1982* (Westview, 1983), pp. 234–48.

14. Ohlson and Stedman, *The New Is Not Yet Born*.

15. Tessy D. Bakary, "Political Polarization over Governance in Côte d'Ivoire," in Zartman, *Governance as Conflict Management*.

16. Pierre Landell-Mills, "Governance, Cultural Change and Empowerment," *Journal of Modern African Studies*, vol. 30 (December 1992), pp. 543–68; and Naomi Chazan, "Engaging the State: Associational Life in Sub-Saharan Africa," in Joel S. Migdal, Atul Kohli, and Vivienne Shue, eds., *State Power and Social Forces, Domination and Transformation in the Third World* (Cambridge University Press, 1994).

17. This conceptualization draws from the original discussion of input and output functions in Gabriel A. Almond and James S. Coleman, eds., *The Politics of Developing Areas* (Princeton University Press, 1960); and earlier from Alexis de Tocqueville, *Democracy in America* (Vintage Books, 1945).

18. I. William Zartman, ed., *Elusive Peace: Negotiating an End to Civil Wars* (Brookings, 1995).

19. Marina Ottaway, "Eritrea and Ethiopia: Negotiations in a Transitional Conflict," in Zartman, *Elusive Peace*.

20. Ohlson and Stedman, *The New Is Not Yet Born*, pp. 113–27; and Ibrahim Msabaha, "Negotiating an End to Mozambique's Murderous Rebellion," in Zartman, *Elusive Peace*.

21. See Ohlson and Stedman, *The New Is Not Yet Born*, especially chap. 7; Powelson, *Institutions of Economic Growth*; and Douglas North, *Institutions, Institutional Change and Economic Performance* (Cambridge University Press, 1990).

22. See Zartman, *Collapsed States*.

23. Alex Gboyega, "Governance in Nigeria: The Management of Conflict in a Plural Society," in Zartman, *Governance as Conflict Management*.

24. See Edmond Keller, "Remaking the Ethiopian State," and Hussein M. Adam, "Somalia: A Terrible Beauty Being Born?" in Zartman, *Collapsed States*, pp. 125–42, 69–90.

25. Ernest Gellner, *Saints of the Atlas* (University of Chicago Press, 1969); and E. E. Evans-Pritchard, *The Nuer: A Description of the Modes of Livelihood and Political Institutions of a Nilotic People* (Oxford University Press, 1940).

26. Ohlson and Stedman, *The New Is Not Yet Born*.

27. Ibid.

28. Immanuel Wallerstein, "Voluntary Associations," in James S. Coleman and Carl G. Rosberg, Jr., eds., *Political Parties and National Integration in Tropical Africa* (University of California Press, 1964), pp. 318–39; and I. William Zartman, ed., *Elites in the Middle East* (Praeger, 1980).

29. Ohlson and Stedman, *The New Is Not Yet Born*, p. 247.

30. The tribe of one of the authors, the Pennsylvania Dutch, disliked government intensely. They fled Germany to avoid it and on arrival in America found it to be practiced by the Pennsylvania English, another foreign tribe. They settled at the edge of the cultivable world, on the east bank of the Susquehanna River, and ran their own affairs—acephalously, in Africanists' terms. When government encroached, they fled west, to the old Northwest, then to the new northwest, then to the east bank of the Pacific, where they gave in. See James Michener, *Centennial* (Random House, 1974).

31. Beliefs of the Pennsylvania Dutch tribe notwithstanding.

32. On a culture of violence as a characteristic of Latin American polities, see Kumar Rupesinghe and Rubio Correa Marcial, eds., *The Culture of Violence* (United Nations University Press, 1994).

33. For a related discussion, see Ohlson and Stedman, *The New Is Not Yet Born*, pp. 244–54; and Samuel P. Huntington, *Political Order in Changing Societies* (Yale University Press, 1968), chap. 1.

34. On the difference between a program constitution, which sets out ongoing rules of the game, and a policy constitution, which lays out future goals, see Maurice Duverger, *Constitutions et documents politiques* (Paris: Press Universitaires, 1957).

35. Ohlson and Stedman, *The New Is Not Yet Born*.

36. Rahma Bourqia and Nicholas Hopkins, eds., *Le Maghreb: Approches des mécanismes d'articulation* (Casablanca: Al Kalam, 1991).

37. Larry Diamond, Juan J. Linz, and Seymour Martin Lipset, eds., *Democracy in Developing Countries*, vol. 2, *Africa* (Lynne Rienner, 1988), p. 165.

38. Martin Lowenkopf, "Liberia: Putting the State Back Together," in Zartman, *Collapsed States*.

39. See I. William Zartman, "Local Negotiations in South Africa," in Stephen John Stedman, ed., *South Africa: The Political Economy of Transformation* (Lynne Rienner, 1994); and Kimberly Lanegran, "South Africa's Civic Association Movement," *African Studies Review*, vol. 38 (September 1995), pp. 101–26.

40. See Zartman, *Governance as Conflict Management*.

41. John Waterbury, "The Political Management of Economic Adjustment

and Reform," in Joan M. Nelson, ed., *Fragile Coalitions: The Politics of Economic Adjustment* (New Brunswick, N.J.: Transaction Books/Overseas Development Council, 1989), p. 53.

42. *The Kampala Document: Towards a Conference on Security, Stability, Development, and Cooperation in Africa* (New York: African Leadership Forum, 1991).

43. Ohlson and Stedman, in *The New Is Not Yet Born*, p. 249, speak of learning as a necessary ingredient.

44. See A. Adu Boahen, "Governance and Conflict Management in Ghana since Independence," in Zartman, *Governance as Conflict Management*. See also Donald Rothchild, ed., *Ghana: The Political Economy of Recovery* (Lynne Rienner, 1991).

45. See Celestin Monga, "Did the National Conferences Take Place?" paper presented at Democratization: Phase Two, a conference held at Johns Hopkins University, School of Advanced International Studies, 1994.

46. See Michael Schatzberg, "Hijacking Democratization: Zaire's 'Transition' in Comparative Perspective," in Marina Ottaway, ed., *Democracy in Africa: The Hard Road Ahead* (Lynne Rienner, forthcoming).

47. See Samuel G. Amoo and I. William Zartman, "Mediation by Regional Organizations: The Organization of African Unity (OAU) in Chad," in Jacob Bercovitch and Jeffrey Z. Rubin, eds., *Mediation in International Relations, Multiple Approaches to Conflict Management* (St. Martin's, 1992); Carol Lancaster, "The Lagos Three: Economic Regionalism in Sub-Saharan Africa," and I. William Zartman, "Inter-African Negotiations," in John W. Harbeson and Donald Rothchild, eds., *Africa in World Politics: Post-Cold War Challenges*, 2d ed. (Westview, 1995); Pamela Chasek, Lynn Wagner, and I. William Zartman, "The Internationalization of North African Environmental Concerns," in Will D. Swearington and Abdellatif Bencherifa, eds., *The North African Environment at Risk* (Westview, 1996).

48. Bertram I. Spector, Gunnar Sjöstedt, and I. William Zartman, eds., *Negotiating International Regimes: Lessons Learned from the United Nations Conference on Environment and Development (UNCED)* (London: Graham and Trotman, 1994); James K. Sebenius, *Negotiating the Law of the Sea* (Harvard University Press, 1984); Robert L. Friedman, *Negotiating the New Ocean Regime* (University of South Carolina Press, 1993); I. William Zartman and Victor A. Kremenyuk, eds., *Cooperative Security: Reducing Third World Wars* (Syracuse University Press, 1995); and Zartman, *Collapsed States*.

Chapter Three

1. Fredrick Barth, ed., *Ethnic Groups and Boundaries: The Social Organization of Culture Difference* (Little, Brown, and Company, 1969), pp. 10–11.

2. Crawford Young, *The Politics of Cultural Pluralism* (University of Wisconsin Press, 1976) p. 20.

3. Nelson Kasfir, "Peacemaking and Social Cleavages in Sudan," in Joseph

V. Montville, ed., *Conflict and Peacemaking in Multiethnic Societies* (D. C. Heath and Company, 1991), pp. 365–66.

4. Ibid., p. 366. As Peter Woodward has argued, "although there may be considerable plasticity in identity, it is not something that is entirely malleable." See *Sudan 1898–1989: The Unstable State* (Lynne Rienner, 1990), p. 7.

5. Young, *The Politics of Cultural Pluralism*, pp. 43–44.

6. Ibid., p. 49.

7. In a discussion with senior Burundi officials, the question as to whether they could always tell a Tutsi from a Hutu received the ambiguous response of "yes, but with a margin of error of 35 percent." In Rwanda, the prime minister bragged that the country was the most fortunate of all African countries as it was not divided by racial or ethnic differences. Arguing that Rwanda had no tribes, nor cultural, linguistic, or religious differences, he claimed that the Tutsi-Hutu dichotomy was an artificial one, imposed upon the country by outsiders. The irony of this description of the country which has suffered the worst genocide since World War II cannot escape anyone. But there is a validity to the underlying assumption that myths or fictions of identity have been injected into the idea that Tutsis and Hutus are fundamentally different groups of people, a perception which does not tally with the facts of the situation. Conversations with Francis M. Deng. For Deng's reports on Burundi and Rwanda to the Commission on Human Rights, see Economic and Social Council, UN Commission on Human Rights, *Report of the Special Representative Mr. Francis Deng on Internally Displaced Persons: Profiles and Displacement: Burundi*, E/CN.4/1995/50/Add.2 (United Nations, 1995), and *Report of the Special Representative Mr. Francis Deng on Internally Displaced Persons: Note on Mission to Rwanda*, E/CN.4/1995/50/Add.4 (United Nations, 1995).

8. Olara A. Otunnu, Opening Address to the First Regional Consultation for the Study on Children in Armed Conflict, conducted under Graça Machel, appointed by the UN Secretary General at the request of the General Assembly (Addis Ababa, Ethiopia, April 18–21, 1995).

9. Stephen John Stedman, "Conflict and Conflict Resolution in Africa," in Francis M. Deng and I. William Zartman, eds., *Conflict Resolution in Africa* (Brookings, 1991), p. 376.

10. National Democratic Institute for International Affairs, *Democracies in Regions of Crisis: Botswana, Costa Rica, Israel* (Washington, 1990), p. 105.

11. Thomas Ohlson and Stephen John Stedman with Robert Davies, *The New Is Not Yet Born: Conflict Resolution in Southern Africa* (Brookings, 1994).

12. David D. Laitin and Said S. Samatar, *Somalia: Nation in Search of a State* (Westview, 1987), p. 1.

13. Terrence Lyons and Ahmed I. Samatar, *Somalia: State Collapse, Multilateral Intervention, and Strategies for Political Reconstruction* (Brookings, 1995).

14. Donald Rothchild, "Regime Management of Conflict in West Africa," in I. William Zartman, ed., *Governance as Conflict Management: Politics and Violence in West Africa* (Brookings, forthcoming).

15. Rothchild, "Regime Management of Conflict in West Africa."

16. In this respect, Nkrumah's legacy for Ghana is comparable to that of

Julius Nyerere in Tanzania. Although himself a tribal chief who significantly based his political and economic philosophies on the one-party system, and African socialism on traditional values and institutions, Nyerere succeeded in making the Tanzanians transcend their tribal identities and develop a national consciousness. The fact that he came from a small tribe that did not threaten the others with domination, and acquired his legitimacy through nationwide popularity, facilitated his mission. And yet his background as a tribal chief meant that he was not perceived as hostile to traditional leadership, as Nkrumah was in Ghana. It is, indeed, ironic that Nyerere was more successful than Nkrumah at circumventing tribalism. Nonetheless, Ghana is more nationally united in tribal terms than most African countries because of Nkrumah.

17. A. Adu Boahen, "Government and Conflict Management in Ghana since Independence," in Zartman, *Governance as Conflict Management.*

18. Tessy D. Bakary, "Political Polarization over Governance in Côte d'Ivoire," in Zartman, *Governance as Conflict Management.*

19. Rothchild, "Regime Management of Conflict in West Africa."

20. Donatella Lorch, "Thousand Flee Kenya Ethnic Strife," *New York Times,* September 7, 1993, p. A3.

21. Alex Gboyega, "Governance in Nigeria: The Management of Conflict in a Plural Society," in Zartman, *Governance as Conflict Management.*

22. Ibid.

23. Ibid.

24. Transitional Period Charter of Ethiopia, No. 1, Negarit Gazeta, 50th Year, November 1, July 22, 1991, p. 4.

25. Ali Moussa Iye, "Djibouti," in Hizkias Assefa and Gilbert Khadiagala, eds., "Conflict Resolution in the Horn of Africa," Brookings.

26. Iye, "Djibouti."

27. Ohlson and Stedman, *The New Is Not Yet Born,* p. 257.

28. Ohlson and Stedman, *The New Is Not Yet Born,* p. 39.

29. Ibid.

30. Robert M. Price, *The Apartheid State in Crisis: Political Transformation in South Africa, 1975–1990* (Oxford University Press, 1991), p. 23.

31. Ohlson and Stedman, *The New Is Not Yet Born.*

32. Peter K. Bechtold, "More Turbulence in Sudan: A New Politics This Time," *The Middle East Journal* vol. 44 (Autumn 1990), p. 579; also in John O. Voll, ed., *Sudan: State and Society in Crisis* (Indiana University Press, 1991), p. 1.

33. Abdelwahab El-Affendi, " 'Discovering the South': Sudanese Dilemmas for Islam in Africa," *African Affairs,* vol. 89 (July 1990), p. 371.

Chapter Four

1. For a catalogue of external shocks that afflicted the African countries during this period see Reginald Herbold and Michael Faber, "Sub-Saharan

Africa: Economic Deterioration or Rehabilitation?" in Robert I. Rotberg, ed., *Africa in the 1990s and Beyond: U.S. Policy Opportunities and Choices* (Algonac, Mich.: Reference Publications, Inc., 1988), pp. 33–43.

2. For most of the African countries, statistics of this nature are either unavailable or of poor quality.

3. This phasic pattern in the management of conflict is akin to the changing approaches in pursuing sustainable balance of payments positions in the African countries. In the 1960s and 1970s, it was fashionable to pursue such positions through demand management policies, and IMF stand-by facilities were a handy tool. Reflecting the altered character of the sources of external imbalance, since the mid-1980s, sustainable balance of payments positions have been sought through demand- and supply-oriented policies, and the IMF's Structural Adjustment Facility (SAF), the Enhanced Structural Adjustment Facility (ESAF), and the enhanced ESAF are deemed to be helpful tools. Likewise, socioeconomic policies required for sustained management of conflict at any one period or place could differ, depending on historical or preceding circumstances.

4. There is, of course, nothing immutable about the land ownership terms negotiated at the inception of majority rule. In the case of Zimbabwe, for example, the negotiated option to subsequently redistribute land purchased at fair prices is now somewhat untenable, in view of the concern that such action could send wrong signals to investors and undermine confidence in the economy.

5. The notable exceptions are the United Nations High Commission for Refugees (UNHCR) and the Food and Agriculture Organization (FAO), which can provide some relief relatively quickly to victims of violent confrontations.

6. International assistance extended through other avenues could also help underpin the peace process during the post-chaos phase. For example, the internationally supported, comprehensive, technical assistance program for Namibia helped create conditions for effective macroeconomic management, thereby instilling confidence in the direction of future economic policy. Moreover, the support of the International Monetary Fund for South Africa shortly before the transition to majority rule helped lock in the direction of future policy, thereby strengthening the minority population's confidence in the orientation of future economic policy in that country.

7. The polarization of economic activity does to an important extent, of course, derive from underlying comparative advantage of the subregions. Economic comparative advantage and the phenomenon of polarization are to a significant extent also influenced by the cumulative effect—intended or benign—of economic policies.

8. This is evidenced partly by the rising levels of resources that have been allocated to the European Regional Development Fund and the European Social Fund and partly the unrelenting ongoing efforts to raise the cost-effectiveness of resources devoted to these ends. For a more detailed discussion of these funds, see Willem Molle, *The Economics of European Integration:*

Theory, Practice, Policy (Brookfield, Vt.: Dartmouth Publishing Company, 1990), pp. 417–36.

9. See Peter Nyot Kok, "Adding Fuel to the Conflict: Oil, War and Peace in the Sudan," in Martin Doornbos and others, *Beyond Conflict in the Horn* (Trenton, N.J.: Red Sea Press, 1992), pp. 104–12.

10. Indeed, emotive appeals to the cessation of exploitation of the motherland were a common refrain in virtually all nationalist mobilization presaging independence.

11. Kok, "Adding Fuel to the Conflict," p. 110.

12. In keeping with this approach—recently endorsed by the Lagos Plan of Action—the African countries are working toward a continent-wide economic community.

13. More specifically, the ending of international economic sanctions against South Africa should provide added impetus for the reintegration of its industrially advanced economy into the economies of its less developed neighbors. This reintegration—constituting negative integration through the elimination of extreme nontariff barriers (trade boycotts and sanctions)—might be expected to result in pronounced industrial polarization. Regional and international investment are especially likely to be concentrated in South Africa because of its sophisticated (by regional standards) economic and social infrastructure and of its advantageous position as a supplier to the regional market.

The resulting polarization could be a source of substantial conflict within the southern African region. The more industrially advanced neighbors, notably Zimbabwe, will probably feel most of the pressure initially, but the other countries will in due course also be affected, as their labor-intensive industries become increasingly exposed to competition from similar industries in South Africa. Should such conflicts be managed poorly, they could easily take on a zero-sum character, with the attendant disintegrative forces giving rise to subregional groupings and to enhanced links between these groups with extraregional partners. In this regard, there is ground for concern, so long as there is no mutually agreed institutional framework for ordering economic cooperation and integration efforts in post-apartheid southern Africa. For a detailed discussion of these issues see Sadikiel N. Kimaro, "Economic Cooperation in Southern Africa: A Post-Apartheid Perspective" (unpublished manuscript, October 1992).

14. This tool—presently being used, for example, by Kenya for two products imported from South Africa—would in many cases have required stronger capacity to analyze price and cost elements of trade originating from other countries. In the absence of such a capacity, protective steps could falsely be paraded as antidumping measures.

15. Thus in southern Africa this would require a restructuring of the Southern African Labor Commission to broaden its membership and reorient its goals toward the resolution of conflicts relating to migrant labor. A similar reorientation would at least be needed for the bilateral arrangements regulat-

ing migratory labor issues between South Africa and countries such as Mozambique and Malawi, unless, of course, such arrangements are abolished in favor of an overarching, regionwide arrangement.

16. For helpful insights on this point, see Jagdish Bhagwati, "Global Interdependence and International Migration," in Douglas A. Irwin, ed., *Political Economy and International Economics* (MIT Press, 1991), pp. 367–402.

17. The Comité Permanent Interétats de Lutte Contre la Secheresse dans le Sahel (CILLS) is an organization through which some West African countries coordinate their efforts against drought in the Sahel.

18. South Africa, would seem to be in a much stronger position to exploit the market for weapons in the neighboring countries, because of its relatively developed armaments industry and the premium which the African countries are likely to attach to the sourcing arms in a nearby market.

19. In the case of Liberia, the ECOWAS protocol on security provided the institutional basis for Nigeria's intervention.

20. There is a distinct possibility that many guns that are now owned by South Africans will sooner or later find their way into the neighboring countries.

21. Other flows (say, exports earnings, labor, and private capital) and policies (exchange rate management, producer pricing, and taxation) also have a bearing on the management of conflict. Such interrelationships are often not direct or systematic; because of the shortage of space they will not be explored in this section.

22. Carol Lancaster, *African Economic Reform: The External Dimension* (Washington, D.C.: Institute for International Economics, June 1991), p. 57.

23. "Camdessus Welcomes Activation of Enlarged ESAF and Broad-Based Support," *IMF Survey*, March 21, 1994, p. 84.

Chapter Five

1. For a review of the concept see William R. Thompson, "The Regional Subsystem: A Conceptual Explication and a Propositional Inventory," *International Studies Quarterly*, vol. 17 (March 1973); pp. 89–117. For an early and important use of the concept see Louis J. Cantori and Steven L. Spiegel, *The International Politics of Regions: A Comparative Approach* (Prentice-Hall, 1970). For the views discussed here, see also I. William Zartman, "Africa as a Subordinate State System in International Relations," *International Organization*, vol. 21 (Summer 1967), pp. 545–64; and Kenneth W. Grundy, "The Impact of Region on Contemporary African Politics," in Gwendolen M. Carter and Patrick O'Meara, eds., *African Independence: The First Twenty-Five Years* (Indiana University Press, 1985), pp. 97–125.

2. Barry Buzan, *People, States, and Fear: The National Security Problem in International Relations* (University of North Carolina Press, 1983), p. 106. For an early classic discussion see Karl W. Deutsch and others, *Political Community*

and the North Atlantic Area: International Organization in the Light of Historical Experience (Princeton University Press, 1957).

3. Raimo Väyrynen, "Regional Conflict Formations: An Intractable Problem of International Relations," *Journal of Peace Research*, vol. 21, no. 4 (1984), pp. 337, 344–47.

4. Buzan, *People, States, and Fear*, p. 106.

5. Stephen John Stedman, "Conflict and Conflict Resolution in Africa: A Conceptual Framework," in Francis M. Deng and I. William Zartman, eds., *Conflict Resolution in Africa* (Brookings, 1991), p. 378. A typology of regional security complexes is provided by Keith Krause, "Constructing Regional Security Regimes and the Control of Arms Transfers," *International Journal*, vol. 45 (Spring 1990), pp. 386–423.

6. Robert Jervis and Jack Snyder, eds., *Dominoes and Bandwagons: Strategic Beliefs and Great Power Competition in the Eurasian Rimland* (Oxford University Press, 1991).

7. This point is made with relation to South Africa in Peter Vale, "Reconstructing Regional Dignity: South Africa and Southern Africa," in Stephen John Stedman, ed., *South Africa: The Political Economy of Transformation* (Lynne Rienner, 1994), pp. 154–55.

8. Thomas Ohlson and Stephen John Stedman, with Robert Davies, *The New is Not Yet Born: Conflict Resolution in Southern Africa* (Brookings, 1994); Olatunde J. B. Ojo, "Nigeria and the Formation of ECOWAS," *International Organization*, vol. 34 (Autumn 1980), pp. 571–604; and Pauline Baker, "A Giant Staggers: Nigeria as an Emerging Regional Power," in Bruce E. Arlinghaus, ed., *African Security Issues: Sovereignty, Stability, and Solidarity* (Westview, 1984), pp. 76–97.

9. Terrence Lyons, "The Horn of Africa Regional Politics: A Hobbesian World," in W. Howard Wriggins, ed., *Dynamics of Regional Politics: Four Systems on the Indian Ocean Rim* (Columbia University Press, 1992), pp. 158–64.

10. René Lemarchand, "On Comparing Regional Hegemony: Libya and South Africa," in René Lemarchand, ed., *The Green and the Black: Qadhafi's Policies in Africa* (Indiana University Press, 1988), pp. 167–81.

11. Leonard Binder, "The Middle East as a Subordinate International System," *World Politics*, vol. 10 (April 1958), pp. 408–29; and Zartman, "Africa as a Subordinated State System, pp. 545–64.

12. Barry Buzan, "Third World Regional Security in Structural and Historical Perspective," in Brian L. Job, ed., *The Insecurity Dilemma: National Security of Third World States* (Lynne Rienner, 1992), pp. 167–89; see also W. Howard Wriggins, "Conclusion," in Wriggins, *Dynamics of Regional Politics*, pp. 297–300.

13. Richard Rosecrance, "Regionalism and the Post–Cold War Era," *International Journal*, vol. 46 (Summer 1991), pp. 373–93.

14. George Modelski, "Kautilya: Foreign Policy and International System in the Ancient Hindu World," *American Political Science Review*, vol. 58 (September 1964), pp. 549–60. See also W. Howard Wriggins, "The Dynamics of Regional Politics: An Orientation," in Wriggins, *Dynamics of Regional Politics*, pp.

6–9; I. William Zartman, "Internationalization of Communal Strife: Temptations and Opportunities of Triangulation," in Manus I. Midlarsky, ed., *The Internationalization of Communal Strife* (Routledge, 1992), p. 34; and Hedley Bull, *The Anarchical Society* (Columbia University Press, 1977).

15. Ahmed Samatar, "Under Siege: Blood, Power, and the Somali State," unpublished manuscript.

16. Lyons, "The Horn of Africa Regional Politics," pp. 155–209.

17. I. M. Lewis, *A Modern History of Somalia: Nation and State in the Horn of Africa* (Westview, 1980), p. xi.

18. David D. Laitin and Said S. Samatar, *Somalia: Nation in Search of a State* (Westview, 1987), pp. 69–70.

19. Ali Ahmed Saleem, "An Introduction to IGADD," in Martin Doornbos and others, eds., *Beyond Conflict in the Horn: Prospects for Peace, Recovery, and Development in Ethiopia, Somalia, Eritrea, and the Sudan* (The Hague: Institute of Social Studies, 1992), pp. 114–15.

20. "Regional Politics, Economics Wrapped Up at IGADD Summit," Voice of Ethiopia in Amharic, translated in Foreign Broadcast Information Service-*Africa*, September 21, 1993, p. 1 (Hereafter FBIS).

21. Francis M. Deng, "Mediating the Sudanese Conflict: A Challenge for the IGADD," *CSIS Africa Notes*, no. 169 (February 1995), pp. 1–7.

22. For some background see Jeffrey A. Lefebvre, "Post–Cold War Clouds: The Eritrea-Sudan Crisis," *Middle East Policy*, vol. 4 (September 1995), pp. 34–49; and Francis M. Deng, "Egypt's Dilemmas on the Sudan," *Middle East Policy*, vol. 4 (September 1995), pp. 50–56.

23. Colin Legum, "Horn of Africa: Sudan's Neighbours Say No More Games," *Third World Reports*, November 7, 1995, p. 2.

24. Terrence Lyons and Ahmed I. Samatar, *Somalia: State Collapse, Multilateral Intervention, and Strategies for Political Reconstruction* (Brookings, 1995).

25. Allen L. Springer, "Community Chronology," in Christian P. Potholm and Richard A. Fredland, eds., *Integration and Disintegration in East Africa* (Washington: University Press of America, 1980), pp. 11–15. See also Donald Rothchild and Robert L. Curry, Jr., *Scarcity, Choice, and Public Policy in Middle Africa* (University of California Press, 1978), pp. 234–41; J. S. Nye, "Patterns and Catalysts in Regional Integration," in Joseph S. Nye, Jr., ed., *International Regionalism: Readings* (Little, Brown, 1968), pp. 333–41; and Joseph S. Nye, Jr., *Pan-Africanism and East African Integration* (Harvard University Press, 1965), pp. 59–171.

26. "The Treaty for East African Co-Operation," Article 2, reprinted in Donald S. Rothchild, ed., *Politics of Integration: An East African Documentary* (Nairobi: East African Publishing House, 1968), p. 304.

27. P. Anyang' Nyong'o, "Regional Integration in Africa: An Unfinished Agenda," in P. Anyang' Nyong'o, ed., *Regional Integration in Africa: Unfinished Agenda* (Nairobi: Academy Science Publishers, 1990), p. 5; John Ravenhill, "The Theory and Practice of Regional Integration in East Africa," in Potholm and Fredland, *Integration and Disintegration in East Africa*, pp. 38–61; see also Arthur Hazlewood, "The End of the East African Community: What Are the Lessons

for Regional Integration Schemes?" *Journal of Common Market Studies*, vol. 18 (September 1979), pp. 40–58.

28. For an analytical overview of Uganda's role in the East Africa regional system see Gilbert M. Khadiagala, "Uganda's Domestic and Regional Security since the 1970s," *Journal of Modern African Studies*, vol. 31, no. 2 (1993), pp. 231–55. For additional information see Gilbert M. Khadiagala, "State Collapse and Reconstruction in Uganda," in I. William Zartman, ed., *Collapsed States: The Disintegration and Restoration of Legitimate Authority* (Lynne Rienner, 1995), p. 38; and David Throup, "Kenya's Relations with Museveni's Uganda," in Holger Bernt Hansen and Michael Twaddle, eds., *Changing Uganda* (Ohio University Press, 1991), pp. 187–96.

29. "Museveni, Moi, Mwinyi in 'Secret' Plan for Joint Army," *The Monitor* (Uganda), January 7–11, 1994, reprinted by *Africa News Service*, vol. 40 (January 31, 1994); Horace Awori, "East Africa-Politics: Positive Steps Taken for Cooperation," InterPress Service, May 3, 1994.

30. Cited in Paul Chintowa, "Rwanda-Burundi: Regional Summit Planned to End Violence," *Africa News Service*, April 7, 1994.

31. Onapito-Ekolomoit, "East Africa-Rwanda: Opposite Sides of a Shaky Fence," InterPress Service, October 9, 1995.

32. Ohlson and Stedman, *The New Is Not Yet Born*, pp. 3–4.

33. Coralie Bryant, ed., *Poverty, Policy, and Food Security in Southern Africa* (Lynne Rienner, 1988).

34. Ohlson and Stedman, *The New Is Not Yet Born*, pp. 26–30.

35. Carol B. Thompson, *Harvests under Fire: Regional Co-operation for Food Security in Southern Africa* (London: Zed, 1991); and Peter Vale, "Reconstructing Regional Dignity," p. 159.

36. Gilbert M. Khadiagala, "Southern Africa's Transitions: Prospects for Regional Security," in Stedman, *South Africa*, pp. 171–75.

37. "Southern Africa Dreams of Unity," *Economist*, September 2, 1995, p. 35.

38. Ohlson and Stedman, *The New Is Not Yet Born*, p. 125.

39. Lewis Machipisa and Gumisai Mutume, "Southern Africa-Politics: Conflict-Free Zone," InterPress Service, September 19, 1995; and "Mozambique: The People for Peace," *Africa Confidential*, vol. 35 (November 4, 1994).

40. Baker, "A Giant Staggers," pp. 76–97.

41. S. K. B. Asante, "Regional Economic Cooperation and Integration: The Experience of ECOWAS," in Anyang' Nyong'o, *Regional Integration in Africa*, pp. 99–137.

42. S. K. B. Asante, *The Political Economy of Regionalism in Africa: A Decade of the Economic Community of West African States (ECOWAS)* (Praeger, 1986), pp. 145–46.

43. Clement Emenike Adibe, "ECOWAS in Comparative Perspective," in Timothy M. Shaw and Julius Emeka Okolo, eds., *The Political Economy of Foreign Policy in ECOWAS* (St. Martin's, 1994), pp. 194–96; "Illegal Immigrants Depart," *West Africa*, May 13, 1985, p. 965; "Stranded Immigrants Riot," *West Africa*, May 20, 1985, pp. 988–89.

44. S. K. B. Asante, "ECOWAS/CEAO: Conflict and Cooperation in West Africa," in Ralph I. Onwuka and Amadu Sesay, eds., *The Future of Regionalism in Africa* (St. Martin's, 1985), pp. 74–95; John M. Ostheimer, "Cooperation among African States," in Arlinghaus, *African Security Issues*, p. 166.

45. Asante, *The Political Economy of Regionalism in Africa*, pp. 156–62.

46. "Convergence of Policies," *West Africa*, July 19–25, 1993, p. 1247.

47. Cited in *Africa Research Bulletin* (Economic, Financial, and Technical Series), vol. 30 (July 16–August 15, 1993), p. 11339.

48. The divisions between Anglophone and Francophone states in West Africa were apparent in the 1994 ECOWAS summit that only two Francophone heads of state attended. See "The Abuja Summit," *West Africa*, August 15–21, 1994, pp. 1425–26.

49. I. William Zartman, *Ripe for Resolution: Conflict and Intervention in Africa* (New York: Oxford University Press, 1985), p. 126.

50. On Zaire generally see Crawford Young and Thomas Turner, *The Rise and Decline of the Zairian State* (University of Wisconsin Press, 1985); and Michael G. Schatzberg, *Politics and Class in Zaire* (New York: Africana, 1980).

51. See, for example, John Darnton, "Zaire Drifting into Anarchy As Authority Disintegrates," *New York Times*, May 24, 1994, p. A1.

52. Claire Spencer, *The Maghreb in the 1990s: Political and Economic Developments in Algeria, Morocco and Tunisia*, Adelphi Paper 274 (London: International Institute for Strategic Studies, 1993).

53. Zartman, *Ripe for Resolution*, chap. 2.

54. Spencer, *The Maghreb in the 1990s*, p. 43. See also John Damis, "Morocco and the Western Sahara," *Current History* (April 1990), pp. 165–68, 184–86; Bruce Maddy-Weitzman, "Conflict and Conflict Management in the Western Sahara: Is the Endgame Near?" *Middle East Journal*, vol. 45 (Autumn 1991), pp. 594–607.

55. Spencer, *The Maghreb in the 1990s*, p. 45.

56. William J. Durch, "Building on Sand: UN Peacekeeping in the Western Sahara," *International Security*, vol. 17 (Spring 1993), pp. 151–71; "Differences Narrow on Voting Criteria," *UN Chronicle*, vol. 30 (September 1993), p. 29; Alfred Hermida, "The Forgotten Front," *Africa Report*, vol. 38 (May–June 1993), pp. 40–43.

57. Ramesh Jaura, "North Africa-Economy: Maghreb Union Hampered by Divergent Policies," InterPress Service, December 26, 1994.

58. Ted Robert Gurr, "The Internationalization of Protracted Communal Conflicts since 1945: Which Groups, Where, and How," in Midlarsky, *The Internationalization of Communal Strife*, pp. 4–5.

59. Mohammed Ayoob, "Regional Security and the Third World," in Mohammed Ayoob, ed., *Regional Security in the Third World: Case Studies from Southeast Asia and the Middle East* (Westview, 1986), p. 14.

60. Christopher Clapham, "The Political Economy of Conflict in the Horn of Africa," *Survival*, vol. 32 (September–October 1990), p. 411. See also Ann Mosely Lesch, "External Involvement in the Sudanese Civil War," in David

Smock, ed., *Making War and Waging Peace: Foreign Intervention in Africa* (Washington: U. S. Institute of Peace, 1993), pp. 89–100.

61. Alex Shoumatoff, "Flight from Death," *New Yorker*, June 20, 1994, p. 44.

62. Ohlson and Stedman, *The New Is Not Yet Born*, pp. 187, 256–57; "Sierra Leone: The Military Prepares to Go, Again," *Africa Confidential*, vol. 34 (August 13, 1993), pp. 2–4; "USC Forces Raid Kenya," FBIS, *Africa*, April 28, 1992, p. 7; "SLA Condemns Kenya's Aid to Barre 'Remnants,'" FBIS, *Africa*, July 27, 1992, p. 6; "Aidid Decries Kenya's Treatment of Refugees," FBIS, *Africa*, August 19, 1992, p. 5; Peter J. Schraeder, "Ethnic Politics in Djibouti: From 'Eye of the Hurricane' to 'Boiling Cauldron,'" *African Affairs*, vol. 92 (April 1993), pp. 203–21; and John Sparrow, *Under the Volcanoes: Special Focus on the Rwandan Refugee Crisis* (Geneva: International Federation of Red Cross and Red Crescent Societies, World Disasters Report Special Focus, 1994).

63. Gil Loescher, *Refugee Movements and International Security*, Adelphi Paper 268 (London: Brassey's, for the International Institute for Strategic Studies, 1992).

64. Richard P. Y. Li and William Thompson, "The 'Coup Contagion' Hypothesis," *Journal of Conflict Resolution*, vol. 19 (March 1975), pp. 63–88; Stuart Hill and Donald Rothchild, "The Contagion of Political Conflict in Africa and the World," *Journal of Conflict Resolution*, vol. 30 (December 1986), pp. 716–35; and James M. Lutz, "The Diffusion of Political Phenomena in Sub-Saharan Africa," *Journal of Political and Military Sociology*, vol. 17 (Spring 1989), pp. 93–114.

65. Quoted in Colleen Lowe Morna, "Nyerere's Turnabout," *Africa Report*, vol. 35 (September–October 1990), p. 24.

66. I. William Zartman, "Introduction," in I. William Zartman, ed., *Governance as Conflict Management: Politics and Violence in West Africa* (Brookings, forthcoming).

67. Samuel P. Huntington, *The Third Wave: Democratization in the Late Twentieth Century* (University of Oklahoma Press, 1991), pp. 100–06.

68. Gilbert M. Khadiagala, "Security in Southern Africa: Cross-National Learning," *The Jerusalem Journal of International Relations*, vol. 14, no. 3 (1992), pp. 82–97. On the consequences of the elections in Namibia and Zambia, see Ohlson and Stedman, *The New Is Not Yet Born*, p. 13. On lesson-drawing, see Richard Rose, "What is Lesson-Drawing?" *Journal of Public Policy*, vol. 11 (January–March 1991), pp. 3–30; and David Brian Robertson, "Political Conflict and Lesson-Drawing," *Journal of Public Policy*, vol. 11 (January–March 1991), pp. 55–78.

69. Nicola Jefferson, "Rwanda: The War Within," *Africa Report*, vol. 37 (January–February 1992), p. 64; "Uganda/Rwanda: No Room," *Africa Confidential*, vol. 32 (March 22, 1991), pp. 6–7; and Donatella Lorch, "Rwanda Rebels: Army of Exiles Fights for a Home," *New York Times*, June 9, 1994, p. A10.

70. "Mauritania: On the War-Path," *Africa Confidential*, vol. 30 (September 22, 1989), pp. 3–4; "Senegal: Crisis in Casamance," *Africa Confidential*, vol. 31 (November 23, 1990), pp. 1–2; Ron Parker, "The Senegal-Mauritania Conflict

of 1989: A Fragile Equilibrium," *Journal of Modern African Studies*, vol. 29, no. 1 (1991), p. 163; and Gilbert K. Bluwey, "Mauritania," in Shaw and Okolo, *The Political Economy of Foreign Policy in ECOWAS*, pp. 92–94.

71. Zartman, *Ripe for Resolution*, pp. 118–19.

72. W. Cyrus Reed, "The New International Order: State, Society, and African International Relations," paper prepared for conference "The End of the Cold War and the New African Political Order" (University of California, Los Angeles, February 17–19, 1994), p. 4.

73. Zartman, *Ripe for Resolution*, chap. 4.

74. Crawford Young, "Zaire: The Unending Crisis," *Foreign Affairs*, vol. 57 (Fall 1978), pp. 169–85.

75. Zartman, "Internationalization of Communal Strife," p. 27.

76. Lyons, "The Horn of Africa Regional Politics," pp. 178–80.

77. Zartman, "Internationalization of Communal Strife," p. 40.

78. George Modelski, "The International Relations of Internal War," in James N. Rosenau, ed., *International Aspects of Civil Strife* (Princeton University Press, 1964), p. 20.

79. Lewis A. Coser, "Conflict with Out-Groups and Group Structure," in Jonathan Wilkenfeld, ed., *Conflict Behavior and Linkage Politics* (New York: David McKay, 1973), pp. 15–24. On conflict as a strategy to deflect attention from domestic problems, see Jack S. Levy and Lily I. Vakili, "Diversionary Action by Authoritarian Regimes: Argentina in the Falklands/Malvinas Case," in Midlarsky, *The Internationalization of Communal Strife*, pp. 118–21.

80. Ohlson and Stedman, *The New Is Not Yet Born*, pp. 55–56, 99–101.

81. Lansana Fofana, "Sierra Leone-Politics: Crippling Bush War Enters Its Fourth Year," InterPress Service, March 24, 1994.

82. Hrach Gregorian, "Plowshares into Swords: The Former Member States and the 1978–1979 War," in Potholm and Fredland, *Integration and Disintegration in East Africa*, pp. 167–91. On the Tanzanian invasion see Tony Avirgan and Martha Honey, *War in Uganda: The Legacy of Idi Amin* (Westport, Conn.: Lawrence Hill, 1982), chap. 5.

83. Lyons, "The Horn of Africa Regional Politics," pp. 178–80.

84. Ohlson and Stedman, *The New Is Not Yet Born*, pp. 64–71, 94–99.

85. Zartman, *International Relations in the New Africa*, pp. 105–19.

86. For a discussion of "structural conflict" see Buzan, *People, States, and Fear*, p. 78.

87. I. William Zartman and W. Scott Thompson, "The Development of Norms in the African System," in Yassin El-Ayouty, ed., *The Organization of African Unity after Ten Years* (Praeger, 1975); and Saadia Touval, *The Boundary Politics of Independent Africa* (Harvard University Press, 1972), pp. 83–84.

88. Ted Gurr, "Tensions in the Horn of Africa," in Feliks Gross, *World Politics and Tension Areas* (New York University Press, 1966), pp. 316–34.

89. Touval, *The Boundary Politics of Independent Africa*, p. 235. See also Zartman, *Ripe for Resolution*, pp. 89–90.

90. Lyons, "The Horn of Africa Politics," p. 175.

91. Robert Buijtenhuijs, *Le FroLiNaT et les Revoltes Populaires du Tchad* (The Hague: Mouton, 1978).

92. René Lemarchand, "Libyan Adventurism," in John W. Harbeson and Donald Rothchild, eds., *Africa in World Politics* (Westview, 1991), pp. 152–58; René Lemarchand, "The Case of Chad," in Lemarchand, *The Green and the Black*, pp. 106–24; Virginia Thompson and Richard Adloff, *Conflict in Chad* (Berkeley, Calif.: Institute of International Studies, 1981), pp. 119–28.

93. 93. Benjamin H. Hardy, "What Can Oil Do for Troubled Chad?" *CSIS Africa Notes*, no. 159 (April 1994), pp. 1–2; and "Chad/Libya," *Africa Report*, vol. 39 (May–June 1994), p. 7.

94. Colin Legum, "Out of Africa Some Good News: A Peaceful Settlement of the Aouzou Strip Conflict," *Third World Reports*, March 23, 1994.

95. "Nigeria/Cameroon: Blundering into Battle," *Africa Confidential*, vol. 35 (April 15, 1994), pp. 4–6; "Cameroon/Nigeria," *Africa Report*, vol. 39 (May–June 1994), p. 7; and Bola Olowo, "The Bakassi Timebomb," *West Africa*, March 28–April 3, 1994, pp. 540–41.

96. Zartman, *Ripe for Resolution*, p. 10.

97. Machipisa and Mutume, "Southern Africa-Politics."

98. Ohlson and Stedman, *The New Is Not Yet Born*, pp. 264–69.

99. This list could be expanded further. Other dimensions would include the struggle between different leaders and factions for control of the Eritrean movement, and the external patron-client rivalries of the cold war.

100. Zartman, *International Relations in the New Africa*.

101. William J. Foltz, "The Organization of African Unity and the Resolution of Africa's Conflicts," in Deng and Zartman, *Conflict Resolution in Africa*, pp. 352–54.

102. Jeffrey Herbst, "The Creation and Maintenance of National Boundaries in Africa," *International Organization*, vol. 43 (Autumn 1989), p. 676.

103. Crawford Young, "Self-Determination, Territorial Integrity, and the African State System," in Deng and Zartman, *Conflict Resolution in Africa*, p. 332.

104. John Ravenhill, "Redrawing the Map of Africa?" in Donald Rothchild and Naomi Chazan, eds., *The Precarious Balance: State and Society in Africa* (Westview, 1988), p. 286.

105. Ravi L. Kapil, "On the Conflict Potential of Inherited Boundaries in Africa," *World Politics*, vol. 18 (July 1966), pp. 656–73; I. William Zartman, "Issues of African Diplomacy in the 1980s," *Orbis*, vol. 25 (Winter 1982), p. 1028; and Yassin el-Ayouty and I. William Zartman, eds., *The OAU after Twenty Years* (Praeger, 1984).

106. Berhanykun Andemicael, "OAU-UN Relations in a Changing World," in Yassin El-Ayouty, ed., *The Organization of African Unity after Thirty Years* (Praeger, 1994), pp. 126–27.

107. Quoted in Robert H. Jackson, "Negative Sovereignty in Sub-Saharan Africa," *Review of International Studies*, vol. 12 (October 1986), p. 253; and Zdenek Cervenka and Colin Legum, "The Organization of African Unity in 1979,"

in Colin Legum, ed., *Africa Contemporary Record: Annual Survey and Documents, 1979–1980* (New York: Africana, 1981), p. A62.

108. Ayoob, "Regional Security and the Third World," pp. 18, 20; F. Gregory Gause, III, "Gulf Regional Politics: Revolution, War, and Rivalry," and Evelyn Colbert, "Southeast Asian Regional Politics: Toward a Regional Order," in Wriggins, *Dynamics of Regional Politics*, pp. 23–88, 213–73.

109. Ohlson and Stedman, *The New Is Not Yet Born.*

110. Amitav Acharya, "Regionalism and Regime Security in the Third World: Comparing the Origins of the ASEAN and the GCC," in Job, *The Insecurity Dilemma*, p. 149.

111. "Regional Politics, Economics Wrapped Up at IGADD Summit," Voice of Ethiopia Network in Amharic, translated in FBIS, *Africa*, September 21, 1993, p. 1.

112. Nhial Bol, "Sudan-Politics: Bashir Accuses Uganda of Backing SPLA Rebels," InterPress Service, September 21, 1994; and Nhial Bol, "Sudan-Politics: Junta Leader Vows to Crush Rebels," InterPress Service, September 28, 1994.

113. " 'We Have Changed Nigeria'—Babangida," *West Africa*, February 22–28, 1993, p. 282.

114. Julian Samboma, "Liberia-Nigeria: Minister Defends Lagos' 'Laudable' Role," *Africa News Service*, March 1, 1994.

115. Ben Asante, "Peace Looms in Liberia," *West Africa*, July 26–August 1, 1993, pp. 1292–94.

116. Christopher R. Mitchell, "Asymmetry and Strategies of Regional Conflict Reduction," in I. William Zartman and Victor A. Kremenyuk, eds., *Cooperative Security: Reducing Third World Wars* (Syracuse University Press, 1995).

117. E. A. Erskine, "Security and Its Management in Africa," in Olusegun Obasanjo and Felix G. N. Mosha, eds., *Africa: Rise to Challenge* (Africa Leadership Forum, 1992), pp. 62, 63.

118. Abass Bundu, "ECOWAS Comes of Age," *West Africa*, July 19–25, 1993, pp. 1253, 1255; and Peter Da Costa, "A New Role for ECOWAS," *Africa Report*, vol. 36 (September–October 1991), pp. 36–40.

119. Terrence Lyons, "Great Powers and Conflict Reduction in the Horn of Africa," in Zartman and Kremenyuk, *Cooperative Security*, and "The Transition in Ethiopia," *CSIS Africa Notes*, no. 127 (August 1991).

120. Reidulf K. Molvaer, "Environmental Cooperation in the Horn of Africa: A UNEP Perspective," *Bulletin of Peace Proposals*, vol. 21, no. 2 (1990), p. 142.

121. Horace Awori, "Sudan-Peace: African Leaders Meet to End the War in Sudan," InterPress Service, March 15, 1994; and Horace Awori, "Sudan-Politics: Belligerents Agree to Let Relief Convoys Through," InterPress Service, March 17, 1994. For Eritrean attitudes, see Martin Plaut, "Eritrea: In the Eye of the Storm," *World Today*, vol. 51 (February 1995), pp. 26–28. Continued conflict may benefit neighboring states because they are engaged in the legal provision of food aid or illegal provision of arms to the insurgents. On the conflicting agendas of IGADD members regarding the conflict in southern

Sudan see John Prendergast, *Sudanese Rebels at a Crossroads: Opportunities for Building Peace in a Shattered Land* (Washington: Center of Concern, May 1994), pp. 18–21.

122. Joseph S. Nye, Jr. *Peace in Parts: Integration and Conflict in Regional Organization* (Lanham, Md.: University Press of America, 1987), p. 16. See also Jeggan C. Senghor, "Theoretical Foundations for Regional Integration in Africa: An Overview," in Anyang' Nyong'o, ed., *Regional Integration in Africa*, pp. 17–31; and David Mitrany, *A Working Peace System* (Chicago, Ill.: Quadrangle, 1966).

123. Amitai Etzioni, "The Dialectics of Supranational Unification," *American Political Science Review*, vol. 56 (December 1962), pp. 927–35.

124. Nye, *Pan-Africanism and East African Integration*, p. 171; Joseph S. Nye, Jr., "Comparing Common Markets: A Revised Neo-Functionalist Model," *International Organization*, vol. 24 (Autumn 1970), pp. 831–32; and Asante, *The Political Economy of Regionalism in Africa*, p. 142.

125. Rothchild and Curry, *Scarcity, Choice and Public Policy in Middle Africa*, pp. 233–61.

126. John W. Harbeson, "The International Politics of Identity in the Horn of Africa," in Harbeson and Rothchild, *Africa in World Politics*, p. 120.

127. See Robert Axelrod and Robert Keohane, "Achieving Cooperation under Anarchy: Strategies and Institutions," *World Politics*, vol. 38 (October 1985).

128. I thank Gilbert Khadiagala for this phrasing.

129. P. Anyang' Nyong'o, "Introduction," and S. K. B. Asante, "Regional Economic Cooperation and Integration: The Experience of ECOWAS," in Anyang' Nyong'o, *Regional Integration in Africa*, pp. 8, 131.

130. For similar ideas as applied to the Horn of Africa, see Terrence Lyons, "Crises on Multiple Levels: Somalia and the Horn of Africa," in Ahmed I. Samatar, ed., *The Somali Challenge: From Catastrophe to Renewal?* (Lynne Rienner, 1994), pp. 189–207.

Chapter Six

1. Francis M. Deng, "Africa and the New World Dis-Order: Rethinking Colonial Borders," *Brookings Review*, vol. 11 (Spring 1993), p. 34.

2. On the notion of the mutually hurting stalemates, see I. William Zartman, "Conflict Reduction: Prevention, Management, and Resolution," in Francis M. Deng and I. William Zartman, eds., *Conflict Resolution in Africa* (Brookings, 1991), pp. 306–07.

3. Thomas Ohlson and Stephen John Stedman with Robert Davies, *The New Is Not Yet Born: Conflict and Conflict Resolution in Africa* (Brookings, 1994); Terrence Lyons and Ahmed I. Samatar, *Somalia: State Collapse, Multilateral Intervention and Strategies for Political Reconstruction* (Brookings, 1995); and Francis M. Deng, *War of Visions: Conflict of Identities in the Sudan* (Brookings, 1995).

4. I. William Zartman, ed., *Governance as Conflict Management: Politics and Violence in West Africa* (Brookings, forthcoming).

5. Itamar Rabinovich, "Smile When You Say Peace," *New York Times*, May 19, 1993, p. A19.

6. Stephen John Stedman, *Peacemaking in Civil War: International Mediation in Zimbabwe, 1974–1980* (Lynne Rienner, 1991), pp. 5–9. For confirming data, see Roy Licklider, "The Consequences of Negotiated Settlements in Civil Wars, 1945–1993," *American Political Science Review*, vol. 89 (September 1995), pp. 683–84.

7. For a successful case of colonial mediation involving racial and ethnic interests, see Donald Rothchild, *Racial Bargaining in Independent Kenya: A Study of Minorities and Decolonization* (Oxford University Press, 1973).

8. Daniel Frei, "Conditions Affecting the Effectiveness of International Mediation," *Papers of the Peace Science Society* (International), vol. 26 (1976), p. 70; see also Paul R. Pillar, *Negotiating Peace: War Termination as a Bargaining Process* (Princeton University Press, 1983), pp. 5–7.

9. See Boutros Boutros-Ghali, *An Agenda for Peace* (New York: United Nations, 1992), p. 9.

10. H. E. Salim Ahmed Salim, *Resolving Conflicts in Africa: Proposals for Action* (Addis Ababa: Organization of African Unity, 1992), p. 17.

11. I. William Zartman, Testimony to the Africa Subcommittee of the House Foreign Affairs Committee, March 31, 1993, 103 Cong. 1 sess. (Government Printing Office, 1993), p. 8.

12. S. Res. 94, daily ed., *Congressional Record*, April 3, 1993, p. S4508.

13. On the South African negotiations, see Ohlson and Stedman, *The New Is Not Yet Born*; and Timothy D. Sisk, *Democratization in South Africa: The Elusive Social Contract* (Princeton University Press, 1995); on the Sudan, see Bona Malwal, "Abuja Two: Who Wants It and What Can Be Achieved?" *Sudan Democratic Gazette*, no. 36 (May 1993), p. 1; and "Sudan: In the Sights of the New World Order," *Africa Confidential*, vol. 34 (April 2, 1993). p. 1.

14. Anna Simons, *Networks of Dissolution: Somalia Undone* (Westview, 1995), p. 69.

15. *The Kampala Document: Towards a Conference on Security, Stability, Development and Cooperation in Africa* (New York: Africa Leadership Forum), p. 11.

16. Organization of African Unity, *Declaration of the Assembly of Heads of State and Government on the Establishment within the OAU of a Mechanism for Conflict Prevention, Management, and Resolution*, AHG/DECL. 3 (XXIX) (Cairo, 1993), p. 4.

17. Letter from Dr. Y. Gershoni to Donald Rothchild, September 5, 1991. See also BBC Monitoring Service, ME/0788 (June 12, 1990), p. ii; and "Liberia: No Ceasefire Agreement," *Africa Research Bulletin* (Political Series), vol. 27 (July 15, 1990), pp. 9734–35.

18. Donald Rothchild and Caroline Hartzell, "The Peace Process in the Sudan, 1971–1972," in Roy Licklider, ed., *Stopping the Killing: How Civil Wars End* (New York University Press, 1993), p. 82.

19. On U.S.-Soviet cooperation regarding the peace talks, see "Ethiopia: Talks Start at Last," *Africa Confidential*, vol. 30 (August 25, 1989), p. 3.

20. "EPLF's Afewerki on Battles, Arab Relations," Al Sharigah Al-Khalij,

Ethiopia, July 10, 1990, in Foreign Broadcast Information Service, *Daily Report: Sub-Saharan Africa*, July 12, 1990, p. 7. (Hereafter FBIS, *Sub-Saharan Africa*.)

21. Hizkias Assefa, *Mediation of Civil Wars: Approaches and Strategies—The Sudan Conflict* (Westview, 1987), p. 141.

22. Confidential interview by Donald Rothchild, Nairobi, March 1, 1991; and Witney W. Schneidman, "Conflict Resolution in Mozambique: A Status Report," *CSIS Africa Notes*, no. 121 (February 1991), p. 6.

23. See Cameron Hume, *Ending Mozambique's War* (Washington: U.S. Institute of Peace Press, 1994).

24. "Mozambique: Funding for Peace," *Africa Confidential*, vol. 34 (May 14, 1993), pp. 3–4; and Chris Alden, "Bringing Peace to Southern Africa: The United Nations and the Resolution of Conflict in Mozambique," paper delivered at the British International Studies Association Conference, University of York, England, 1994, p. 28.

25. U.S. Institute of Peace, *Conflict and Conflict Resolution in Mozambique*, report of a conference held in July 1992 (Washington, 1993), p. 26.

26. Interview by Donald Rothchild, Hannes Siebert, Washington, April 29, 1993.

27. Daniel Williams and John M. Goshko, "Reduced U.S. World Role Outlined but Soon Altered," *Washington Post*, May 26, 1993, p. A1.

28. On the aspect of mediator leverage, see Ohlson and Stedman, *The New Is Not Yet Born*, p. 88.

29. Jeffrey Davidow, *A Peace in Southern Africa: The Lancaster House Conference on Rhodesia, 1979* (Westview, 1984), p. 117.

30. Jeffrey Herbst, *State Politics in Zimbabwe* (University of California Press, 1990), pp. 232–33.

31. For further details, see Donald Rothchild and Caroline Hartzell, "Interstate and Intrastate Negotiations in Angola," in I. William Zartman, ed., *Elusive Peace: Negotiating an End to Civil Wars* (Brookings, 1995), chap. 8.

32. William J. Foltz, "The Organization of African Unity and the Resolution of Africa's Conflicts," in Deng and Zartman, *Conflict Resolution in Africa*, pp. 350–51.

33. Nicola Jefferson, "Rwanda: The War Within," *Africa Report*, vol. 37 (January–February 1992), pp. 62–64; and "Varying Accounts of Tutsi Massacre," report by Brussels Radio, August 14, 1991, in FBIS, *Sub-Saharan Africa*, August 15, 1991, p. 5.

34. *Business Times* (Dar es Salaam), February 22, 1991, p. 4.

35. Jim Cason, "Africa's Top Statesman Minces No Words," *Africa News*, vol. 38 (March 22–April 4, 1993), p. 4.

36. Colin Legum, "Rwanda: A Military Invasion That Has Gone Right," *Third World Reports*, R.J/1 (April 14, 1993), p. 3; and Catharine Newbury, "Background to Genocide: Rwanda," *Issue: A Journal of Opinion*, vol. 23, no. 2 (1995), p. 15.

37. United Nations, Security Council, Resolution 846, June 22, 1993.

38. Economic and Social Council, Commission on Human Rights, "Question of the Violation of Human Rights and Fundamental Freedoms in Any Part

of the World with Particular Reference to Colonial and Other Dependent Countries and Territories," E/CN.4/1995/7 (United Nations, June 28, 1994), p. 7.

39. Zartman, "Conflict Reduction," p. 310.

40. See Gilbert Khadiagala and Hizkias Assefa, eds., "Conflict Resolution in the Horn of Africa," Brookings.

41. Department of State, Bureau of Public Affairs, "The U.S. and Sudan: Peace and Relief" (Washington, 1989), pp. 1–3.

42. Colin Legum, "Horn of Africa: Super-Powers' Curious New Initiative," Third World Reports, L.F/2 (February 8, 1989), p. 1.

43. Interview by Donald Rothchild with Herman J. Cohen, Washington, June 13, 1993.

44. Eddie Becker and Christopher Mitchell, Chronology of Conflict Resolution Initiatives in Sudan (George Mason University, Institute for Conflict Analysis and Resolution), p. 139.

45. "Breathing New Life into the American Initiative?" Sudan Democratic Gazette, no. 14 (July 1991), pp. 4–5.

46. Terrence Lyons, "The Transition in Ethiopia," CSIS Africa Notes, no. 127 (August 27, 1991), p. 5.

47. Terence Lyons, "Great Powers and Conflict Reduction in the Horn of Africa," in I. William Zartman and Victor A. Kremenyuk, eds., Cooperative Security: Reducing Third World Wars (Syracuse University Press, 1995), p. 254.

48. See the discussion in Ohlson and Stedman, The New Is Not Yet Born, p. 105.

49. This section draws heavily on Rothchild and Hartzell, "Interstate and Intrastate Negotiations in Angola," chap. 8; Chester A. Crocker, High Noon in Southern Africa: Making Peace in a Rough Neighborhood (W. W. Norton, 1992), p. 363; Robert S. Jaster, The 1988 Peace Accords and the Future of South-Western Africa, Adelphi Papers 252 (London: International Institute for Strategic Studies, 1990); and Michael McFaul, "Rethinking the 'Reagan Doctrine' in Angola," International Security, vol. 14 (Winter 1989–90), pp. 99–135.

50. On the concept of ripe moments, see I. William Zartman, Ripe for Resolution: Conflict and Intervention in Africa (Oxford University Press, 1985), p. 9.

51. Raymond W. Copson, "Peace in Africa? The Influence of Regional and International Change," in Deng and Zartman, Conflict Resolution in Africa, p. 40; and Saadia Touval, "Why the U.N. Fails," Foreign Affairs, vol. 73 (September–October 1994), p. 54.

52. For a useful background on the issues and players in this conflict, see I. William Zartman, Ripe for Resolution: Conflict and Intervention in Africa, updated ed. (New York: Oxford University Press, 1989), pp. 19–81. For another interpretation see Yahia H. Zoubir and Daniel Volman, "The Western Sahara Conflict in the Post–Cold War Era," in Daniel Volman and Yahia H. Zoubir, eds., International Dimensions of the Western Sahara Conflict (Greenwood, 1993).

53. United Nations, General Assembly, Question of Western Sahara: Report of the Secretary-General, A/43/680 (October 7, 1988), p. 5.

54. UN Chronicle, vol. 27 (September 1990), p. 12.

55. *UN Chronicle*, vol. 28 (September 1991), p. 4.

56. "South Africa: Boipatong Massacre," *Africa Research Bulletin* (Political, Social, and Cultural Series), vol. 29 (June 1–30, 1992), p. 10622.

57. "ANC's Mandela Addresses UN Security Council," SAPA, July 15, 1992, in FBIS, *Sub-Saharan Africa*, July 16, 1992, p. 6.

58. *National Peace Accord*, p. 27. This accord was enacted into law by the South African Parliament, Act 135, 1992. Timothy Sisk reports that as of June 1993, eleven regional and sixty-five local committees are functioning and another thirty to forty local committees are planned. See his memo, " South Africa: The National Peace Accord and the International Community," Washington, U.S. Institute of Peace, 1993, p. 1.

59. United Nations, Security Council, Resolution 765 (July 16, 1992), p. 2.

60. Prior to this, the UN high commissioner of refugees had been active in South Africa, assisting refugees to return home. Because of the professional and nonpartisan way he had conducted his affairs, he had broken the ice and made it easier for the South African government to accept UN monitors. The government continued to make it clear, however, that while it was not opposed to UN monitors, it did not think there was a need for formal mediation by an outsider. Statement by the Constitutional Development Deputy Minister, Dr. Tertius Delport, "Delport Sees No Need for Formal Outside Mediation," SAPA, in FBIS, *Sub-Saharan Africa*, July 8, 1992, p. 5.

61. United Nations, Security Council, Resolution 772 (August 17, 1992).

62. Interview by Donald Rothchild, Hannes Siebert, Washington, April 29, 1993.

63. Interview by Donald Rothchild, Chris Spies, Washington, June 9, 1993.

64. Bill Keller, "A Tide of Violence Swells in Zulu Area as Vote Nears," *New York Times*, March 28, 1994, p. A6.

65. Marrack Goulding, "The Evolution of United Nations Peacekeeping," *International Affairs*, vol. 69 (July 1993), pp. 451–64.

66. Mohamed Sahnoun, *Somalia: The Missed Opportunities* (Washington: U.S. Institute of Peace Press, 1994), pp. 6–7.

67. This agreement appears in United Nations Security Council, "The Situation in Somalia," *Report of the Secretary-General*, S/23693 (March 11, 1992), pp. 24–25.

68. For an enlightening discussion of the events leading up to this decision, see Herman J. Cohen, "Intervention in Somalia."

69. United Nations, Security Council, Resolution 794, December 3, 1992.

70. For African endorsement of the decision to deploy an additional 3,500 security forces by the UN Operation in Somalia (UNOSOM), see African Group Press Release, NY/OAU/AG/1/92, New York, 1992.

71. Robert Oakley, "Remarks to the HFAC [House Foreign Affairs Committee] Africa Conference," March 31, 1993, p. 2. Mimeo.

72. Raymond W. Copson and Theodros S. Dagne, *Somalia: Operation Restore Hope* (Washington: Congressional Research Service, 1993), p. 1; and Jane Perlez, "Expectations in Somalia," *New York Times*, December 4, 1992, p. A1.

73. See Hussein M. Adam, "Somalia: Militarism, Warlordism, or Democ-

racy?" *Review of African Political Economy*, no. 54 (1992), p. 18; Rakiya Omaar, "Somalia: At War with Itself," *Current History*, vol. 91 (May 1992), p. 233; and Lyons and Samatar, *Somalia: State Collapse*.

74. John W. Harbeson, Donald Rothchild, and Naomi Chazan, eds., *Civil Society and the State in Africa* (Lynne Rienner, 1994). On human rights organizations as demand-bearing groups, see Zartman, "Introduction," in Zartman, *Governance as Conflict Management*.

75. Lyons and Samatar, *Somlia: State Collapse*, p. 68.

76. "Factions Agree on Interim Government, Treaty," London International Radio, March 28, 1993, in FBIS, *Sub-Saharan Africa*, March 29, 1993, p. 1. On this, Donald Rothchild has also benefited from discussions with Professor Abdi I. Samatar, Berkeley, April 24, 1993.

77. Interview with President Ibrahim Babangida, *West Africa*, no. 3935 (February 22–28, 1993), p. 282.

78. "Liberia: The Battle for Gbarnga," *Africa Confidential*, vol. 34 (May 28, 1993), p. 2.

79. William O'Neill, "Liberia: An Avoidable Tragedy," *Current History*, vol. 92 (May 1993), p. 217. For his part, Taylor rejected "the ceding of the sovereignty of the Republic of Liberia to an external force under the governorship of a military commander." Letter from Charles G. Taylor to President Félix Houphouët-Boigny, April 7, 1992.

80. United Nations, Security Council, Resolution 788, November 19, 1992.

81. Lindsay Barrett, "Liberia: Dilemma of Neutrality," *West Africa*, no. 3940 (March 29–April 4, 1993), p. 503.

82. "Liberia: The Battle for Gbarnga," pp. 1–2.

83. Baffour Ankomah, "Liberia: UN Turns Blind Eye To ECOMOG's Atrocities," *New African*, no. 308 (May 1993), p. 16.

84. Sawyer's interim government was recognized by the OAU summit meeting in Abuja, Nigeria, June 1991.

85. On the Yamoussoukro negotiations, see Nnamdi Obasi, "The Negotiation Process," in Margaret A. Vogt, ed., *The Liberian Crisis and ECOMOG: A Bold Attempt at Regional Peace Keeping* (Lagos: Gabumo Publishing Co., Ltd., 1992), pp. 190–202.

86. Peter Da Costa, "Liberia: Good Neighbors," *Africa Report*, vol. 36 (November–December 1991), p. 22.

87. Brenda M. Branaman, *Liberia: Issues for the United States* (Washington: Congressional Research Service, 1992), p. 7.

88. United Nations, Security Council, Resolution 788, November 19, 1992.

89. United Nations, Security Council, Resolution 813, March 26, 1993. UN Special Representative Trevor Gordon-Somers reported that several of the warring parties favored the deployment of some 200 UN observers to serve, along with ECOMOG, following the signing of the cease-fire agreement. The UN observers are to take up positions between the combatants as well as at ports and border crossing points. United Nations, Security Council, *Report of the Secretary-General on the Question of Liberia*, S/25402 (New York, March 12, 1993), p. 9.

90. Kwabena Ofosuhene and Amma Osafo-Mensah, "Lay Down Your Arms," *Daily Graphic* (Accra), November 22, 1994, p. 1.

91. *Africa Research Bulletin*, vol. 32 (August 1–31, 1995), p. 11955.

92. Tunde Asaju, "Peace in Sight?" *Newswatch* (Lagos), September 4, 1995, p. 19.

93. Stephen John Stedman, "Conflict and Conflict Resolution in Africa: A Conceptual Framework," in Deng and Zartman, *Conflict Resolution in Africa*, p. 397.

94. Stephen John Stedman, "Mediation in Civil War," in Michael E. Brown, ed., *The International Dimensions of Internal Conflict* (Massachusetts Institute of Technology Press, forthcoming); and Donald Rothchild, "On Implementing Africa's Peace Accords: From Defection to Cooperation," *Africa Today*, vol. 43 (First–Second Quarters 1995), pp. 8–38.

95. *The Protocol of Estoril* (Peace Accords for Angola), sec. I(9), translated by Department of State, Office of Language Services, LS 134967 (Washington, n. d.).

96. Ibid., VI (9).

97. "An Exit Interview with 'Hank' Cohen," *CSIS Africa Notes*, no. 147 (April 1993), p. 5.

98. National Democratic Institute for International Affairs, *Nation Building: The U.N. and Namibia* (Washington, 1990), p. 74; and Gabriele Winai Strom, "United Nations Intervention and Supervision: The Role of the United Nations in the Namibian Conflict," paper presented at the International Studies Association, 1992, p. 24.

99. "Angola: The Toothless Watchdogs," *Africa Confidential*, vol. 34 (March 5, 1993), p. 1.

100. Robert S. Jaster, "The 1988 Peace Accords and the Future of Southwestern Africa," *Adelphi Papers* 253 (Autumn 1990), p. 35.

101. United Nations, Security Council, *Further Report of the Secretary-General of the United Nations Angola Verification Mission (UNAVEM II)*, S/25840 (May 1993), p. 9. Emphasis added.

102. Statement by Jardo Muekalia, UNITA chief representative to the United States, at the Carnegie Endowment for International Peace, December 7, 1994.

103. Statement by James L. Woods, Hearings before the Subcommittee on Africa of the House Committee on Foreign Relations, 103 Cong. 1 sess. (GPO, 1994), p. 3.

104. Ibid., p. 8.

105. Remarks by Aldo Ajello at the International Workshop on the Successful Conclusion of UNOMOZ, New York, March 27, 1995.

106. Ernest Harsch with Roy Laishley, "Mozambique: Out of the Ruins of War," *Africa Recovery*, no. 8 (May 1993), p. 2; and "Mozambique: Looking to Luanda," *Africa Confidential*, vol. 35 (March 18, 1994), pp. 6–7.

107. U.S. Institute of Peace, *Special Report on Mozambique*, May 18, 1993, p. 1.

108. Giuseppe Di Palma, *To Craft Democracies: An Essay on Democratic Transitions* (University of California Press, 1990), p. 153.

Chapter Seven

1. Opening statement by Olara A. Otunnu to the First Regional Consultation to the Study of the Impact of Armed Conflict on Children, Addis Ababa, April 17–19, 1995.

2. I. William Zartman, "Guidelines for Preserving Peace in Africa," in David R. Smock and Chester A. Crocker, eds., *African Conflict Resolution: The U.S. Role in Peacemaking* (Washington, D.C.: United States Institute of Peace Press, 1995), pp. 95–104.

3. For a holistic analysis of security see Barry Buzan, *People, States and Fear: The National Security Problem in International Relations* (University of North Carolina Press, 1983), pp. 245–58.

4. Gilbert Khadiagala, "Conclusion: The Future of Conflict Resolution in the Horn," in Gilbert Khadiagala and Hizkias Assefa, eds., "Conflict Resolution in the Horn of Africa," Brookings.

5. William J. Foltz, "The Organization of African Unity and the Resolution of Africa's Conflicts," in Francis M. Deng and I. William Zartman, eds., *Conflict Resolution in Africa* (Brookings, 1991), p. 352.

6. Crawford Young, "Self-Determination, Territorial Integrity, and the African State System," in Deng and Zartman, *Conflict Resolution in Africa*, pp. 320–46.

7. Chester A. Crocker, "What Kind of U.S. Role in African Conflict Resolution?" in Smock and Crocker, *African Conflict Resolution*, pp. 121–31.

8. *The Kampala Document: Toward a Conference on Security, Stability, Development, and Cooperation in Africa* (Kampala, Uganda, May 19–22, 1991), p. 7.

9. Terrence Lyons and Ahmed I. Samatar, *Somalia: State Collapse, Multilateral Intervention, and Strategies for Political Reconstruction* (Brookings, 1995).

Index